Scotty, in his early twenties, as a Marine Paratrooper
during shore leave (San Diego, 1944).

Full Service

First published in the United States of America in 2012 by Grove/Atlantic Inc.

First published in Great Britain in 2012 by Grove Press UK,
an imprint of Grove/Atlantic Inc.

This paperback edition published in Great Britain in 2013
by Grove Press UK, an imprint of Grove/Atlantic Inc.

5 7 9 8 6 4

A CIP record for this book is available from the British Library.

ISBN 978 1 61185 580 7

Printed and bound by CPI Group (UK) Ltd, Croydon, CR0 4YY

Grove Press, UK
Ormond House
26–27 Boswell Street
London
WC1N 3JZ

www.groveatlantic.com

Cover image of Katharine Hepburn: Photo Columbia Pictures /
Collection Sunset Boulevard / Corbis

All other cover photographs : Getty Images

Full Service

My Adventures in Hollywood
and the
Secret Sex Lives of the Stars

Scotty Bowers
with Lionel Friedberg

Grove Press UK

For Don, Donna, and my beloved baby, Maxie—Scotty Bowers

For all who have the honesty and courage to be different—LF

Authors' Notes:

This manuscript is based on my memory and,
to the very best of my ability, reflects actual incidents
and personalities as I recall them.
—*Scotty Bowers*

This manuscript is based on roughly 150 hours of recorded
interviews with Scotty Bowers. I have added only factual details
regarding studios, productions, and various film shoots
to augment Scotty's recollections, specifically where he
could not remember exact details himself.
—*Lionel Friedberg*

Preface

Although I'm not a shy man I have always been reticent to reveal details about what I have done, mainly to respect the privacy of those whose lives have intersected with mine. But, if the truth be told, over the years many people have told me to write about my experiences and share them with others. A few decades ago my good buddy Tennessee Williams began writing his own account of my life but before it saw the light of day I told him to destroy it. Now, as I take stock of myself in my twilight years—I'll be eighty-nine on my next birthday—I feel compelled to share my story.

I reached this decision not long ago as I was driving east along Hollywood Boulevard. I had been to see a friend in Westwood and I was on my way to one of the two houses I own to pick up my mail. It was a perfect Southern Californian summer afternoon. The traffic wasn't too bad and my dog, Baby, happily bounded from one side of the rear seat to the other, thrusting her nose out of the windows. We passed Mann's Chinese Theatre, where throngs of tourists gathered in the courtyard to gaze at autographs and handprints of their favorite stars enshrined in concrete. People dressed up as characters from a multitude of blockbuster movies wafted among the crowds.

Farther along the block, visitors gathered in the forecourt of the Kodak Theatre to admire the grand gallery where, once every year, the famous red carpet welcomes stars to the Academy Awards presentation. The El Capitan Theatre across the road was a riot of twinkling lights and more surging multitudes. It was just another average day in Hollywood.

Even for me, after all these years, the very name of Hollywood conjures up images of a fantastic world of make-believe. It's a world that throbs with energy, excitement, indulgence, even decadence. This is a crazy, zany, wonderful, topsy-turvy town sandwiched between a blistering desert and the vast Pacific Ocean. It has been my home for nearly seven decades. I have enjoyed a fabulous life here ever since I put down my roots following my discharge from the U.S. Marines at the end of World War II. I love this place and all the people in it. The story that I am going to tell could only have happened here. This is a gathering place of lost souls, of eccentrics, of people who don't follow the mainstream of anything.

As my car purred along Hollywood Boulevard I crossed Highland Avenue. I glanced around and realized how much things have changed since the early days. The old clanging streetcars are long gone. The shows that run in places like the Pantages Theatre are very different from what they used to be. Buildings have come and gone. The sidewalk still shimmers with inlaid terrazzo and brass stars that honor the many talented people who have worked in the film, television, radio, and music industries. Where bejeweled and fur-clad women once strolled arm in arm with tall, handsome men in tuxedos, there are now mainly tourists during the day and, after sundown, drunks, drug pushers, and the homeless. I drove on for a couple of miles. The crowds thinned out until the sidewalks were empty. When I reached Van Ness Avenue I pulled over. As Baby's face appeared over my shoulder she licked my ear. She was curious. Why had we stopped? Her wagging tail thudded against the seat behind me. How could I explain it to her? I tugged at her muzzle and stared at the intersection, now the site of major construction work.

A new fire station for the Los Angeles Fire Department was rising there. Like a floodgate suddenly opening, a million memories enveloped me. This very spot, this place where cranes, concrete mixers, and metal scaffolding now stand, is where it all began for me. A little gas station once occupied that corner. Shortly after I first got here I worked there as a young pump attendant. But it didn't take me long to learn to do more than just pump gas. Through a series of extraordinary incidents I became enmeshed in a wild world of sexual intrigue the likes of which few people can even begin to imagine.

Over the years more Hollywood personalities secretly congregated at that little gas station than anywhere else in town. It was a scene that saw as much furious action as the busiest studio back lot. The place became a magnet for those in quest of carnal thrills and escapism of every kind. A cavalcade of movie stars and others were attracted to the station like the proverbial moth to a flame. I became the go-to guy in town for arranging whatever people desired. And everybody's needs were met. Whatever folks wanted, I had it. I could make all their fantasies come true. No matter how outrageous or offbeat people's tastes, I was the one who knew how to get them exactly what they were after. Straight, gay, or bi; male or female; young or old—I had something for everyone. The vice squad and the press were constantly lurking on the periphery, eagerly waiting to pounce. But I always managed to elude them.

The gas station was the portal that eventually took me into an exclusive world where high-class sex was everything. I've had many occupations during my life but, to be honest, what really drove me was a desire to keep people happy. And the way I did that was through sex. Arranging sexual liaisons for folks from all walks of life became my raison d'être. When I first arrived here the stars were owned by the studios, which were heavily invested in them. Naturally, they needed to protect their investments. But people still wanted to have sex. And I was there to help them get it. Also, you have to remember that there were lots of gay people working at the studios at the time. Those behind the camera could be more open in their private lives but the actors and major directors and producers had "morals" clauses in their contracts, which they would have violated by being openly known as gay or bisexual.

Eventually I changed jobs. I moved on from the gas station to become one of the busiest bartenders in Los Angeles. In that capacity I gained access to the inner sanctums of Hollywood royalty. I moved in the highest of circles. Nothing was out of bounds for me. Those were amazing, intoxicating days, wildly erotic and carefree. Such a time can never come again. The lusty activities and vagabond lifestyle we once enjoyed in this town were unique to our time.

As I sat in the car that summer afternoon with Baby I became aware of the passing of an incalculable number of years. I felt myself reminiscing about dear and wonderful friends, all long departed. Oh, Kate, Spence, Judy, Tyrone, George, Cary, Rita, Charles, Randolph, Edith, Vivien, I thought . . . where are you all now? Do you look down at me from wherever you are and chuckle as you watch me mulling over how our lives intersected? What should I make of all those incredible adventures we enjoyed together? What do you beautiful souls think of the nostalgia now welling up within me? Am I resurrecting moments from yesterday simply because I want to dust them off and discard them or because I want to burnish them more brightly and hold on to them more endearingly?

Baby licked my ear again and I came out of my reverie. I reminded myself that there weren't only movie stars in my past. There were politicians, judges, bankers, doctors, industrialists, newspaper columnists, even kings and queens. Not all were rich and famous. There were also plain, regular men and women whose names I shall never be able to recall. But I knew them all. Intimately.

I started the car and drove off. I realized that wherever I look, the suburbs, the boulevards, the side streets, the studios, the nightclubs, the fancy homes in the hills, there is a sliver of my past in all of it. There is so much to recall. There are apparitions and memories of myself everywhere. My mind lazily ambled through endless mental files containing images of glamorous parties, of wild poolside orgies, of weekends in fancy hotels, of studio dressing rooms, of crowded sound stages, of dark places where bodies collided with electrifying vigor, of ghostly gatherings of gorgeous women and virile young men, of a magnificent variety of passionate sex of every kind.

Frankly, I knew Hollywood like no one else knew it.

I

Dream Factory

In 1946 I was twenty-three years old and the city of Los Angeles was witnessing a major spurt of postwar development. Even though the metropolitan district boasted a comprehensive bus and streetcar system, the era of the freeway was about to begin. To supply the war effort no new cars had been made since 1942. Now production was ramping up again. The automobile was about to become king, setting a trend that would make the City of Angels grow up around the car and its vast network of freeways. Gas stations were soon to become an iconic emblem on the landscape and were already springing up everywhere. Many became meeting places for young servicemen recently discharged from the armed forces. With their bustling late-night, brightly lit driveways and soda pop dispensing machines, they were ideal places for unemployed guys to hang around with their girlfriends, kill time, and meet up with friends.

Russ Swanson, an ex–Marine Corps buddy of mine, worked at a Union Oil gas station on Wilshire Boulevard. He occasionally asked me to help out at the pumps from 8:00 a.m. to 4:30 p.m., just before I went to work at my own evening gas station job on Hollywood Boulevard. One morning I got a call from him saying that he needed me to fill in for him for a couple of hours so I headed down to his station and manned my post at the pumps. It was a lovely, clear sunny day and I wasn't expecting much traffic. In that kind of weather folks usually headed for the beach; they weren't going to spend much time riding around in hot, stifling automobiles. I resigned myself to a potential day of boredom.

When Russ returned at about noon I spent a while chatting with him. Then, just as I was about to leave, a shiny Lincoln two-door coupe drove up. It was a big, swanky, expensive car. Only someone rich and famous drove something like that. Russ was busy in the office so I said I'd take care of the customer. When I approached the car the driver's side window slid down revealing a very handsome middle-aged male face that I was certain I had seen before.

"Can I help you, sir?" I asked.

The man behind the wheel smiled, looked me up and down, and said, "Yes, I'm quite sure you can."

It was the voice that instantly gave him away. My God, I realized, this guy's none other than Walter Pidgeon, the renowned movie star. I remembered him from films like *How Green Was My Valley*, *Mrs. Miniver*, and *Madame Curie*. That distinctive deep, smooth, very intelligent-sounding voice was instantly recognizable. I thought it best to pretend that I didn't know who he was, so I bumbled a response.

I pumped the amount of gas that he requested and when I came back to the driver's window Pidgeon had his hand on the sill. He was holding a few dollars for the gas between his thumb and forefinger and squeezed between his middle and index fingers was another crisp bill. I couldn't make out how much it was but I stopped when I saw it. His gaze remained locked on me.

"What are you doing for the rest of the day?" he asked in a very friendly tone, his face remaining expressionless.

Well, it wasn't too hard to guess what he wanted. I got the message immediately.

I took the money, thanked him, then went to tell Russ that I was leaving. A couple of minutes later I found myself on the passenger's side of the comfortable leather bench seat of Walter Pidgeon's vehicle. With neither of us saying anything he pulled out of the station and headed west on Wilshire Boulevard. After a couple of awkward, silent minutes he offered me his right hand and said, "Name's Walter."

"Scotty," I said, and shook his hand.

And that was that, the sum total of our introductions. The rest of it was all pleasantries and idle chitchat. We talked about the war that had ended the previous year and we discussed my role in it as a U.S. Marine. He wanted to know how old I was, where I was from, whether I knew many people in town.

About twenty minutes later we were driving up Benedict Canyon in Beverly Hills. He swung the car onto a paved drive that led to a large house. As he turned the wheel he pointed out the imposing gates on the other side of the street.

"You like movie stars?" he asked.

"Sure, why?" I replied.

He gestured toward the opposite driveway and told me that it was the home of Harold Lloyd, the famous silent movie actor.

I cooed in mock wonder. I wanted him to feel that celebrities impressed me but I had to keep my act up about not recognizing Pidgeon himself. As the car crunched up the gravel and pulled up outside a large expensive-looking house he glanced at me and told me that the guy who lived here was his friend. *Yeah, right,* I thought. Whoever he was he would certainly be more than a "friend." Nevertheless, I kept my thoughts to myself. The extra bill he had given me—all twenty dollars of it—meant a lot to me. I could certainly use the cash. Whatever Walt and his friend were into I decided to play along.

I swung my legs out of the car, shut the door, and joined Pidgeon on the porch as he rung the bell. When Jacques Potts opened the front door he was surprised to see me standing there.

He greeted Pidgeon, then looked me up and down as though he were studying a piece of merchandise. I got the feeling that he liked what he saw. Potts led us through his palatial home to the pool in the backyard before he turned around and disappeared inside the house. Pidgeon walked over to me and said, "It's hot, Scotty. Hop in for a swim. I'll join you in a minute."

He turned to go inside but not before throwing me a quick remark. "No need for a suit. There's no one else here."

What the hell? I thought. *Who cares?* So I got undressed, threw my clothes over a deck chair, and dove stark naked into the sparkling water. It felt great. I swam a lap or two before Potts reappeared, followed by Pidgeon, who was naked except for a towel tucked around his waist. They each chose a chaise lounge, lay back, and watched me.

"So, tell me about your new friend here, Pidge," Potts said.

Apparently all of Pidgeon's friends called him Pidge. I was being assessed, studied, sized up. I was a plaything being carefully examined before being brought into the playpen. And, to be honest, I was enjoying every moment of it.

After an hour of some really hot sex, preceded by both of them taking turns performing fellatio on me, we all unwound, and relaxed around the pool. By then, of course, Walter Pidgeon had revealed his true identity to me. I had feigned complete surprise. I hemmed and hawed and made a great fuss, doing my best to appear both humbled and excited by his mere presence which, to be honest, I really was. As for Jacques Potts, I soon learned that his real name was Jack, and that Jacques was a fancy French name conjured up to match his profession as a well-known milliner to the stars.

It turned out that both men were married. Pidgeon's wife was Ruth Walker, whom he had wed back in 1931. Before I left that day, he swore me to secrecy, begging me not to mention anything to anyone about what had transpired between us. I told him I was quite capable of being as discreet as necessary and I instinctively knew he believed me. Potts's wife was out of town. And because he and Pidge had agreed to see one another that day the servants and the gardener had been given the day off. It was a perfect opportunity to play under a blazing Southern Californian sun.

Pidge and Potts were two very nice, sweet, highly likeable guys. They were both smart, well groomed, and very rich. Their manners were impeccable. Neither of them exhibited even a hint of effeminate behavior. They were both in remarkably good shape, too, especially when you consider their ages. Walter Pidgeon must have been at least fifty at the time. Potts could have been a bit older. They were totally masculine in all their mannerisms and in the way they moved, talked, and behaved. The only thing that made them a little different than straight men is the fact that they enjoyed having sex with other men as well as with women. And, quite frankly, I saw absolutely nothing wrong with that.

As a result of that encounter, Pidge and I would see each other off and on over the ensuing years, always for sex followed by a handsome tip. His preference was to suck me off while masturbating. He would reach his orgasm just as I reached mine. On the rare occasion in later years when we got together with Jacques Potts the three of us would engage in some inventive ménage à trois antics. Sometimes I would just be a voyeur while the two of them did their thing, with Jacques acting as a "bottom" to Pidge's "top." Do you get what I mean? I'm sure I don't have to explain. The fact is that whatever we did and whenever we did it, we always had a lot of fun together.

2

Gas Station
on Hollywood Boulevard

There was no such thing as self-service at gas stations in 1946. My job at the Hollywood Richfield gas station was to welcome each customer with a big smile and a friendly greeting, pump as much fuel as they ordered into the gas tank, wash the windscreen, empty the ash trays, check the oil and water, ensure that tire pressures were correct, and generally see to it that every car and every customer got the red carpet treatment. I enjoyed the interaction with people and I did my best to make everyone feel special. And I didn't mind the late hours. In fact, it gave me an excuse to chase some tail and get up to a little mischief after I locked up around midnight. It seemed like the older I got the greater my sex drive became. I *had* to have it. Every night. Or day. And sometimes multiple times at that.

My live-in girlfriend Betty never questioned me, even when I got home after dawn. With a regular paycheck coming in we were able to move to a nice little apartment not too far from the station. Although we never took the plunge by getting married, within a couple of months Betty was pregnant. We were both thrilled about it and moved into a slightly bigger place, one that had an extra bedroom for the new baby.

One afternoon before going over to the station I decided to pay a call to a little office that had been set up in the fashionable Crossroads of the World shopping center on Sunset Boulevard. The government-funded facility, run by a woman whose name I no longer recall, had become a popular and vital contact point for ex-military personnel who were trying to obtain information about buddies, friends, and family members in the months that had elapsed since the war ended. It functioned as a kind of clearing house, a meeting place and a database where ex-servicemen could leave their names, telephone numbers, and addresses for people to find them or, conversely, where they could look up the names and whereabouts of others who had served in the military with them. It was a very important service that helped a lot of people reconnect after the war. As an ex-Marine who saw service in the Pacific I was curious to find out if they knew where any of my old fellow Marines were. I went in there, filled out a small card, left the lady my name and work address, and thought no more about it.

At the time I could never in my wildest imagination have foreseen the ramifications of filling out that little card.

ONE LATE AFTERNOON, not too long after I had first been picked up by Walter Pidgeon, I arrived at the gas station to start my five o'clock shift. As I drove up and parked my car I was delighted to see two Marine Corps buddies of mine sitting waiting on the curb for me. We hadn't met up since we had been discharged from service in Seattle. We shook hands warmly, then hugged, and kibitzed around for a couple of minutes. It was a lot of small talk, but I was glad to see them. Once a Marine, always a Marine. It was great to make the connection again. I offered them each a soda from the refrigerator outside the office and then I asked them how they had found me. I hadn't given my work address to anyone.

"C'mon, Scotty. 'Course you did."

"Where? When?" I asked.

And then they reminded me about the ex-servicemen's contact office down at the Crossroads of the World in Hollywood.

"You filled out a card, dumb head," they chided.

Of course! It had been a couple of weeks since I'd filled out the card. Amazingly, another Marine compatriot showed up a couple of days later. And then another. And another. Within a fortnight I'd been contacted by at least a dozen of my old buddies from the Corps. Over the next few weeks one or two of them would show up at the station every day or so. And it wasn't long before it became a daily ritual. Small groups of them began congregating just as I arrived for work at five o'clock. Many of them had found girlfriends and they would bring them along, too. The guys just wanted to shoot the breeze with one another for an hour or two, talk about ball game scores and catch up on news and events before they all went their separate ways as the evening wore on. A couple of them had bought cars—old jalopies mainly—that they brought in and filled up with gas. Others rode motorcycles. All of them bought gas and oil from me and occasionally they would bring their vehicles in for a service and an oil change. A guy by the name of Wilbur McGee—or "Mac" as he was better known—manned the service bay during the day but in the evenings I took care of all the jobs for my friends. I did lubes, changed oil, put in new spark plugs, charged batteries, rotated tires, changed brake linings, fixed radiator leaks.

As time went by my Marine pals would bring their civilian friends over and so the circle constantly widened. Soon the station took on the role that the shopping mall plays in the lives of kids today. The Richfield gas station on Hollywood Boulevard became *the* fashionable place for guys and gals between the ages of eighteen and twenty-five to hang out. The place buzzed, business boomed, and my boss, Bill Booth, who leased the station from the Richfield Gas Company, was as happy as a pig in clover.

BECAUSE THE GAS station was in the heart of Hollywood, many of the rich and famous also stopped by to purchase gas from me. One of them was playwright Jerome Lawrence along with his writing partner Robert E. Lee. Jerry was the other half of the famous team, Lawrence and Lee. They wrote thirty-nine works together including the librettos for *Dear World* and *Auntie Mame*. They also wrote *The Night Thoreau Spent in Jail*, *First Monday in October,* and the classic courtroom drama, *Inherit the Wind*. Jerry would stop by, fill up his tank, and then chat for a half hour or so.

Another good customer was an exceptionally talented and very handsome young and upcoming author by the name of Gore Vidal. Gore was one of the nicest, brightest men I knew. He would go on to become a towering force in the world of modern literature, screenwriting, and sociopolitical commentary. He has remained a close friend ever since we first met. Actor Glenn Ford became a regular. So did producer Harry Cohn, head of Columbia Pictures, which was just down the road. Hermes Pan the choreographer came to the station, too. He once claimed that he had choreographed every single musical starring that royal dancing duo, Fred Astaire and Ginger Rogers, including their final partnering in *The Barkleys of Broadway*. Actor Lionel Barrymore often came to the station, as did Bing Crosby and Bob Hope. Rock Hudson and one of his young gay lovers drove in one night in a brand-new 1947 Chevrolet Coupe, of which he was very proud. He filled up and we chatted; every second or third day after that he came back and had me pump five dollars worth of gas into his car. He was living in North Hollywood at the time and, in due course, he and I would get to know one another pretty well.

* * *

ON FEBRUARY 1, 1947, Betty gave birth to our darling baby daughter. We named her Donna, in honor of my brother Donald. Now that I had another mouth to feed I needed to earn extra money, so I took odd day jobs trimming a tree here, patching up a fence there, fixing a leaking roof, doing a bit of carpentry, painting gutters, cleaning pools, gardening, or doing whatever (or whoever!) came along. My family was never short of anything, and our little daughter thrived. But my life with Betty was pretty dull. Yes, we lived together at the same address, we still had great affection for one another, we still enjoyed sex now and then, but, in actual fact, we began to drift into living separate lives. For one thing my work kept me very busy and, to be quite frank, I was seeing other people, both women and men, frequently.

Betty was no fool. Even though she never brought it up in conversation she knew what I was up to. And she learned to live with it. She even took phone messages for me at home and not once did she ever ask what my relationship with the caller was. She was such a sweet, considerate woman that she never questioned my whereabouts on those many nights when I didn't come home. That's the unique kind of woman that Betty was.

One evening at the gas station something happened that would herald a whole new enterprise for me. While a group of my friends and other young folks, both male and female, were hanging around, a big car pulled in. I ran out, flashed my big Richfield Oil smile at the driver, and asked him what I could do for him.

"Fill her up, please," he said.

"Sure thing, sir," I replied.

While I was wiping down his windshield I noticed him staring at my friends huddled together in a group at the end of the driveway. When I finished I went around to the driver's side window to collect payment for the gas. The guy must have been in his fifties. He was fiddling with a pile of bills that he had pulled from his wallet. I told him what he owed me for the gas. He didn't respond and continued fidgeting with the wallet while staring at the group of young folk. He couldn't take his eyes off them.

"Will there be anything else, sir?" I asked.

He nodded in the direction of the group. Speaking very softly and in a carefully honed American yet very British-sounding accent he asked, "That boy over there, he a friend of yours?"

"Which one?" I responded.

"The tall one, the blonde," he replied.

I looked over at my pals.

"How old is he?" he asked.

I began to suspect where all this was going. I told him that the guy was twenty and asked him whether he would like to meet him. He nodded as he handed me the money for the gas, not taking his eyes off my friend. Then I went over to the group and pulled my buddy aside, walking him over to an area where no one could see or hear us.

"Want to earn some cash tonight, pal?" I asked.

"Sure thing," he said. "How?"

I wandered back over to the car. The driver was clearly anxious to hear what I had to say and seemed a little nervous.

"He'll go with you," I said. "But it's going to cost you twenty bucks."

The man said nothing. He immediately pulled out his wallet again and started counting out some bills.

"Oh, no, sir," I said. "Not for *me*. For him. You can pay him later."

He looked at me and nodded. I went back to my blonde friend. I told him to get into the car with the guy, go with him, and do whatever he wanted. Although at first he was unsure of what I was asking of him, he immediately brightened when I told him that it would earn him twenty bucks. Because he was a Marine I knew that he was quite capable of defending himself if the guy turned out to be a weirdo, though it was obvious that he was a harmless queen who probably only wanted to suck my buddy's cock.

None of our friends noticed as he slipped into the front passenger seat and closed the door. The man behind the wheel glanced momentarily at me and flashed me a grateful smile. I grinned back at him. The driver looked away, put his foot down on the accelerator, and the car pulled out onto the boulevard and into the night.

The next evening my friend showed up again. He wasn't gay, or at least I never thought of him as being that way. Nevertheless, he wasn't the least bit embarrassed to tell some of the other guys who were hanging around what had happened the night before. I never expected him to be so open and honest about it. If I'd had my way I would have kept the whole thing under wraps, mainly to protect the reputation of the driver of the car, whoever he was. But this guy wanted to tell all.

"Easiest fuckin' twenty bucks I ever earned," he confided to us. "You were right, Scotty. The old geezer only wanted to give me a blow job, and I wasn't gonna say no to *that*. He was good, too! "

Some of the guys were mildly amused by the story but most of them thought it hilarious and burst into raucous applause. I could detect a note of envy among one or two of them. One of the youngest ones detached himself from the group and pulled me aside, asking me if I could arrange something like that for him, too. He was desperate for some extra cash.

"So you're up to doin' tricks, too?" I asked, playfully slapping him on the back.

"Hell, yeah," he said. "For money? You kidding?"

I thought for a moment.

"Okay, fellas, stick around," I said to the entire group. "You never know. *Your* turn may come soon."

More laughter followed that remark but I must have foreseen exactly what was going to happen. Having heard my buddy's account of what transpired with the trick I arranged for him wasn't the end of the story. It was only the beginning. Because one thing you can be sure of: if you ever ask a middle-aged queen to keep a secret you can be absolutely sure that it will spread like wildfire before you can say Jack Robinson. It turned out that the guy who drove off with my friend was a senior makeup artist at Warner Bros. The ambling studio complex was located in Burbank, just a few miles from the gas station. He had obviously told his colleagues about the cute little number he'd picked up at the Richfield gas station on Hollywood Boulevard because within two days three or four cars driven by gay men from the studio were pulling in every night for a few dollars worth of gas and a request for me to set them up with a trick. It happened so fast. Before I could take stock of the situation, I was becoming the go-to guy in Hollywood for arranging tricks.

To be honest, though, none of this was completely new to me. I hadn't had the most sheltered of childhoods and had discovered sex at an early age. In fact, I was just a kid in Illinois when it all began.

3

Awakenings

The year was 1930.

Like a dependable, precision timepiece my body instinctively knew it was time to get up. Throwing off the heavy blanket and the frayed homemade quilt, I swung out of my warm bed and padded over to the window. Drawing the curtains aside I stared at the dark landscape that lay beyond. Even though the sun would not rise for another two hours I could make out that the world was covered in snow. A feeble light spilled into the gloom of the tiny bedroom. The thought of going outside made me tremble in anticipation of the freezing weather, but I had no choice. There was work to be done.

I shuffled over to my brother Donald's bed and gave him a shake. He grunted and then turned over to face the wall, clutching the blankets more tightly around his shoulders. But I knew he would not remain in bed for long. I could already hear Momma banging pots and stoking the big wood-burning stove in the kitchen downstairs. She would soon be knocking on our door to make sure we were up. I yawned and went over to the porcelain jug and washbasin that sat on the dresser. I poured out some icy water, splashed it on my face, pulled on my bib overalls, slipped on a sweater, and stepped into my muddy work boots.

Giving Momma a peck on the cheek as I passed her in the kitchen, I stepped outside into the icy air. The temperature was probably around ten or fifteen degrees Fahrenheit, typical of midwinter in this part of Illinois. Through the damp haze that swirled around the yard I caught sight of my sister Phyllis going to collect eggs in the hen house. Yearning for something hot that I knew would be offered at the breakfast table a couple of hours later I slushed my way over to the big cowshed. Using all my strength I dragged one of the heavy doors slightly ajar, slipped inside, and shut it behind me.

A strong whiff of manure, methane, dust, hay, and mildewed timber filled my nostrils. But I was used to it. I did this every morning and had been doing it ever since I could remember. I greeted Dad and Willy, our hired hand. They were already hard at work milking the cows. There were forty of them. My brother Don and I were responsible for assisting with the task.

Walking over to a corner in the shadows I picked up an empty metal pail and went over to the first stall, where one of our oldest and most dependable Holstein milk producers watched me with her innocent, oily brown eyes. When Don and I returned from school later in the afternoon we would help with the milking again. This was a twice-a-day operation, seven days a week, 365 days a year.

As my fingers tugged on the cow's soft teats, her warm milk squirted into the pail. It was a comforting sound, imparting a sense of continuity to life on the farm. After breakfast I would ride my pony Babe down the unpaved road to the schoolhouse half a mile away. Sometimes Don or Phyllis would hop on her back with me and we would ride together. We couldn't afford a saddle so we always rode bareback. There would be some homework to do when I returned that afternoon, then more farmyard chores, and then, weather permitting, I would hop over the fence to the Peterson's property down the road. I enjoyed slopping through the snow and mud to their farmhouse, which was about a ten-minute walk away. The Petersons had a boy and a girl who were close in age to me. Their company made for a pleasant contrast to my own brother and sister. In winter their mother—Ma Peterson we called her—usually managed to serve up a cup of warm cocoa at around four o'clock. And whenever he was around, old man Joe Peterson always set aside a few minutes for me, curious to hear what I'd been up to since my last visit.

It was a simple life on the farm, but a tough one. In fact, nobody had it easy those days. I was only seven years old so I never fully understood the hows and whys of it but from overhearing teachers' and adults' conversation I knew that a disaster had befallen the nation the year before. All of us kids were aware that in October 1929 a place called Wall Street in New York City had "crashed." People usually referred to the event as "That dang Black Tuesday," and then they would cuss and fume and walk away shaking their heads, mumbling, "Sure cut us up good and well."

We were now in the grip of something folks called the Great Depression. There was a shortage of everything: work, money, customers for our produce, even hope. Some people had even packed up their meager belongings and moved away, completely abandoning their farms. Where they went heaven only knew. One thing was for sure—the Depression had ruined lives and had redefined everything on the farmlands of the Midwest. But this was where I lived. It was the only place I knew.

I had been born on the farm on July 1, 1923. The property was 280 acres and was owned by my paternal grandmother, Anna Boltman. She was originally married to a man named William Bowers, who had died a few years before I was born. She then married a man named Boltman, became widowed again, and ended up living alone in a house in the nearby town of Ottawa. The little hamlet lay at the confluence of the Illinois and Fox rivers, about seventy-five miles southwest of Chicago.

Grandma Boltman's second husband had left her his farm but she preferred to remain in town and let Dad run the place. As the matriarch of the family no one ever took issue with her and she invariably had the final word on everything. When I came along in 1923 she decided to call me George while Momma added the name Albert in memory of her late father. Although Momma detested it with a vengeance, George was the name that stuck. I didn't much like it either but that's how I was known. Well, at least at that time anyway. I didn't become "Scotty" until much later on.

Momma was born Edna Ostrander, in 1900. Her father, Albert, was of Dutch descent. Her mother, Sarah, was a local girl from Ottawa. Momma was a slim, petite yet strong woman, and very even-keeled. She always had her dark brown hair pulled back in a tight bun and wore dresses that she made herself. She managed to ride out many storms and would live to within a few days shy of her hundredth birthday. A kinder, more decent and more caring woman you couldn't find. Donald, Phyllis, and I all loved her dearly.

My father's name was Glen. Born in 1901, he was a good man, a hard worker with solid values and rigid scruples. He was a big, muscular guy with a shock of black hair and blue eyes. In temperament he was more volatile than Momma and wouldn't tolerate any insolence or misbehavior from us kids. But we loved him very much, too. We were lucky. We enjoyed a good relationship with our parents. Unfortunately, things between the two of them weren't so good. Although they did their best to hide it from us kids, their marriage was foundering.

My brother Donald was two years older than me, and my sister Phyllis two years younger. We all got along pretty well, especially considering Momma and Dad's wavering relationship and the harsh economic difficulties of the times. The workload on the farm was pretty heavy for kids of our age. Dad was really struggling to hold everything together and my parents began to squabble. On many a night I lay awake listening to them arguing behind the closed door of their bedroom. Whenever Grandma Boltman came from town to visit she tried mediating between them as best she could, but she was under great stress, too. Dwindling finances brought us close to losing the farm. But what did we kids know of such things? We had other matters on our minds. We did our chores, we went to school, and we grew up. Poverty deprived us of any toys or games to play with. Don and I didn't even have so much as a football to toss around. We had no hoop, no basketball, no baseball bat. Phyllis had no dolls, no puzzles, no pretty frilly dresses to sew ribbons onto. We didn't even have an indoor toilet! When I occasionally visited the neighbor's kids the situation was much the same. They were as short of everything as we were.

In the natural course of events every young boy experiences a physical phenomenon that he simply takes for granted and regards as something perfectly normal. I refer, of course, to erections. If you were in a group of young guys splashing around in the water or romping around a green field you couldn't care less if you developed a hard-on. However, we wouldn't want to be caught dead being seen with an erection in front of a parent or, even worse, a girl. Of course, every farm boy knows exactly what erections are for. Sex is around you all the time. I knew that once a boar had an erection and mounted a sow, a litter of piglets would be born just under four months later. From a very early age I saw frisky stallions galloping around paddocks and corrals sporting an erect penis more than three-feet long. Sometimes farmers would pay a breeder to bring a young stallion over to his farm to mate with one or more mares for the purpose of producing a foal. Intercourse was everywhere. Oh, what the heck, let's call it what everyone calls it: fucking. Fucking was everywhere. Our dogs and cats were always doing it. Roosters mounted hens, rabbits mated in the fields, goats coupled in the barnyard. Bulls, birds, and bees did it, so sex was nothing new to me. As a matter of fact, before they started fighting, we kids occasionally heard Mom and Dad doing it, too. If their bedroom door was just a tiny crack open we'd take a peek. And why not? As far as I was concerned, they were only doing what nature intended them to do. But for some reason society seemed to follow more antiquated values.

Like generations before us, we boys were eager to find out as much as we could about the female of the species. I vividly remember during a school picnic or a social outing when we crossed the boundary into forbidden territory according to the rules of church, school, and society's norms. A couple of guys and girls would sneak behind the bushes and expose their private parts to one another, playing the "I'll show you mine if you show me yours" game. Lots of giggling would follow the briefest of glimpses. Of course, we hid such activities from parents and teachers but it was all in good fun and we never went as far as physically touching one another. We just looked. And every time I did so I would have to cover myself up because of my hard-on.

One warm September day I returned home from school on Babe's back and led her to the stable where I watered and fed her. Watched over by Momma's all-seeing eyes, Don, Phyllis, and I had lunch together and then got on with our homework seated around the kitchen table. As always, I was impatient to go outside. As soon as I completed the last mathematical problem in my homework book I looked up at Momma, grinned from ear to ear, slammed the book shut, and was dismissed from the table. While Don and Phyllis enviously scowled at me as they continued to scribble away at their assignments I ran outside and went racing across the yard, free as a bird. I sprinted over the fence and headed toward the Peterson's house to find out what my friends next door were doing.

We managed to get up to some benign and forgettable mischief and then went racing across the folds of rich green grass that undulated around the farm. Toward late afternoon, satisfactorily exhausted, we returned to the house where Ma Peterson offered us refreshments. Just as I was about to return home to help with the evening milking her husband Joe walked in. He greeted me in his usual friendly manner.

Joe Peterson was a gentle, jovial sort of guy. Big and burly with bright eyes, he never talked down to the kids like so many adults did.

We chatted for a few minutes and then I said I really had to go. Don would already be helping with the milking of the cows and would no doubt be wondering why I wasn't home yet. Peterson got up from his chair and offered to see me part of the way home.

He came over, ruffled my hair, and, with his arm loosely slung over my shoulder, walked me outside. We went around the side of the house and continued to make small talk. I suddenly realized that I had an urgent need to urinate. I sheepishly told Peterson that I needed to pee and quickly slipped behind a tree to relieve myself. As I struggled with one of the buttons of my fly I looked up and was surprised to see him standing just a foot or two away from me. I hadn't even heard him approach. He was staring at me with a look that I couldn't quite figure out.

The next thing I knew Peterson came over and helped me unbutton my fly and then, to my surprise, thrust his hand inside my overalls. Before I could say anything he grabbed my penis, pulled it out, and then let go.

"There," he said. "Go ahead and do what you have to do, son."

I thanked him and began to urinate, but I couldn't help noticing the intensity with which he was staring at me. He said that he thought I had a very nice penis. I didn't know what to say so I merely shrugged my shoulders and smiled back. I'd never thought about it before. I finished, buttoned up, and excused myself by saying that I really had to run off right away or I would be in deep trouble not only with Don but also with Dad.

I thought no more about what had just happened. All I knew was that I was in for a solid hollering when I got to that cowshed.

A week or so later I was over at the Petersons again, cavorting around the property with their kids. At the end of the day we were sitting in the kitchen eating cookies and gulping down milk when Joe Peterson strode in and sat down. Once again he made small talk with me and then called my attention to the fact that darkness was falling outside. He said it was probably time I started out for home.

I had been having such a good time that I hadn't noticed how late it was getting. Once more I began to panic about not being at home to help Don, Dad, and the hired hand with the evening milking. Joe Peterson got up and in a very friendly manner said that he'd walk me across the road. Turning to his wife and kids he said he wouldn't be gone long.

As his family started to prepare the table for dinner Peterson briefly looked at me and winked. I don't know why but something clicked inside me. Was he trying to tell me something? I wasn't sure, but the answer came as soon as we stepped outside.

He told me to follow him to the woodshed, where he said he wanted to show me something. He gently laid his hand on the nape of my neck and steered me toward the shed. He took me inside and closed the wooden door behind us. Then, in the nicest of ways, he invited me to sit down next to him on a large flat chopping block that filled the middle of the floor. He laid his hand on my knee. Looking me straight in the eye he whispered in a low voice and told me that he had something to say. I wasn't sure what would come next but because of Peterson's tender, reassuring demeanor I didn't feel frightened or threatened. His tone and composure made me feel completely relaxed. I listened carefully as he searched for words, telling me that he liked me in a very special way, a way that I was to keep a closely guarded secret between us. He told me things I had never heard anyone say before. Within a few minutes I became aware of the fact that he had opened my fly, button by button, softly confessing how attractive I was to him. The next thing I knew he was fondling me. Our eyes were locked together as I felt strange sensations in my loins and my body. After a few minutes, Peterson closed my fly, gave me a pinch on the cheek, and then demurely leaned over and laid a kiss on my forehead. He made me swear not to tell anyone what had happened and I nodded in agreement.

I guess you could call that my very first sexual encounter. I was far too young to fully comprehend the implications of what had happened but that little session was my first personal portal into the mysterious world of human sexual dynamics.

In the weeks and months that followed, unbeknownst to anyone, Peterson and I had innumerable secret meetings. In fact, he replaced my father as the dominant male figure in my life. Unlike with Dad, Peterson and I could talk to each other on many levels. He cared about how I felt, what I thought, what my views were. Dad never had time for stuff like that. Peterson kept reminding me never to mention anything to anyone, especially my parents.

As the seasons came and went our private encounters became a little more open, with any prevailing inhibitions now cast aside. We would both undress completely and he encouraged me to touch his genitals as he played with mine. One winter's day as a small fire crackled in the little stove in the corner of the shed he touched himself as he fondled me. Then he began to masturbate. With his eyes squeezed tightly shut, his mouth wide open, and his head thrust backward he groaned as he reached his climax. Although I had watched animals do it over the years, it was the first occasion that I had witnessed what happens when a human male experiences an orgasm. When it was over he looked at me as if either he was unsure of what he had just done in front of me or felt guilty about it. But then he relaxed, smiled, wiped himself off, and lightly kissed me on my forehead. I wasn't in the least bit shocked or disgusted by what I had seen. Quite the contrary, I was grateful to Joe Peterson for opening up a whole new chapter of learning for me.

SUMMER CAME, but it was a summer I would rather forget. It was 1932. I was nine years old and the Great Depression was at its height. One day Grandma Boltman was driven over to our farm by her attorney. Donald and I slowly stalked around his big, shiny black car like wild animals encircling their prey. We didn't dare touch the gleaming metal and chrome of that beautiful machine but we stood on tiptoe and peered inside, enchanted. Momma and Phyllis were in the kitchen while we boys hung around outside. Then Dad, Grandma, her attorney, and Momma went to sit in the parlor and were soon engaged in serious discussion. None of them looked happy. Through the curtains I caught sight of Momma wiping away tears. Don and I had no idea what was going on. We sauntered over to the porch stairs, then sat on the steps. Phyllis remained in the kitchen, busying herself with plates and cups and whatnot. That evening over supper, after Grandma had left to return to town, the subject of the adults' big discussion was revealed to us. Dad informed us that economic reality would force us off the farm. Grandma Boltman had no alternative. She could not afford to keep the place going. She had explored every option, had searched the depths of her soul, and had no recourse but to sell off all the livestock and give the farm over to farmers from neighboring areas. They would work the land and if any profits were realized they would share half the income with her. The mere thought of leaving our home was devastating. That night both Don and I quietly sobbed into our pillows, crying ourselves to sleep. As for Phyllis, she spent the night lying next to Mom in her bedroom, both of them howling loudly while Dad sat in the parlor all alone, contemplating our fate and our future. Deep down inside I knew he was frantic. What was he going to do? What would we do? Where were we going to live? More importantly, how was Dad going to earn a living? Grandma Boltman was stone broke. She couldn't help us at all.

When Joe Peterson heard about our plight a couple of days later he came over with Ma Peterson to express their sorrow and sympathies. But Peterson admitted that he, too, was on the verge of closing down his own farm. It was the first I'd heard of it. On his way out that evening he gave me a look that I will never forget. It was one of genuine love, of pity, of remorse, of affection for me. But he couldn't say anything and neither could I. Deep down I knew I was going to miss him. He was a warm, tender man, and in a very special way I knew that he cared for me. But all that was soon to be over.

Fortunately, Dad had a few good friends in Ottawa. As luck, fate, and providence would have it—I don't know which was more applicable —one of them came through with help. I don't recall the guy's name but Dad told us that he worked for the Stateville Penitentiary near the town of Joliet, about halfway between Ottawa and Chicago. He had managed to find Dad a job as a guard with the prison service. Dad was overjoyed, but when he came home and told Momma about it she simply accepted it without showing too much enthusiasm.

The worst part about the whole business was having to say good-bye to our beloved animals and livestock. It was sad enough finding good homes for the cats and dogs but I was heartbroken the day I watched my beloved pony Babe being shipped off in a horse trailer to her new owner. She and I had grown up together and had spent many happy years trudging down the dirt road to school, come rain, hail, sunshine, or snow. I felt my heart being torn to pieces as I heard her hoofs echoing on the metal floor of the trailer as she clip-clopped into it, and then there was that dreadful thud as the door was closed. We were sad to see the chickens and the hogs go, too. Each one of them had a name and a distinctly individual personality. Especially upsetting was seeing the cows and the horses go. Momma sobbed as they were taken away. Don and I, the ones who knew them best, were horribly cut up about it. I hugged my favorite cow before she was coaxed up the ramp onto the trailer that took her and five of the others to the farm of our friends the Jones's, ten or twelve miles away.

But that was that. Our days on that glorious piece of Midwestern farmland were over. And the day Dad, Mom, Don, Phyllis, and I drove off for the last time I knew I had left a piece of me behind.

4

Full Service

Hollywood was probably about the most different place from my Illinois hometown that I could have ever chosen to move to. And I ended up spending my days right in the very heart of it. Because car culture was so dynamic and essential to the city, a gas station was the best place I could possibly be to arrange tricks for people from all tiers of society. And my gas station became the focal point for everyone looking for a trick. It became the crossroads of the city's sexual underbelly.

The station was ideally located, convenient to most of the major movie production centers in town: Warner Bros., Universal Studios, Republic Pictures, and Walt Disney Studios in Burbank. It was just a couple of miles away from Paramount Pictures, RKO Radio Pictures, Samuel Goldwyn Studio, Columbia Pictures, General Service Studios, and the Charlie Chaplin Studios in Hollywood. Slightly farther away, between Santa Monica Boulevard and West Pico Boulevard, lay the sprawling studio complex of Twentieth Century Fox. A few miles beyond that in an area known as Culver City was the vast Metro-Goldwyn-Mayer complex, Hal Roach Studios, and another huge RKO studio lot that was once home to Selznick International

Pictures, makers of *Gone with the Wind*. With the war over and the American economy booming, film production was at an all-time high. The town was buzzing. And, like a glowing oasis offering something very special in this frenzied firmament was the little gas station where I worked on Hollywood Boulevard.

I still don't quite understand how it all happened so rapidly, but it did. Whenever anyone was on the prowl for sex, my gas station was the place to head.

"Need a trick for tonight?" someone would say. "Well, go see Scotty Bowers at Richfield Gas on Hollywood Boulevard. He'll set you up."

These folks included creative types, executives, and technicians. The majority of the men who sought male partners were in the makeup, wardrobe, or hairdressing departments, but there were also production designers, art directors, set decorators, dialogue directors, casting people, and writers. Some were gay, some straight, and some bisexual. Most of the technicians who worked with heavy equipment in the lighting, camera, grips, sound, construction, and transportation departments were straight and in search of the perfect young lady. Well, I could help them out, too. I began to cater to all tastes, all sorts, all interests.

The queens were the most demanding. A straight guy would merely ask for a blonde or a brunette or a girl with a cute figure or big tits or one who was good at some specific sexual technique like giving a fantastic blow job, but gay guys were a lot choosier. They not only wanted someone tall or blonde or very good-looking, he also had to be suntanned or hairy or smooth or muscular. He had to have a big cock, be circumcised or uncircumcised, have big feet, long toes, hairy toes, blue eyes, long hair, or whatever. The list could go on and on. And you know what? I was able to provide them with precisely what they wanted. Soon enough such a varied and eclectic group of people were flocking to the gas station to get their name into my little black book of contacts, or "tricks," that I was able to get anyone the person of their dreams. My little book listed only names and numbers. I wanted things to remain discreet. Everything that people liked, including the type of person they wanted to do it with, was committed to memory. I kept all those details in my mind, safely hidden from view.

Most of the folks who made themselves available for tricking were very average, ordinary people. The majority of them were unmarried. Few, if any, of them were starstruck. If I arranged a trick for a guy or a girl with a major movie star or celebrity they invariably couldn't care less. They were in it only for a quick trick and a bit of cash. Money was tight in those days. Young people between the ages of eighteen and twenty-five would do anything to earn some extra cash.

Eventually, lesbians also began dropping in. I could get them exactly what they wanted, too. Word quickly spread within the lesbian community and I managed to make them all happy. As an aside, I must admit that I was disturbed about the way square, bigoted, and homophobic members of society nastily referred to a lesbian as a dyke. Many people simply tossed the derogatory word around with the express purpose of humiliating, criticizing, and demeaning certain women. At first I disliked the term but I eventually had to get used to it, especially when I heard it being used so often in conversation among members of the gay and lesbian community itself. "Dyke" seemed to be as commonly used as "queen."

When it came to my own sexual liaisons, I was always more than happy to pocket the tip that anyone offered me for a night of sex. But I never charged for my matchmaking services when hooking up other people. I would set up the trick and then the two of them went off together and money changed hands between them. It was only fair. My operation—if you want to call it that—was not a prostitution ring. I was simply providing a service to those who wanted it and, as recorded history has shown, throughout the ages there has always been a need for good, old-fashioned, high-quality sex. As I've said before, I don't think there is anything wrong with that. I never thought so and I still don't.

Everyone I chose to introduce to my gas station customers was someone I knew from my circle of contacts. They were people I trusted, and it was a circle that widened all the time. I never took in total unknowns from the street. I was wary of anybody who simply walked in and offered himself or herself as someone "for hire." Those in my black book were all young, honest people who, in the vast majority of cases, really needed the money that a little fun in the sack could provide. There were thousands of young guys and women who found themselves at loose ends after the war. Some were looking for jobs while others were trying to get started in new careers. Many were earning pittances as waiters, waitresses, barmaids, and the like. As far as I was concerned I was doing them all a favor.

I was very fond of tricking people myself, and could always make good use of the twenty bucks that was handed over to me afterward. I jumped at the opportunity to go off with either a man or a woman who was attractive and who wanted to make whoopee with me, just as long as it didn't interfere with my normal working hours.

I was blessed with a very healthy sexual appetite. I wanted sex every day. I was proud of my dick and I was happy to share it. Not once did I ever have trouble getting an erection and I always came. Always. I was proud of the size of my load, too, even after I had already come two or three times earlier on the same day or evening. I was blessed with a great sexual constitution. Why hide it?

During my years at the gas station I would invariably spend the night with someone, either male or female, often not even going home to Betty and my daughter Donna. I was beginning to live a very gypsylike lifestyle. I would be out all night sleeping in a different bed, then go home, do my laundry, change my clothes, make sure my two girls had everything they needed, throw a sandwich together, and then head back to the gas station for my evening shift.

* * *

AFTER THREE OR FOUR months working at the gas station I began to establish contact with many of my old Hollywood friends from my boot camp days, as well as those I had met during a month-long series of flings while on shore leave in 1944. Among them were Cary Grant and Randolph Scott. I saw Marion Davies—William Randolph Hearst's girlfriend—again. And I looked up many others with whom I had earlier been sexually involved. These included two wonderfully talented guys by the names of Sydney Guilaroff and Edwin B. Willis. Both men are unknown today but back then they were legends in their profession. Syd was the chief hairstylist at MGM from 1934 until the late 1970s. His hair styles graced stars like Greta Garbo, Greer Garson, Elizabeth Taylor, Joan Crawford, Norma Shearer, Hedy Lamarr, Ava Gardner, Lana Turner, Lena Horne, Grace Kelly, Debbie Reynolds, Kathryn Grayson, Ann-Margret, Marilyn Monroe, Claudette Colbert, Lucille Ball, and Judy Garland. He was the one who gave Judy her lovely braids in *The Wizard of Oz*. He had the distinction of making legal history in the United States by becoming the first unmarried man allowed to adopt a child when he became the legal father to a one-year-old boy he named Jon, after one of his favorite actresses, Joan Crawford. Later he adopted a second son, Eugene, named after his late father. The behind-the-scenes stories he would tell made it seem like nobody is as close to an actor as his or her hair stylist and makeup artist. Sydney could keep me engrossed for hours with his stories.

Ed Willis was another MGM man, one of the top set decorators in Hollywood. During a career that spanned thirty-five years and over six hundred films he picked up no less than eight Academy Awards, including for *Somebody Up There Likes Me, Julius Caesar, The Bad and the Beautiful, An American in Paris, Little Women, The Yearling,* and *Gaslight.* Ed was very fond of me, primarily, I think, because I had been a Marine. He had been a Marine, too, in World War I. Although openly gay to gay men, he never publicly admitted it, and he always looked and behaved as though he were straight. He once told me that he had found it very difficult being in the Marines and had cultivated a very masculine image to avoid harassment.

Another guy in town who had an absolute passion for Marines was the composer and lyricist Cole Porter, the man responsible for writing the hit musicals *Anything Goes, Silk Stockings, Can-Can,* and *Kiss Me Kate,* as well as some of America's best loved songs such as "Night And Day," "I Get a Kick Out of You," "In the Still of the Night," "I've Got You Under My Skin," "Just One of Those Things," "Easy To Love," "What Is This Thing Called Love?," and "De-Lovely." Cole was married to divorcée Linda Thomas from 1919 until her death in 1954 but it was a marriage of convenience, or what in those days was sometimes referred to as a "professional marriage." Cole was openly gay and undeniably promiscuous. He never made any attempt to hide it. I don't remember exactly when he called me out of the blue at the gas station one evening. He said he'd heard that I knew a lot of Marines and asked me if I could come over to his place with two or three of them at around midnight on the following Saturday night. He didn't beat around the bush. He knew I had been a Marine myself and he wanted me to bring a few buddies around. Short and sweet. I knew exactly what he wanted and I was only too happy to oblige. I did have other plans for the upcoming Saturday evening but I cancelled everything. I mean, after all, this was the legendary Cole Porter, for crying out loud.

Porter was renting a home with a large secluded pool just off Sunset Boulevard in Brentwood. It was owned by my old friend Bill Haines, whom I'd first met during my boot camp days back in 1942. When I arrived at Porter's place on that Saturday night with three ex-Marines a party was already in progress. There wasn't a woman in sight. Porter was probably in his late forties or early fifties at the time. Most of his guests were younger men, one more strikingly handsome than the next. Linda, Porter's wife, was not there (I later learned that the couple lived apart most of the time). The lower portion of Porter's right leg had been amputated because of a horse riding accident on the East Coast. He was in constant pain and found it difficult to get around, relying mainly on crutches.

I soon learned that Cole's passion was oral sex. He could easily suck off twenty guys, one after the other. And he always swallowed. There are many people, both male and female, who really enjoy the taste of semen. Porter was one of them. On one later occasion I took about nine of my best-looking young guys over to his place and he sucked off every single one of them in no time. Boom, boom, boom and it was all over.

Over the years I fixed him up with many tricks and he valued my friendship. In some odd sort of a way he eventually looked upon me as a sort of confidant. The ceaseless pain in his leg turned him into a bit of a recluse. Cole shared a lot of his innermost dreams, desires, and fears with me. He was insecure and uncertain about a lot of his friends, often suspecting them of maintaining a friendship purely because of his fame. He wanted so much to be liked simply for who he was. He was especially introspective after he and I had indulged in a night of sex. Cole loved to suck me off and then have me fondle him until he reached his own orgasm.

One day he asked me to help him find out how his closest clique of so-called allies really felt about him. The plan was that he would throw a dinner party at his home, offering an ideal opportunity for him to find out what he wanted to know. He invited a group of twelve or fourteen people comprised of married couples and single men and women, all of whom had known him for a long time. I was one of them.

Cole's home was opulently furnished. He had a huge dining room table that could easily seat all the guests with room to spare. He asked me to come over in the afternoon and help with the preparations for the dinner and for his exercise in plumbing the true depths his friends' love and loyalty. To achieve this he intended to hide and eavesdrop on them. But how to do it? The plan we came up with was to cover the dining room table not with a conventional tablecloth but with three large white bed sheets. We laid out the sheets and then covered them up with flowers, place settings, tableware, glassware, and other accoutrements to conceal the pleats in the sheets. The sheets were made to hang very low over the sides of the table, reaching right down to the floor. No one could see anything underneath the table, where there was room enough for someone to hide undetected. It was arranged that when the guests arrived that evening they would be welcomed by the butler, who would show them into the drawing room for drinks prior to dinner. Apologies would be made by the butler at the front door for Cole's absence. Each guest was to be informed that Cole was a little overworked, that he was feeling tired, and would join us all at the table later for dinner.

While we chatted over cocktails the large doors to the dining room remained closed. Unseen by his guests, just prior to dinner, Cole secretly hobbled into the dining room through another door and crawled beneath the table. Squatting as comfortably as he could, he positioned himself so that he could overhear everything that would be said around the table. Then the butler threw open the doors between the dining room and the drawing room. He cleared his throat and announced that Cole was still not feeling well but that, as dinner was ready, we should take our seats around the table and that Cole would join us in time for dessert.

By then everyone was suitably loaded, happy, hungry, and more than ready to sit down and dine, despite the absence of the host. Nameplates indicated where everybody was to be seated. I was placed at the left center of the table and as soon as I sat down, Cole, unseen beneath the table, inched himself over by my feet. The food was brought in and we began to eat. By prior arrangement Cole and I had figured out a complex system whereby he would pinch me or touch me on the ankle or calf if anyone spoke about him. Depending on how and where he touched me I would enter the conversation and try to elicit more details from the person speaking. If he wanted me to encourage someone to expand on what was being said about him he would only have to touch me on my knee and I would try to throw the discussion open to all those present. From his invisible place on the floor Cole was directing nothing less than an inquisition into the loyalty of his friends. As the wine flowed inhibitions and discretions were cast aside and everybody talked quite a lot about their host.

Most of the remarks were complimentary. There was much praise for him. But every now and then a critical or bitchy remark would be made. Needless to say, Cole remained under the table, taking it all in. By the time dessert was served he had still not made an appearance, but by then nobody cared. For Cole it turned out to be a most revealing evening. His only complaint as I woke up in bed beside him the following morning was that he was suffering from excruciating pain in the stump of his leg from crouching beneath that table for almost two hours. I no longer remember what judgments or opinions he made about his guests that night. The fact that I cannot recall the details is not only because so much time has passed since that evening, but because secrets and seclusion were typical of Cole. But despite his insecurities and doubts I always found him to be an easygoing kind of guy. However, even though he confided in me, I don't think I ever really fully understood him. I don't think anyone did.

For whatever reason, people have always found me easy to trust. I guess I'm a good listener, and I always take people on their own terms. Maybe some of that comes from being exposed to quite a wide variety of people at an early age. I was an adventurous kid in a big city.

5

Big City

After we left the farm in Illinois we spent a few months in Joliet, where Dad was working at the Stateville Penitentiary. But it wasn't long before he and Momma decided to get a divorce. In 1933, me, Momma, Donald, and Phyllis moved to Chicago, which was probably the most exciting metropolitan area in America at the time. It had undergone major reconstruction and development since the Great Fire of 1871. Streetcars clanged everywhere. New buildings pierced the skyline downtown and on the wide boulevard that snaked along the shore of Lake Michigan. Although we were still in the throes of the Depression, and money was as tight as anywhere else in the country, in the Windy City life crackled in all its infinite variety. Yes, there were breadlines and soup kitchens and beggars, but in addition to all the hardships that everyone endured many folks still managed to eke out a living and some even found cause to laugh and to look on the bright side of things. Chicago was a great place for an inquisitive, healthy young fellow like me to begin to discover big-city life. We took up residence in a small apartment on Oakwood Boulevard near Thirty-ninth Street, which was in a relatively poor neighborhood in the South Side.

Our new home was barely big enough for the four of us. Don and I shared a bedroom, tinier than anything we had before. Phyllis and Momma shared an equally cramped room. Don and I kept our secondhand bikes chained up downstairs in the dimly lit lobby of the building. The hallways were stuffy and moldy and a timer turned the lights off after ten minutes. A rickety staircase led up to our apartment, where Momma took on work as a seamstress. She also found piecemeal employment outside as a cleaning lady or by doing sewing and baking for people in their private homes.

We kids were enrolled at Oakenwald Elementary School on South Lake Park Street. I adapted quickly enough, but I was itching to help Momma bring in an extra dime or two. I couldn't stand seeing the way she had to slave away to support us. I really wanted to go out and find some kind of work of my own to augment her income. That's when I discovered my entrepreneurial side. A few weeks after arriving in the city I got myself a part-time job delivering and selling newspapers. This job allowed me to visit many areas in and around Chicago, some very wealthy, and others not at all. I carried the *Chicago Tribune* and the *Chicago Herald Times,* each of which sold for two cents. The profit margin for me was so small that I had to sell at least a dozen papers before I made a single penny. But I was thrilled to be earning something. I worked hard at it every single day after I got out of school. I would race Don home on my bike, forego lunch, hurriedly finish my homework, and set out on my beat. I was good at what I did. I sold a lot of newspapers and soon I began including the *Saturday Evening Post* in my inventory. This bumped up my profits but it was hardly enough to help Momma buy the groceries we needed so I expanded my activities. I saved up a little bit of cash and invested in a shoe-shine box, brushes, and shoe polish, making my services available as a combination newspaper deliverer and shoe-shine boy.

This double role started taking me to new and interesting places. With Momma's permission I began going downtown, where I stood outside bars and movie theaters, shining shoes for a nickel. Because I brought in much-needed cash Momma allowed me to stay out late at night. As my profits accumulated I could give Momma enough money to buy food for the whole family and still have some change left over to indulge in a few of the things I enjoyed doing.

My buddies and I loved the movies, but a ticket cost ten cents. So a dozen of us would hang around outside the theater on a Saturday afternoon just before the matinee began. One of us would buy a ticket while the rest of us hid outside the emergency exits on the side or at the back of the building. As soon as the guy with the ticket had distracted the attention of the doorman the others would yank open the emergency-exit doors and dash inside. This invariably set off alarm bells but once inside the dark auditorium we were very difficult to spot. If the ushers went in with flashlights to find us some of us might occasionally get caught and thrown out but most of us would settle low into our seats and stay for the whole show. I loved the movies. I secretly harbored a wish about one day getting to meet those larger-than-life movie stars who stared down at me from the big silver screen. I especially fantasized about Greta Garbo, Katherine Hepburn, Joan Crawford, and Mae West. Watching those beautiful women made my crotch bulge.

ACROSS THE STREET from where we lived on Oakwood Boulevard stood the Holy Angels Catholic Church. The priest who ministered there began to appear outside the church to watch me as I set out on my shoe-shine and newspaper route every day. He had obviously taken an interest in me. Leaning against the jamb beneath the cornice of the doorway, casually attired in slacks and his clerical collar, he would stare at me as I passed by. He was a slim, plain-looking man, probably in his early forties. At first I tried to avoid his gaze but it didn't take more than a few days before our eyes met, and then he smiled. Somehow I knew there was more behind that friendly gesture than a mere greeting. That hunch was borne out the next day as he motioned to me to come over.

"How's it going, son?" he asked.

"Oh, fine, Father, thank you," I replied, setting down my load of shoe-shine box and newspapers.

Approaching me, he said that he thought I worked too hard. We shook hands, introduced ourselves, and then made small talk for a couple of minutes. As I picked up my things to leave he invited me to come over that evening for some soup.

I told him that I might be too late for that as I usually only got back around midnight. This didn't deter him at all. He told me that he would be up, working on next Sunday's sermon. He said I should come in through the side door of the rectory. He'd leave it unlocked for me.

That invitation opened up a whole new world for me. Young and healthy enough to be driven crazy by his oath of abstinence, the Father ached for release. I mean, just think about it. What's a poor celibate priest going to do? Bark at the moon and jack off in the backyard? No, the guy yearned for company, for some kind of sexual partner. And so it was that night after night when I came back from my newspaper delivery rounds and my shoe-shine gigs I would slip in through the back door of the rectory of the Holy Angels Church. In the privacy of his quarters the priest would fondle me and then have me stroke him to orgasm. He also liked to have me lie naked in front of him and slowly caress my own stiff cock while he masturbated. Eventually he plucked up enough courage to introduce me to a form of sensual pleasure that I had not been aware of until then. Even Jim Peterson never went as far as that with me on the farm. I speak of fellatio or, to dispense with formalities, cock sucking. I was still not sexually mature so I could not reach orgasm when he tried it on me, but he still loved nothing better than to suck on my penis.

Just as I had felt about my experiences with Joe Peterson on the farm I found none of the priest's likes or preferences in any way abhorrent. I never questioned them. They seemed perfectly normal to me. I figured that if it felt good and provided pleasure, why not enjoy it? That only seemed logical. Do you get what I mean?

At the end of the evening the sweaty, satisfied priest would saunter over to his trousers, which he had carefully hung up on a rack at the foot of his bed, dig into his pockets, and, smiling, hand me a few coins as a token of his gratitude. The change came in very handy. Very handy, indeed. In fact, it always amounted to a lot more than I had earned selling newspapers and shining shoes that evening.

I felt no shame, no guilt, no remorse for what I had done. In fact, I derived an undeniable sense of satisfaction knowing that I had brought a little joy into someone's life. I saw nothing wrong in that. As far as I could see, our bodies were designed in a certain way and there was no doubt in my mind that sex was essential for one's emotional, psychological, and physical health. Hell, even priests needed it.

News traveled fast, especially in a tightly knit community of sexually starved young and middle-aged men who had sworn themselves to celibacy. Within weeks of my first session at Holy Angels Church, nearly every Catholic man of the cloth in town knew about me. It wasn't long before I was seeing more than twenty of them, each and every one in desperate need of sexual gratification. They all willingly handed over small piles of loose change just so that they could spend a little time with me. As my reputation within the archdiocese of Chicago spread, the range of activities in which I became involved diversified. Other than fellatio the most popular sex act that I engaged in was what I can only refer to as "mock penetration." A lot of male homosexual sex invariably involves anal penetration. I was far too young to anally accommodate an erect adult penis at that time so I resorted to the next best thing. If the priest was very excited I simply pinched my legs tightly together and he would thrust his dick backward and forward between them. If there was time I would try to increase his pleasure by smearing Vaseline, cold cream, or baby oil on the insides of my thighs. This always ended in the desired result.

Though hiding it from their congregations and the outside world as best they could, those inventive clergymen engaged in a wide range of erotic behavior. I learned a lot and I enjoyed keeping everybody happy, myself included, since I was making really good money. I came away from every session with an eagerly anticipated handful of coins and even the occasional dollar bill or two.

Momma never questioned where the cash came from. As far as she knew I was earning all of it by shining shoes and delivering and selling newspapers. My brother, Donald, never once suspected what I was up to, either. Each night I would creep into our tiny bedroom where he had already been asleep for hours, silently undress, and fall into bed, utterly exhausted, catching just enough shut-eye to be up in time for school in the morning. I had my private little world, and my family was none the wiser.

You might think that all that same-sex activity would have suggested that I was gay, but I was much more interested in females. Around the time I turned twelve, I discovered a sweet blue-eyed curly-haired blonde of about my age who lived in a small apartment building near us. She used to take her little black Scottish terrier dog for a walk every day. One afternoon just as I was preparing to go out on my newspaper and shoe-shine rounds I saw her approaching. I quickly dumped my newspapers and other paraphernalia in the hallway of our building, ran a comb through my hair, slicked it down, straightened out my windbreaker, and, as casually as I could, stepped out onto the sidewalk to intercept her. Falling into step next to her I introduced myself and, to my delight, she was happy to engage in conversation. She told me that her name was Gillian. As we walked, her Scotty dog huffed and puffed and pulled frantically on the leash, urging us on. Our conversation topics ranged from the weather to the school we each attended to who our favorite movie stars were. We had a nice thing going and became the best of friends. Unfortunately, much to my disappointment, she never permitted our acquaintanceship to blossom into anything that would allow us to explore one another's bodies. Try as I might, there were never any sexual overtures between us. But she and I would meet up to walk that cute little black dog of hers on more occasions than I can remember. Folks eventually got to know us as we passed by, and pretty soon they would say to one another, "Here come the Scotties."

As we passed by they would smile and call out "Hi, Scotty!"

The name caught on. Everyone began referring to Gillian and me as Scotty—even my friends and my brother, Donald. When Momma first heard Don call me Scotty she thought it so appealing that she immediately dropped the name George that Grandma Boltman had bestowed upon me. To her, Scotty was imminently preferable. Gillian eventually moved away from the neighborhood and I would never find out what became of her, but thanks to her I had a new name.

THOUGH THE PRIESTS proved to be a great source of additional cash, I could not entirely rely on their payments as a primary source of income. Once the novelty wore off for them they didn't see me as regularly as they once did. My shoe-shine service and newspaper route remained active, but the job came with hurdles. Chicago winters were brutal. Not only did I face heavy snowstorms, icy sidewalks, and sleet- and wind-whipped flurries as I went about my work, but I had the arduous task of delivering papers to subscribers' front doors. It wasn't simply a case of tossing them into the front yard of a house or throwing them onto a porch. Tenement blocks and apartment buildings were especially difficult. In some cases I would have to walk up many flights of stairs to reach an address so that I could leave the paper neatly folded on a mat outside the front door.

One day I was on my way to drop off a *Tribune* at the apartment of a guy called Frank Risnick. I usually got to his place at around five thirty every afternoon. Mr. Risnick was a friendly, stocky, middle-aged guy in his fifties with jet-black hair and a babyish face.

He was originally from Europe and spoke with a thick accent. He lived alone, had few friends, and verged on what we would nowadays refer to as a "nerd." He worked for the Buell Horn Company, a local small-industrial plant that made loud horns for trucks, trains, boats, and buses.

Mr. Risnick was always very kind to me. Knowing that by the time I got to him I had already been doing my rounds for a couple of hours he always used to await my arrival and then invite me in for a glass of milk and a cookie or a sandwich. He could hear me coming as I plodded up the stairs to his apartment. The door would be left open and I would go in, drop my pile of papers and shoe-shine equipment in the hall, then spend six or seven minutes seated with him at his small kitchen table gulping down the refreshments on offer while he scanned the day's headlines. One day, out of the blue, he suddenly put down his newspaper as I slurped some milk and ate the peanut butter and jelly sandwich he had prepared for me. He just sat there, an elbow on the table, his chin resting in the palm of his hand, staring at me.

Then he got up, came around to where I was sitting, dropped down on all fours, unbuttoned my fly, and took out my cock. It took me completely by surprise. Because of my priestly liaisons I was familiar with this kind of thing but certainly not with Frank Risnick. With peanut butter and jelly smeared all over my face I stared down at him as he took my penis in his mouth and then, as gently as he could, began sucking on it. I was speechless. The guy was good, belying anything that I might ever have expected of him. I became awash in the most incredible sensations as his soft, warm tongue worked its magic. I spread my legs wider, then gripped the seat of the chair with both hands and leaned backward. Waves of unbelievable pleasure that I had never felt before surged through my body. Those recently awakened seminal vesicles were pulsing with energy. Elsewhere within me, muscles were contracting, glands were pumping. With his other hand Risnick had unbuttoned his own fly and began masturbating. Within a couple of minutes I could not hold back any more and reached a state of overwhelming ecstasy. The session ended in a cataclysmic mutual climax. My heart was pounding like a sledgehammer as I looked down at Risnick. He smiled up at me, kissed my penis, and handed me a napkin. It was the first time I had experienced an ejaculation. It was a defining moment in my life, signifying that I had finally reached sexual maturity. In retrospect I'm glad it happened in the company of Frank Risnick. He was such a decent, gentle, unthreatening man. Nothing would ever be the same again. Regular masturbation would now result in a couple of very satisfying ejaculations every day, something that I had been looking forward to ever since my buddies and I talked about it in the school playground back in Ottawa.

6

Star Treatment

One evening during my days as a pump jockey at the gas station in Hollywood a man I had never seen before pulled up in a brand-new four-door sedan. I can no longer recall the make, but the driver was a slightly stocky fellow in his late forties with dark hair and thin wire-framed glasses. He was grasping the steering wheel like a nervous elderly lady would do. When I asked him what I could do for him his eyes flicked up and down, taking me in as he made a quick assessment of me. Then he asked me to fill up the tank. We got to chatting about the weather and how he liked his new car. He struck me as being a bit worn out and crabby so I asked him whether he'd had a rough day or had just been working late. He admitted that he was exhausted. He had just come off the set of a picture that he was shooting on a soundstage over at Universal. He said that he was the director.

I can't remember the exact details of our conversation but he told me his name was George Cukor. I also know that he was directing *A Double Life* at the time. The film starred Ronald Colman, Edmond O'Brien, and Shelley Winters. Cukor was a legend in the motion picture industry. He had directed *Camille*, starring Greta Garbo, a movie

I loved when I saw it as a teenager in Chicago. He also made *Romeo and Juliet* and one of my all-time favorites, *The Philadelphia Story.* Another of his more recent films at that time was *Gaslight,* featuring Ingrid Bergman and Charles Boyer in the starring roles.

I quickly warmed to the guy. He definitely seemed a bit odd, and nervous, but there was something fascinating about him. There was a lot about him to like. The feeling was obviously mutual because, even though I cannot remember exactly how or why it happened, he invited me over to his home in West Hollywood the following Sunday. He gave me his address and drove off, saying, "See you on Sunday, about noon."

My normal working routine included Sundays from ten in the morning until midnight. I would have to ask Mac McGee, the mechanic, to stand in for me. Mac was a sweetheart of a guy. He usually worked in the service and repair bay on weekdays only, but I expected that he'd fill in for me at the pumps on Sunday. In retrospect I don't know how much Mac ever really knew about what was going on in my life or at the gas station itself after dark. He was a square no-nonsense kind of a guy who pretty much stuck to himself and to his nine-to-five weekday work schedule.

As I went back into the office that night I began to think about Cukor. I had to stifle a chuckle. He had a very strange manner of speaking. Every word he had said he articulated unusually clearly. He had bared his teeth, hissing as he precisely pronounced each syllable. It was as though he were trying to enunciate the exact way to say something in a complex foreign language, his face becoming very expressive and animated as he spoke. It was hilarious, but in looking back on it now I figure that it was his way of imparting his innermost feelings, thoughts, directions, instructions, and ideas to people who worked under him. Perhaps that was how he managed to get such superb performances out of all his stars.

On Sunday I drove over to Cukor's place on Cordell Drive in West Hollywood. The property consisted of a beautiful orange grove in the middle of which stood an ambling white house, surrounded by a high wall and gates. There was a large yet secluded pool at the side of the house. The main house was a single-story structure but because the grounds sloped downward to accommodate the pool area, the guest suite beneath the main house was on the same level as the pool. It was all very well-planned and beautifully executed, in keeping with George's tastes and personality. When I arrived just before noon, lunch had already been laid out around the pool and Cukor was entertaining a small group of people. I didn't recognize anyone and felt a little out of place as I walked up to the crowd. As soon as he saw me Cukor broke away from his guests and welcomed me with a very friendly, "Hello, there, dear boy. So glad you could come."

He insisted that I call him George, asked me to remind him what my name was, and then he paraded me around, introducing me to everyone. I cannot remember who they all were, just that they were all famous and influential people. I do recall that they did their best to politely welcome me into their fold. I almost never touch alcohol, I just don't enjoy the taste of the stuff. Ditto for tea and coffee. I was fascinated to learn that, like me, George was also a teetotaler, so there was no alcohol around except for a couple of bottles of champagne that one of his visitors must have brought along.

Although I didn't recognize her until we were introduced, among the guests was Katharine Hepburn, who on-screen seemed so feminine. And yet here was a woman with a severe short hair cut, tightly cropped and combed with a boyish side part. She was wearing a suit with trousers and had no makeup on at all. She looked infinitely more masculine than feminine. I thought of her in *The Philadelphia Story* and could barely make the connection.

Because Hepburn was such an illustrious individual with a really sparkling personality I only recall talking to her that afternoon, though I'm sure I spoke to others. She intrigued me. There was, no doubt, considerable intellect behind her stark yet fascinating facade. She strutted around, cocksure; she was clearly cognizant of the fact that she was a rapidly rising superstar.

By three o'clock the summer heat had become stifling. It was time for the party to break up. Everyone had adequately partaken of George's hospitality, bid their good-byes, and was slowly starting to drift away. Hepburn was one of the last to leave. As I watched her go, George tapped me on the shoulder. He whispered that she didn't know how to behave in public. When I questioned him about that he replied, "It's not that she's a dyke. I have no trouble with that. But the studio does. They've been pleading with her not to advertise the fact in public but she ignores them."

I waited for more. He fussed around with plates and leftovers and then went on, telling me that Hepburn was very arrogant. He said that she thought she knew best about everything. I wasn't going to comment. What did I know of any of this? It was the first time that I'd met her and I really didn't know anything about her behavior, her personality, or her lesbianism until that day. My first impression was simply that George didn't like her very much. He went on to tell me that Hepburn had once been married to a guy named Ludlow Ogden Smith but the marriage had lasted just five years and they had divorced in 1934. He said he thought she ought to be more discreet about her sexual orientation.

In time I was to be proved wrong about George's dislike of Hepburn. During the years that followed I would remain close to both of them and throughout that period George and Hepburn would turn out to be the very best of friends. They understood one another. I would eventually also learn that Hepburn relied heavily on George's opinions about her career. She hardly ever made a film without consulting him about her performance.

After Hepburn had left, as the afternoon wore on, George suggested we take a dip in the pool. Afterward, I followed him upstairs to his bedroom. He closed the door behind us and we undressed, dried off, and flopped onto his bed. He moved over to me, began to fondle my balls, then rapidly stroked me to a full erection. In no time at all he started to suck on my erect penis. He was so good at what he was doing that before I knew it I was dizzy with ecstasy and simply lay back until I experienced an absolutely exquisite orgasm. As soon as it was all over George daintily hopped off the bed, disappeared into the bathroom, and took a shower. When he came out he politely asked me to take a shower, too, and then, putting it as nicely as he could, intimated that it was time for me to leave.

I learned that this was George Cukor's strictly adhered to modus operandi when it came to sex. There was never any foreplay or necking. There was no preamble, nor was there ever any form of penetration. Anal sex was out of the question. To put it crudely, just like my friend, Cole Porter, George just wanted to suck dick. And he would do it with a quick, cold efficiency. Unlike other men, including Cole, as soon as George had finished there was no time set aside for his partner to bask in the afterglow of orgasm or to reciprocate the favor. He also insisted on slipping me a few bucks when I left. It wasn't long before I realized that George always paid for sex, no matter who his partner was. As the ensuing months and years went by we became extremely close friends and frequently had sex together. I would often fix him up with other young guys, too. He always paid them well but he seldom asked me to bring the same person over more than once.

George was an early riser and usually went to bed at nine o'clock in the evening. He wasn't a night owl at all. Whenever he threw a party it was either a luncheon or a small informal dinner for a select group. There were no midnight gang bangs or orgies for him. Sex was purely a brief diversion from his all-consuming passion, which was his work. His films included *A Star is Born,* the classic drama starring Judy Garland and James Mason. That 1954 production caused him untold headaches. Because of her erratic behavior on set it also fostered his intense dislike of Garland.

"That dreadful woman!" he once confided in me. "What a bitch she is. I'll *never* work with her again. Ever!"

One day, during the making of *A Star is Born*, George and his crew were shooting a very difficult scene on one of the biggest sound-stages on the Warner Bros. lot. There was a huge interior set and the lighting and camera work were unusually complicated. It was ten o'clock in the morning and they had just done one run-through of the scene. There were at least a hundred technicians involved and Sam Leavitt, the director of photography; Gene Allen, the production designer; Malcolm Bert, the art director; and various members of the lighting, camera, grips, sound, and construction crews had a lot of minor tweaking and last-minute alterations to take care of before George could call for a take. Despite the amount of work that needed to be done, the delay was expected to take no more than fifteen or twenty minutes. As everyone knows, when it comes to motion picture production, time is money. Lots of money. Long delays could cost the studio a small fortune. The assistant director announced to everyone over the megaphone that there would be a short wait. Judy Garland plopped down on her chair, sighed, fanned herself with her script, then got up and told the assistant director that she needed to go to the bathroom. She promised that she wouldn't be away for more than ten minutes. Her dressing room and private bathroom were just off to the side of the soundproofed studio. So, off she went. Fifteen minutes later when the assistant director called out, "Places, please, everyone!" there was no sign of Judy.

Major stars always have what are known as stand-ins on the set. It's their job to take the place of the star while camera crews and lighting technicians make adjustments to ensure that the lighting and lens focus on the actors are exactly as the director and the director of photography want them. Judy's stand-in was immediately dispatched to Judy's dressing room to make sure that she was all right and to ask her to kindly return to the set. But a couple of minutes later she returned with the disturbing news that Miss Garland was neither in her dressing room nor her bathroom. Panic rippled through the entire cast and crew. Where could she be? Three assistant directors ran off in various directions to look for her. But Judy was nowhere to be found. Pandemonium broke out. Frantic phone calls were made to other soundstages, to the administration building, to the makeup, hairdressing, and wardrobe departments. But no one had seen Judy. George Cukor was the only one who suspected what might have happened. From past experience he knew that Garland occasionally exhibited moody and erratic behavior. And there was a story behind that. As a seventeen-year-old, during the filming of *The Wizard of Oz* at MGM in 1939, she had been kept on what amounted to a starvation diet to maintain her trim figure. She had also been pumped up with caffeine and amphetamines to sustain her energy level. This had kept her wide awake at night so she was given barbiturates to help her sleep. As a result Garland had become addicted to tranquilizers and other drugs. She became unstable, moody, and prone to depression.

"Call all the gates," Cukor ordered. "Ask anyone if they saw her go out."

Sure enough, the guard at one of the main studio security gates reported that he had seen Garland come out of the soundstage, walk over to her car, which was parked in a private bay nearby, and get into it. She had driven up to the gate smiling broadly and waved as the guard opened it to let her out. She had turned onto West Olive Avenue and drove away from the studio, disappearing into traffic. No one could reach her anywhere for the next two days. She wasn't at home and she wasn't with friends; nobody knew where she had gone.

On the third day after her sudden departure she returned to the set. No explanations were given and no apologies were made. She pretended as though nothing had happened. Meanwhile, her absence had caused havoc on the production. Hundreds of people were kept on tenterhooks and the studio absorbed costs that ran into multiple thousands of dollars. As no other sets were ready, the unit could not shoot anything else and the production was now behind schedule. Even when executive producer Jack Warner hauled Garland over the carpet in his office she refused to acknowledge that she had done anything wrong. George told me that this was only one of her many misdeeds during the shooting of the film. He said that she was never on time for her call.

"That cow was never, ever on time. She always kept us waiting. She never explained herself and she never said sorry. Not once. She was an unpredictable, unreliable, untrustworthy, and unrepentant *bitch*!"

IT WAS AROUND this time that I began seeing quite a bit of an old Marine buddy of mine, Tyrone Power. He had just completed what was probably one of his best films, *Captain from Castile,* for Twentieth Century Fox, and was between marriages. He and I would get up to quite a few sexual shenanigans together, and I began arranging tricks for him and some of the other more sophisticated members of the upper echelons of society who were either coming into the gas station or calling me up. These men were not all Hollywood people; some came from the corporate and banking community. I can't think of anyone who would not have jumped at the opportunity to have a fling with Ty Power. He was scandalously handsome. My circle of friends was constantly widening and he was never one to shy away from meeting new people. Women swooned over him and he bedded quite a few of them, but he much preferred men. He would often call me up and ask me to send over a young guy. Some of his sexual tastes were rather odd and offbeat, but none of the guys seemed to mind. He was always meticulously careful about who he saw. He fiercely guarded his reputation at the studio and his position as a highly visible actor, so few outside of a very tight circle could point a finger at him and accuse him of indiscreet behavior.

In addition to seeing to the needs of people in their private homes I was now arranging quick tricks for folks at the gas station itself. This meant that I had to be resourceful. The washroom was situated off to one side of the building, sandwiched between the office, a storeroom, and Mac's service bay. The walls were made of wood and corrugated metal sheeting. I had drilled a little quarter-inch hole about halfway down the wall of the washroom, just below the toilet paper holder. On the other side of the wall was the storeroom. It was a comfortable place to sit and peek through the hole. You could see everything. For five dollars I would allow someone to watch a guy pee or jerk off in there. Penis watching became quite popular and occasionally led to guessing games among voyeurs about who had the longest dick. Sometimes I would arrange for two guys to go into the washroom together and suck each other off, or I would send in a guy with a girl and, unbeknownst to them, while they were enjoying themselves I could make a buck or two on the side by charging folks to watch them perform. I had something for everyone. I catered to them all, be they participants or onlookers.

The single most important component in my growing bag of tricks came as a total surprise. One evening in late 1949 a middle-aged guy by the name of Gene someone-or-other—I can no longer recall his full name—drove into the station. It was just before Bill Booth, the proprietor, took off for the weekend. Gene worked as a lighting technician for Warner Bros. He was constantly on location and was making really good money. He had a wife and nurtured ambitious plans for retiring one day and touring the United States with her. As a treat he had bought himself a big, custom-built trailer, a truly luxurious affair with all modern conveniences. It had a bedroom at either end of it, each equipped with a big double bed. It also boasted a bathroom, a kitchen, a comfortable little living room area, and an entrance in the middle. The trouble was that Gene was away on location so often that he was getting little use out of the trailer and, as an even more pressing problem, he lived on a narrow street high in the Hollywood Hills and had nowhere to park the monster. He realized that he had no option but to store it somewhere. But where? And then he thought of our gas station. Behind the main building and the service bay there was an empty field. It backed up to the lot next door and had been set aside for future development. But for now, it was empty. Was it available for him to park his trailer, he wanted to know. He would be happy to pay us. Would we object to having a trailer parked out there? After he asked Bill Booth about it Bill shrugged his shoulders and looked at me. He said he saw no reason why we couldn't accommodate the guy's request. Bill had already handed over to me so much responsibility in running the gas station that he said he'd leave it to me to decide what to charge the guy. A sum of fifty dollars a month was agreed upon, we shook hands, and that was that.

Gene was overjoyed. Just before he left he pulled me aside and said, "Scotty, I know there are going to be nights when you feel tired or when you work very late and you just don't feel like going home. Well, here's the key to the trailer. Use it whenever you want, pal."

Those words were magic to my ears. A brand-new venue for covert sexual activity had been delivered directly into my hands! The potential was mind-boggling.

In later years many people told me that some of the best memories of their lives were created in that trailer. Once it had been parked on our lot it became one of the busiest places in town. In it I arranged tricks for guys with guys, guys with girls, girls with girls, you name it. There was hardly a night when it wasn't being used.

One person who got good mileage out of that trailer was an extremely good-looking young executive who worked at Warner Bros. I can only recall his name as Dale. He was a well-heeled, important, good-looking guy and had an absolutely gorgeous young wife. A real beauty she was but, alas, not very intuitive. Dale would often call me up and ask me to arrange a quick trick for him in the trailer. He gave me his approximate arrival time and when he got to the gas station I would have a nice girl spread-eagled on one of the beds, raring to go. The thing that makes Dale's story especially interesting is that he would invariably have his wife with him in the car when he came in for his little trick in the trailer. He would pull into the drive, get out of the car, spin a quick tale to her by saying that he was either going to the washroom or to check out some new tires or look at the latest spark plugs in my office, and I would busy myself by washing the windscreen, cleaning out the ashtrays, checking the tires, battery, oil, and water, and generally messing around while he was away. The wife would be preoccupied with her makeup or fiddling around with her compact or brushing her hair and I would be making small talk with her. This always took about ten to fifteen minutes. Meantime, unseen, her husband Dale had quietly slipped behind the gas station and crept into the trailer, eager for the girl he knew was waiting there for him. He was already as hard as a rock and ready to explode by the time he pulled off his trousers. She was so worked up and excited that boom, bang, boom, it was all over within ten minutes. Then he would put his trousers on again, slip the lady twenty bucks, and meander back to his car as if nothing had happened. His wife was none the wiser about what had just occurred. He did this dozens of times and never once did his innocent wife pick up on it!

That trailer proved itself invaluable. But it wasn't always available. If someone was using it when there was more tricking to do in the immediate area I had other venues up my sleeve. Across the street was a bowling alley and next door to that was a two-story brick motel where a sweet, fat old queen was the night manager. If someone came in and picked up one of my young male or female friends while the trailer was occupied, I could call him up and request a room. He would always give me a good discount and I would simply pass the rate on to the evening trick.

Sometimes when business was brisk he would call me up and say, "Hi, Scotty. I see you've got a lot of cars pulling in there tonight. Room three's empty if you want it. It'll be five bucks." Or he'd say, "You can have room seven tonight. Six bucks." I could always send people over there for a half hour. When they were finished he would change the sheets, freshen up the room, call me up, and say, "Three's ready again if you need it."

And so, soon enough, I had quite a slick operation going. I'd always had an entrepreneurial spirit, I guess—I suppose that's what comes from growing up in a household without a lot of money.

7

Turning Tricks

As I reached my teens in Chicago I had become quite a little businessman. My shoe-shine service and newspaper beat were doing well. I had built up a large, steady clientele and people were recommending me to their friends. But admittedly it was not all about shining shoes and selling newspapers. I often went into bars and pool parlors with other objectives in mind. In some of the fancier places a guy would have me buff his shoes until they were gleaming, toss me a two-bit gratuity, and then invite me to come back to his place with him. I never refused and, of course, I always knew that the sole purpose of those little excursions was sex—which meant money. To use the slang term for it, I had begun "turning tricks." The word had many definitions. It could refer to a prearranged sexual encounter, or it might simply imply a casual sexual acquaintance. It could also be used to refer to the person you were having sex with, especially when there was no emotional or romantic bond involved. The word could even be used as a verb, as in a sentence like, "Are you tricking that guy?" or as a noun, as in, "She's my trick tonight." I was learning fast.

Exposure to the effects of alcohol and the heavy drinking of some of the guys in the bars where I plied my trade induced in me a profound distaste for alcoholic drinks. That's when I became an avowed teetotaler.

Momma remarried in 1935. Her new husband was a good-natured Welshman by the name of John Davies. At first he worked in a soybean processing plant owned by the Spencer Kellogg Company, but he subsequently became a truck driver. He was a nice guy and we kids all got along fine with him. However, his income wasn't nearly enough to support us all, so the tips I was making from tricks served our family well. We had already moved twice by this time and after our new stepdad entered the picture we settled in a little apartment at 3801 Ellis Avenue in the South Side. While many people in our neighborhood were struggling during the long years of the Depression our stepdad, Momma, Don, Phyllis, and I always had enough to eat. Our kitchen shelves were fully stocked. In fact, all of our basic needs were met. Momma was able to stop working as hard as she had when we first arrived in the city and, under the difficult circumstances of the prevailing economic climate, things were really not all that bad for us. Amazingly, despite the late nights and other distractions, I never once missed a day of school and I still managed to get pretty good grades. I kid you not. I've always been diligent about everything I do. Sex, science, and shoe-shining all received equal attention!

By 1936 I started taking my shoe-shine box and my pile of newspapers deep into the North Side and the Loop areas of the city. This meant taking streetcars or the "El," the nickname for the extensive elevated railroad rapid-transit system that served downtown Chicago and many of the suburbs.

Many a time a guy would take me home and invite a few friends over to join in the fun. I didn't mind that at all. It was good for business. I would remain in the bedroom and the men would come in to see me one at a time. The sex consisted of a variety of activities. Most of the guys would get their rocks off by thrusting their penis between my lubed-up legs; others would jack off on me, while others would simply want oral sex. On a few occasions when I was invited to someone's home I would see as many as fifteen people in the space of two or three hours. As each of them finished, got dressed, and filed out of the bedroom they would leave me a few coins or as much as a dollar bill. By the time the evening was finished I was substantially better off than when I arrived.

In some dive bars in these parts of town there were poker games going on, usually in a smoke-filled back room. The players were usually fat, middle-aged men, who smoked imported cigars and cussed incessantly. Just about every single one of them wore a wedding ring. When I walked into the room with my newspapers and my shoe-shine box I was always amazed at how quickly the ambience changed. The atmosphere and mood softened. The cussing stopped. The joke that someone was telling suddenly hung suspended in midair.

"Ah, here's Scotty," one would say, and then they would turn to look at me. There would be a nod here, a wink there, a little wave over there. After I had crawled around underneath the table to give each of them a shoe-shine one of them would invariably leave the game by mumbling, "Deal me out, Joe," then get up, lead me into a small anteroom next door, sit down, open his arms, and, still fully dressed, invite me to cuddle up against his hot, sweaty body. With his armpits dank and odorous and the smell of liquor and cigar smoke heavy on his breath he would just sit there and clutch me tightly, either stroking my hair or gently caressing my cheek. He just wanted to hold me close for a few minutes. Then, after a while, with not a word being spoken, he would begin to rub his crotch against me. As his excitement mounted he would unbutton his fly and eventually erupt in an orgasm that made every inch of his fat, flabby frame quiver. I would remain locked up tightly against him as his heart pounded and his breathing slowly returned to normal. Then he would gently maneuver me away from him, look me up and down, force a smile across his stubbly face, and hand me a dollar. Not a word would be said. On a couple of occasions I could detect moisture welling up in the guy's eyes as he looked at me and I can swear that once a tiny tear ran down one of their cheeks.

Sometimes, when a man left the room, another would come in and go through the same motions with me. If not, I would quietly leave, passing the players at their poker game without any of them so much as looking at me. I felt truly sorry for some of those men. I'm certain that despite their loud, gregarious, and aggressive behavior they were extremely lonely. They must have led frustrating, unhappy family lives. Even though they clearly had wives at home, they no doubt all saw hookers regularly for sex, but I guess I brought something else, something indefinable—perhaps a reminder of their own youth—back into their lives. The Depression was like that. It exposed the best and the worst in people, but it also had the effect of tearing out the deepest and most secret recesses of the soul, bringing them out for all to see.

I was totally open-minded and happy to participate in gay sex but I most welcomed those occasions when a guy arranged a ménage à trois with a wife or a girlfriend he wanted me to service or share. Although most of the men I saw were gay, many were bisexual or straight, and quite a few were married. Some of them derived pleasure by simply watching me have sex with their wives. They would sit in a chair in a shadowed corner of the bedroom quietly smoking or sipping a beer, eagerly watching the performance. It was during one of these heterosexual encounters with a man's wife that I experienced my very first vaginal ejaculation. Although I still give credit to Frank Risnick for my first orgasm I suppose that the first occasion that I came inside a woman's vagina was technically and clinically the real moment that I lost my virginity. I sure wish I could remember the lady's name. But I don't. In fact, I'm sad to say that I can't even recollect what she looked like. Nevertheless, it was a life-altering experience; from that moment on I knew what my preference was. I had nothing against gay sex. Far from it. I had no compunction about doing whatever a guy paid me to do, but for me, sex with a woman was always more satisfying.

Even though I was blessed with a very healthy libido and sex drive, and despite all my sexual activity, if the truth be told I had not yet reached full physical maturity. I was still in my midteens. My package was still growing and if my natural equipment was not yet sufficient to satisfy the ladies I would resort to other methods to please them. I was already quite proficient at cunnilingus or, to dispense with cold clinical terminology, "sucking pussy." There were married women who would arrange for me to come over to their homes when their husbands weren't around to perform oral sex on them. They were never hesitant to tell me that the men in their lives nearly always demanded oral sex but seldom reciprocated. So my services in that department were increasingly in demand. In the more fashionable and well-to-do parts of town these ladies would often favor me with generous gratuities far in excess of those handed over by their spouses and gentleman counterparts.

It had long become obvious to me that sex played an enormous role in human affairs. Speaking for myself, I wasn't infatuated with it simply because of money or raging hormones. This wasn't just some passing physical phase that I was going through. To some extent *everyone* had sex on their minds a great deal of the time. It was blatantly clear that it was an integral and essential part of human nature. Sex defines much of who we are and what we do. It exerts immeasurable force on our thoughts and actions. I always wondered why the conventional attitude toward sex was so ridiculously uptight and conservative. I know the Victorians had a lot to do with it, but the ancient Hindus, Greeks, and Romans had dispensed with sexual taboos thousands of years ago. Why couldn't we take a lesson from them? The rigid contemporary attitude toward sex made no sense to me at all. All it did was stifle people's natural drives, causing untold suffering and unnecessary guilt.

DURING THESE YEARS a roaring prostitution trade was under way on the South Side of the city. There were areas where four or five whorehouses jostled alongside one another on a single block. In each of them there were about two dozen pretty, scantily clad young girls with peroxide-dyed hair, wearing little more than lacy, see-through robes. They sat around in groups in the front parlor, their legs either crossed or splayed wide apart as they lounged on enormous couches and padded armchairs. The furniture was piled high with garish plush pillows and the windows were always covered with faded velvet drapes. Most of these alluring ladies would be smoking, painting their toenails, or checking their overdone makeup in the tiny mirrors of their cheap little compacts as they giggled and whispered to one another. The average age of these prostitutes was somewhere between sixteen and twenty. Many were barely out of school. And they all charged a dollar for their services. A portion of that fee went to the madams or owners of the bordellos. But that was the standard price. It was a buck for a fuck. Or for a blow job. You could take your pick.

Streetwalkers, on the other hand, were in a better position to bargain with their clients. Few of them had pimps. The starting price was always a dollar but you could easily talk that down to as low as fifty or thirty-five cents. These ladies of the night were so desperate to earn something that a guy could often get a blow job for as little as a quarter. Sex was a major industry during those lean and troubled years. It not only provided a welcome relief from the harsh reality of everyday life but was also a lifesaver for many young people who simply could not find legitimate work elsewhere.

I wasn't the only kid in town turning tricks. Other guys did it, and so did girls. And many of them tricked women—at first I was surprised to learn about it but it didn't take the brains of a rocket scientist to realize that it was perfectly normal. Some guys liked guys. Some women preferred only women. That's how things were. End of story. I met quite a few lesbians as I moved around the city, and if any of the men I saw wanted a young girl for their gay wives, girlfriends, or sisters, I could always connect them with someone I knew.

* * *

•Turning Tricks•

ONE OF THE FEMALE TEACHERS at the Oakenwald school that Don, Phyllis, and I attended had a brother who everyone knew was gay. I don't remember their names but they lived together, not too far away from the school campus. I had met him at one of the gay group-sex sessions at someone's apartment on the South Side. He was a pleasant enough sort of guy, probably in his early twenties, and quite good-looking. He had taken a shine to me and so I saw him privately now and again, always when his sister wasn't at home, though I suspected that she secretly knew about our little get-togethers. One day while I was over there he was giving me a blow job and she walked in on us. He didn't seem to mind but I was a little uncomfortable about it. After all, this was a teacher at my school. I pulled on my trousers and got ready to make my getaway but as I went through the tiny living room she stopped me at the front door, put her hand on my shoulder, smiled, and calmly invited me to sit down. When I saw her brother sitting cross-legged in one of the chairs, still stark naked and nonchalantly smoking a cigarette, I eased up a bit. He threw me a friendly and reassuring smile. She went on to tell me that it wasn't only her brother who liked people of the same sex, and that she had similar inclinations. In fact, as she offered me a plate of cookies, she confided in me about how she liked young girls.

"Next time you come over, Scotty," she cooed, "do you think you can bring someone for me, too?"

I shrugged and searched for words but before I could say anything she went on.

"Just don't say anything to anyone, okay? Especially at school."

No problem, I thought. I totally got the message.

There was a very pretty, good-natured young girl with long brown hair in my class who I knew came from a very poor family. I heard that her father had been unemployed for years. While he was out looking for work, her mother stood in breadlines, collecting whatever she could to take home to feed her three children. They could certainly do with some extra cash I thought, so, as discreetly as I could, I asked her whether she would be interested in seeing the teacher. I made it very clear that physical intimacy would be involved and that she would receive a monetary reward for it. I held my breath as she took it all in, expecting to be walloped over my head at any moment. She looked away for a couple of minutes and then turned to me and nodded. How could she refuse? She knew the money would come in handy. I hugged her. We now shared a secret, a special thing, and the next time I went over to the teacher's house to see her brother the girl came along, too.

In 1938, at the age of fifteen, I started high school at Tilden Technical School at the corner of Union and Forty-seventh streets, not too far away from the notorious Chicago stockyards. Things would remain much the same for me for the next three and a half years. The Depression continued its throttling hold on society. I pursued my double life at night, accumulating experiences, perspectives, and cash. Within a year war came to Europe and my newspaper sales skyrocketed. Don finally found himself a girlfriend. In time, he, Phyllis, and I gave Momma a secondhand radio that I had bought for a few dollars at a pawnshop downtown for her birthday. With it she listened to all her favorite music, especially the big bands and shows like *The Shadow, The Burns and Allen Show,* and the *Mercury Theater on the Air,* including the famous 1938 Halloween broadcast of Orson Welles's production of "The War of the Worlds." Life went on, and few of us could foresee what was coming.

8

Boot Camp

The Japanese attack on Pearl Harbor gave America an enormous jolt. The only positive thing that came out of the unexpected offensive was the fact that the country was grabbed by the scruff of its neck and forcibly yanked out of its long Depression. We hardly knew what hit us but employment shot up overnight as industry speedily swung into action to create the machinery of war. When we kids gathered around Momma's radio to listen to a scratchy broadcast of President Roosevelt talking about the bombing of the U.S. Pacific Fleet we were not sure what to do. But clearly everyone was being swept into the conflict. Just a couple of weeks after hostilities began I rushed over to my best buddy Bill Nall's house.

Bill was as straight as an arrow. He was a red-blooded, all-American male, but to help him make ends meet I occasionally fixed him up with gay or straight tricks. Like all of us, he needed extra cash. Both of us became caught up in the pervasive spirit of patriotism, eager to join in the fray against the enemy. So one day we headed for the nearest recruiting station and, despite Momma's tearful objections, we signed up. In January 1942 I waved good-bye to my family and a handful of friends who slowly diminished in size as they stood on the platform while my train chugged out of Union Station. I was eighteen years of age, bound for boot camp in San Diego, California.

What really appealed to Bill and me was the potential excitement of frontline action. We were anxious to fight so we had joined the branch of the service that would best fulfill our ambitions, the Marine Corps. Marine recruits were paid $50 a month for serving, but I didn't find this figure very enticing. After all, I was already earning close to that kind of money during my ventures around town. So I opted for something that paid more. I decided to become a Marine Paratrooper. Jumping out of aircraft was deemed such a difficult, dangerous, and demanding occupation that we were paid an extra $50 a month. I didn't care about the dangers. I just wanted that extra fifty bucks. As the train rumbled across the Great Plains and the prairies toward the west my excitement grew. I was leaving the state of Illinois for the first time in my life and a great adventure lay ahead. With mounting eagerness I looked forward to my twelve weeks of military training.

The Paratroopers were a brand-new, highly specialized unit of the United States Marine Corps. They were being honed for a crucial task. As I understood it, their primary purpose was to be dropped from the air to what was known as the Burma Road, a strategically important seven-hundred-mile stretch of roadway cut through the mountainous jungle linking Burma and China. It had fallen into Japanese hands after they invaded the Burmese mainland. In support of troops from the United Kingdom, Australia, and New Zealand, the objective of the Paratroopers was to wrest the road from Japanese control and to reopen critical Allied supply lines.

When boot camp got underway I was so enamored with the handsome pose I struck in uniform that I had a picture taken of myself and sent it to Momma. I think she kept that photo on her dresser for the rest of her life. As an ex–farm boy I had a good, lean, hard body. I felt very comfortable in my own skin. I had brown hair and blue eyes, I stood about five feet ten, and was happy with my physique. A lot of my sexual partners, both male and female, praised my looks but inwardly I didn't feel anything special about myself. As far as I was concerned I was just a regular, clean-cut, all-American boy.

Training was tough and made me fitter than I had ever been. A few weeks elapsed before we were ready to be sent to sea to engage in combat. The Pacific War was raging. All we knew was that our first objective would be to attack a number of Japanese-occupied islands. Needless to say, like most of the other guys, I was nervous about what was coming. How on earth were we Paratroopers going to jump onto those fortified islands that we were hoping to take from the Japanese? Because there weren't any airfields near the islands, we would have to be put ashore by landing craft. Once we got onto the islands how were we going to get off them? A million questions haunted me but I guess, like all the other three thousand young men who had become Marine Paratroopers, I tried to dismiss such thoughts from my mind. What was the point of thinking about it? What was the sense in contemplating failure or capture or death? So, for the time being, we resolved to play as hard as we could before we went into battle. With few exceptions, we had one primary objective in mind: to screw ourselves silly.

As we had some time before being shipped out, a group of us got a weekend pass and decided to take a trip up the coast to visit Los Angeles. After all, the City of Angels was home to Hollywood, the film industry, and all those glamorous movie stars I had admired as a kid. In addition to looking for a little carnal action the prospect of catching even the briefest glimpse of one of those sexy actresses was enough of a reason for me to make the pilgrimage. The only way for us to get there was to hitchhike. Dozens of guys were always standing on the side of the road thumbing rides. Fortunately, folks were only too happy to help out. You never had to wait long to be offered a ride, especially if you were in uniform. The vistas of the glimmering Pacific Ocean were breathtaking as we made our way northward. Halfway up the coast we passed the Del Mar Racetrack, a famous venue renowned for its high stakes horse racing. Back in those days the road between San Diego and Los Angeles hugged the coast all the way, unlike today when traffic speeds along the 405 freeway slightly inland. As we drove by the grandstands, parking lot, and wide, sweeping racetrack I noticed that the place seemed desolate. And then we passed a big hand-painted sign that announced OWNED & OPERATED BY BING CROSBY & PAT O'BRIEN. SORRY, WE ARE CLOSED DURING THE WAR. WE WILL REOPEN WHEN HOSTILITIES ARE OVER.

My heart skipped quite a few beats as I caught my first sight of the famous Hollywoodland sign perched high on Mount Lee in the Hollywood Hills overlooking L.A. After being dropped off in Hollywood we each decided to go our own way. Unfortunately, I didn't see anyone famous as I did the traditional pub crawl through the dives and dens of Hollywood and the Sunset Strip. Aside from being underage, I was a confirmed teetotaler, so I didn't go there to drink. No, what I was looking for that Saturday evening as I prowled Hollywood Boulevard was whatever sexual diversion I could find. With twelve long weeks of boot camp training behind me I was as horny as hell. I was ready to fuck anyone. But nothing happened. Yes, there was the odd hooker here and there, but no starlets ready for action. No glamorous actresses dying to get me into bed with them. Then, just as I was about to give up and look elsewhere, a car horn sounded. I looked over to the boulevard and saw a dark, good-looking guy in his early forties waving from behind the wheel of a fancy convertible. I had no idea who he was so I kept on walking. The horn sounded again.

"Hey, over there!" I heard him shout.

I looked over at the convertible again. Yes, no doubt about it. It was definitely me that he was waving at.

"Excuse me," he called. "May I ask you something?"

Me? I thought. *What could he want?* I wandered over to the edge of the sidewalk where he had stopped his car. I noticed that he was immaculately dressed. *A real dandy,* I thought. He asked whether I was lost. I was going to respond but before I could he stretched over and opened the passenger door for me. Then it hit me. Of course. I was being picked up. He introduced himself to me as Jack. As we pulled away and merged into traffic he came out with the frank admission that he had been cruising the boulevard in search of a trick. Being the car culture city that it is, Los Angeles has always been the quintessential cruising capital of the world.

"I haven't seen you around before," he said. "You cut quite a figure in that uniform of yours, you know."

I was flattered but didn't really know what to say so I just sat back and let whatever was going to happen play itself out. Excitement mounted as we drove down Hollywood Boulevard, passing famous landmarks such as Grauman's Chinese Theatre and the Egyptian Theatre. We drove all the way over to Jack's place in an area called Los Feliz. As soon as we arrived he started pawing me. In no time we stripped off our clothes. After an hour or two of oral and anal sex we sat, pretty well exhausted, in his elegant bedroom. Clearly, this was a man who had taste. And money. Lots of it. He told me his real name was John Kelly and that he had been born in Australia. He said he was a costume designer in the film industry and went by the professional name of Orry-Kelly. Had I heard about him? I was embarrassed to say no, I hadn't. Well, never mind, he assured me. And then he began to rattle off the names of some of the pictures he had worked on. These included the 1933 version of *42nd Street, Gold Diggers of 1933, Gold Diggers of 1937, Hollywood Hotel,* and classics like *Dark Victory; The Private Lives of Elizabeth and Essex; All This, and Heaven Too; The Maltese Falcon; Kings Row; Now, Voyager;* and, the production he was working on at the time of our meeting, a little movie starring Humphrey Bogart and Ingrid Bergman called *Casablanca.* (In later years he would be recognized for the excellence of his craft by winning no less than three Academy Awards.)

Jack knew a lot of people in town and over the next few weekends I got passes from camp and made my way up to L.A. to meet many of them. I began to turn a lot of tricks during those brief getaways and the money I was making from them came in handy. There I was, an unsophisticated farm boy from Illinois, suddenly immersed in the highest circles of Hollywood's creative society. It was amazing. *This is all right*, I thought. I could get used to this lifestyle. Daunted though I may have been, I nevertheless seemed to fit right in. I went with the flow and saw a different guy every time I went up to L.A. Each was more influential, more famous, and richer than the last. The degree of sexual frankness was a real eye-opener. Anything and everything were regarded as the norm. Nothing was too outrageous. I attended innumerable expensive, classy orgies where the participants were all wealthy, famous, and sophisticated. And everyone paid me very well for my services.

This was my first glimpse into a whole other world. I was also learning a completely new language, one that embraced the terminologies and slang words in vogue in the gay world at that time. A gay man was playfully referred to as a "jelly bean." A man who had a preference for oral sex, especially if he had the inclination to suck on another man's dick until he ejaculated in his mouth, was referred to as being "on the stem." A guy who had a smaller than average penis was often amusingly dismissed as a "PTM," which stood for "princess tiny meat."

"Oh, don't bother with her," someone would say. "She's PTM."

Men who were obviously effeminate and who worked in department stores, especially in the ladies' departments, were called "ribbon queens."

"Queen" was a particularly popular word. It was most often used to describe an openly homosexual and more mature man, rather than a youngster in his teens. Although originally intended as a derogatory term for someone who was gay, no one really seemed to mind it. In fact, mature gay men were quite content to refer to one another as queens. Younger gay men, especially teenagers or those in their early twenties, were simply called "twinkies." An older man who preferred a twinkie as a sexual partner was called a "twinkie queen."

One of the queens that I was introduced to by Jack, or Orry-Kelly if you prefer, was William Haines. We all called him Bill. He was a dark, sensuous, good-looking forty-two-year-old guy from Virginia who had enjoyed a very successful career as a movie actor, at one point having been the country's number-one male box office draw. Surprisingly, he had given up acting in the thirties to become an interior designer and decorator. Rumor had it that when he was still acting he had stormed out of Metro-Goldwyn-Mayer mogul Louis B. Mayer's office when he insisted that Bill give up his relationship with his male lover, Jimmie Shields, because if the public heard about his homosexuality it would have generated bad publicity for the studio.

"My happiness with Jimmie is more important than my career in your lousy motion pictures, Mr. Mayer," Bill is reputed to have said. Well, that put a swift end to his acting career. His new life as a designer blossomed and soon Bill was at the top of the heap of interior designers in Hollywood.

One weekend Bill and Jimmie were invited to go up the coast to spend a weekend at Hearst Castle, the legendary retreat of newspaper magnate William Randolph Hearst. They accepted the invitation provided, they told Hearst, they could bring me along with them. Hearst agreed, so, armed with another weekend pass, I rushed up to L.A. and off we went to Hearst's splendid home in Bill's brand new Lincoln.

Everyone who was anyone in Hollywood at the time got an invitation to Hearst Castle. If you were asked over for a weekend it meant that you had made it. It was the dream of every star, every producer, every writer, and every wannabe to be invited there. You would arrive at about midmorning on Saturday, spend the night, and then leave after tea on Sunday afternoon. Hearst himself welcomed us in the library an hour or two after we arrived and then got us settled into our guest bedrooms. He was polite but pretty lukewarm to me, mainly, I guess, because I was still a kid. There were far more important people around for him to fuss over. But his girlfriend, Marion Davies, was charming and welcoming, and she and I struck up a friendship that weekend that would endure for many years.

Hearst's vast, sprawling complex overlooking the Pacific near San Simeon on the Central Coast of California was the inspiration for Xanadu, the fabulous house in Orson Welles's immortal *Citizen Kane*. Not in my wildest imagination did I ever dream that a place like that existed. I was truly out of my depths. My head still swirls when I think back on that incredible weekend. The guest list consisted of Hollywood royalty and there were more movie stars in attendance than I could count. The luxurious bedrooms, the wood paneling, the Italian marble, the imported European fixtures, the paintings, the tapestries, the Roman pool, the extravagant meals with the bewildering array of glassware and cutlery at each place setting, the cavalcade of butlers, waiters, and maids, the fancy food and wine, the stunning fashions, the dancing, the music, the libraries, the private zoo, the beautiful movie theater, the gardens, the lawns, the private airfield, the flashy automobiles, Mr. Hearst's magnificent personal yacht moored at his personal jetty at his personal beach. It is all still a magnificent montage of breathtaking wonders, even now, decades later. The memories I have of it are from a lost era, of another time, of a place relegated to a glorious and irretrievable past.

One Saturday afternoon on another weekend away from camp I was strolling down one of the main arteries through Hollywood when a guy who was out cruising stopped and picked me up. He introduced himself as Frank Horn. We went over to his place, where we spent the weekend together. He was movie actor Cary Grant's private secretary and apparently he was responsible for coercing Grant to leave the East Coast and come to California, where he became one of the most successful and sought-after male romantic stars of all time. Horn was originally a stage manager. He had met Grant when Grant was a sixteen-year-old singer in a variety show in New York. At that time Grant still used his real name, Archie Leach. He had been sent over to Broadway from his native England to perform in the show and Horn had taken him under his wing. Horn was a sassy old queen with a naughty sense of humor. He told me that he often liked to walk his dog around the neighborhood wearing nothing but an overcoat. Whenever he passed a cute young guy or someone he knew he'd flash them and roar with laughter at their horrified reaction. He wanted to know whether I would like to meet Cary Grant and, of course, I agreed, so a couple of weekends later I was back in town and he took me over to Grant's beach house near Malibu.

Cary Grant was as suave in real life as he was on the screen. He was the quintessential Mr. Smooth. He was forty years old when I met him and everything he did was executed in precise, dapper, and debonair style. Perhaps the most well-known films that he had starred in by then were *Gunga Din* and *The Philadelphia Story*. He would walk into the room and the ambience would change immediately. You instinctively felt a presence, an indefinable sense of classiness, whenever he appeared. He was married to Barbara Hutton at the time, although she wasn't around when I met him. That did not surprise me. The day I was introduced to him he was actually sharing the house with another actor, Randolph Scott. Need I say more?

Randy Scott took an instant liking to me. He was a ruggedly handsome man of forty-six who, well over six feet tall, towered over me. He had carved a very successful career for himself primarily in Westerns, with more than fifty films to his credit. He was a big guy but as sweet as can be. He was married to Patricia Stillman, who was also not around that day, and it was patently clear to me that he and Cary Grant were more than mere friends. The proof arrived that first weekend that I spent with them. The three of us got into a lot of sexual mischief together. Aside from the usual sucking—neither of them were into fucking, at least not fucking guys, or at least not me—what I remember most about that first encounter was that Scott really liked to cuddle, and talk, and was very gentle. Grant was nice as well, though Scott was even more of a gentleman. He even drove me back down the coast to Camp Elliott in San Diego on Sunday evening—a four-hour drive each way, undertaken during the difficulties of wartime gas rationing.

I really liked those two men, and they were obviously very good for one another. In future years I would be seeing a lot of them. Theirs was a relationship that would last a long time, with the two of them eventually sharing a home together behind the famed Chateau Marmont Hotel in Hollywood as well as the Malibu beach house. I don't know if their wives ever knew what was going on between them. I never asked.

On another local weekend pass I was on my way to pick up a pretty sixteen-year-old girl I had met in the nearby town of El Cajon, near San Diego. I really had the hots for her and planned on taking her downtown, where I intended to rent a room at a once plush hotel on Broadway called the San Diego. We duly met and went there, both of us eager to hop into the sack. As we walked through the door I was surprised to see my fellow Marine, movie idol Tyrone Power, in the lobby. Ty was in the Marine Air Wing as a trainee pilot. He was a major box-office star and a heartthrob for millions worldwide. My girlfriend was utterly speechless when she saw him. He was already very famous for his roles in films such as *Jesse James* and *A Yank in the R.A.F.* but his real claim to fame was as a swashbuckling hero in historic movies such as *The Mark of Zorro* and *Blood and Sand*. Power was a dark and strikingly handsome man. His brilliant smile could knock you off your feet. The ladies worshipped him and he had a huge international bevy of fans, both male and female. Every woman on the planet wanted to bed him and every man wanted to look exactly like him. Yet here he was, in a joint notorious for renting rooms by the hour.

With my girl clinging to my arm in awestruck wonder, Power and I planned our strategy. We went up to my rented room for a series of exciting ménage à trois sexcapades. Ty Power was married at the time but I had heard rumors that the relationship was on the rocks, mainly because of meddling from the studio bosses at Twentieth Century Fox, where he was on contract. As we romped around that rather grimy little hotel room that night it was patently clear to me that Ty had a healthy and inventive sexual appetite, but one that was infinitely more focused on me than it was on my girlfriend. I felt truly sorry for the poor guy. It must have been very tough for him to have to perpetually hide who he really was. We would get to know one another very well after the war but, at that time, there was still a great battle to be fought.

BACK AT CAMP ELLIOTT, as my pal Bill Nall's and my own departure for the Pacific approached, we grew impatient. In between training we spent hours in camp drumming our fingers and tapping our feet, nervously awaiting our call to duty. Fortunately, on weekends, a lot of the guys would still get passes. On Monday mornings we always had the awkward task of covering for buddies who hadn't made it back in time. At roll call the sergeant would call out names, one at a time. As he did so he'd hear a loud, "Here!," "Here!," "Here!"

When he was finished the sergeant would look around, squint at us suspiciously, and then yell, "You little bastards! I called out sixty names and all of them answered! But look around you! There are only twenty of you bozos on parade! Get down and gimme twenty." And down we would go and do twenty push-ups. Some form of additional disciplinary action would follow, such as cleaning out the latrines and showers, or peeling potatoes, but it was all taken in good spirit. There was no time for unnecessary or excessive punishment. This wasn't a movie; this was the real thing. There was a war on.

In June 1942, we shipped out on the transporter USS *Rocham-beau,* bound for Hawaii. Finally, my role in World War II was about to begin.

9

Into Battle

Our first port of call was Hawaii, where the ship took on more Marines. Adrenaline was building now that we knew we were going into combat. Some of the guys yearned for a little fun and games during the voyage, but any form of sexual hanky-panky was strictly ruled out. And God help anyone in the U.S. Marine Corps who was ever found out to be a homosexual or, in more vulgar lingo, a "queer," "homo," "pervert," "faggot," "fag," or "fairy." Anyone found eyeing up, let alone making a sexual overture toward another man would pay severely for his transgression. He would be beaten to a pulp by his fellow Marines, then subjected to severe military discipline. There was such a stigma against it that heaven help any guy who developed a hard-on while showering with his colleagues. He would be immediately branded a fag and subjected to ridicule and torment. Nevertheless, there were exceptions to this archaic state of affairs. The medical group in the Marine Corps came directly from the Navy. They were known as Navy Corpsmen. As has been the case in navies for centuries, quite a few of them happened to be gay. We called them "pill pushers" or "chancre mechanics." Chancre was the medical term for the ulcerated lesions guys developed during the early stage of syphilis. Some degree of gay behavior among Corpsmen would be tolerated and overlooked by the top brass but they still had to be careful. I was very good at fitting in and fell into line. As some queens say about being with a bunch of straight people, you have to be careful not to tip your hat.

After Hawaii we headed southwest to American Samoa, where we picked up another large contingent of Marines. After that we went to Fiji, where we underwent extensive training by practicing landing on the beaches. By day and by night, carrying a whopping seventy pounds of gear, we ran up the beach from the surf, dove into whatever natural cover we could find, and then dug foxholes. It was tortuous and exhausting, but it was valuable training. From Fiji we boarded a naval vessel carrying Higgins amphibious landing craft. These were thirty-six-feet-long shallow draft vessels made of plywood, with metal shielding on the sides to protect the men inside from enemy fire. They had a flat metal drop-down ramp in front to allow quick access to the beach. Our ship headed for our next destination, the island of New Caledonia. This was a noncombat zone and an important U.S. staging and supply center. It was there that we were told we were being prepared for a big offensive against the Japanese-held island of Guadalcanal. Although we Paratroopers had been trained for deployment from the sky, because of a lack of nearby airfields, the only way we were going to be able to invade the Pacific Islands was from the sea.

The invasion began in the predawn hours. As silently as we could, thousands of us from the First Marine Division prepared to storm the beaches. There wasn't enough time to think too much about anything before the Higgins boats were launched from our transport ship. With their motors growling they swiftly pulled up alongside the ship and we were ordered to scamper down netted ladders that had been thrown over the sides of the transport ship. It was agony trying to climb down those things with our heavy kits and rifles. The ladders swung out as the ship listed, then banged against the side of the gray hull. If you weren't slammed to your death you could easily be crushed between the ship and the Higgins boat. It was a nightmare. Once we were huddled inside the landing craft the engine screamed to full revs and we lurched toward the island. The invasion of Guadalcanal had begun, and there was no turning back.

When the boat reached shore, the front ramp was dropped down and we were ordered to storm the beach. Splashing through the surf, surrounded by a hail of machine gun fire, we ran for our lives. I can hardly remember the details of what happened. It is all a haze now. But somehow or another most of us made it, scampering into the foliage and digging ourselves in. How we survived I still don't know. There were many brutal close encounters with the Japanese all over the island during the weeks that followed. After some gruesome fighting the First Marine Division was withdrawn from Guadalcanal in December 1942. By then, the island was firmly held by units of the U.S. Army. As we shipped out we tallied our casualties. In our division 650 had been killed, 1,278 wounded, 31 were missing in action, and over 8,000 were suffering from malaria. We Marines shared a camaraderie that is unique in America's fighting forces. We went through so much together that watertight bonds were formed. We thought of each other as brothers, and those deaths affected us all on a very personal level. On December 18, I leaned over the railings of our naval transport ship watching the island slip beneath the horizon as we made our way toward Australia. I was fortunate to still be alive and unhurt. I was one of the lucky ones.

AFTER BEING BRIEFLY STATIONED in New Caledonia I joined the Third Division and, for whatever reason, we spent a month back on Guadalcanal where all hostilities had now ceased. We didn't mind the interlude but I still have no idea why we spent so much time there. Surprisingly, the forest and undergrowth had already covered most of the signs that a fierce battle had been fought there. In March 1943 we sailed for the island of Vella Lavella in the Solomon Islands group. By now I had received the exciting news from home that my brother Donald had also joined the Marines. I was really pleased to hear this and hoped that we would not only meet up again soon but see some combat action together. In that same letter I also learned that Momma and Phyllis were both doing well. They had given up the apartment in Chicago and moved back to Ottawa with my stepdad. It made better economic sense for them to be in a small town rather than in the big city. They were renting a small house, not too far from where Grandma Boltman lived. I don't know whether Momma ever saw her anymore now that she and Dad were divorced, and I never ventured to ask. I missed Momma so much, but I knew that she would remain comfortable on the money that was coming in from my Marines pay, augmented by whatever my stepdad was earning

On Vella Lavella we trained on PT boats for three weeks. Intelligence reports revealed that there was a small noncombatant Japanese presence on the island of Choiseul, about fifty miles away, so one night a group of 125 of us were ordered to carry out a raiding party to neutralize them. We set out just after sunset on six PT boats.

By early dawn we reached Choiseul and made contact with an Australian missionary who was stationed on the island. We rendezvoused at an agreed point and he led us to a steep cliff where the locals had secretly knotted together a series of throw-down ladders made from tropical vines. We used these to clamber up the cliffside, reaching the summit before the sun was too high in the sky. The locals were very helpful and led us to a spot where we could observe the Japanese, way on the other side of a thickly forested valley, through our binoculars. It took all day to crawl through that dense and miserable abyss, fighting heat, sweat, mosquitoes, and thirst all the way. Just before we reached the Japanese outpost three of our guys were captured by what must have been a Japanese reconnaissance party. One minute our men were there, and the next minute they were gone.

We were petrified. We didn't know how many more Japanese were around. I could literally hear my heart pounding in my chest. But we pressed on. We approached the Japanese settlement, encircling it as quietly as we could. From thick cover on the perimeter of the clearing we observed a bunch of them sitting at makeshift tables outside a little building made of bamboo. They were laughing and chatting as they ate a meal from little bowls. They were so preoccupied with their food and their conversation that they didn't detect us. We hit them hard with our Thompson submachine guns, Browning automatic rifles, and .45 caliber sidearms. A fierce firefight ensued and then the enemy raiding party that had captured our three buddies appeared out of nowhere and joined in the battle. We fought hard. After a couple of hours not a single Jap remained alive. Six of our own men lay dead. We searched everywhere for the three men who had been captured earlier but they were never found.

Fortunately, we humans have incredibly effective natural defense mechanisms that we aren't even aware of until they are needed. I managed to distance myself enough from all the horrors and suffering and carnage by valuing life and living more than anything else. The device that I used to keep that safety net in place was to believe that I would survive anything and have enough left within me when I got out of that lousy war to enjoy life to the maximum. What I missed most during the war was a nice glass of ice-cold milk and what we Marines called "flat peter," which was nothing more than military slang for pussy. I knew that as long as my penis was intact and my balls in place I was still capable of enjoying the years that I was convinced still lay ahead of me. And I would certainly need that conviction, especially as the war continued. Because the worst was yet to come.

IN 1944 WE RETURNED to the States on the transport ship USS *President Hayes* for a thirty-day furlough. Camp Pendleton, just outside Oceanside on the Southern California coast, had recently become operational and was to be our new base. My pay had dropped by $50 a month because in March 1944 Congress had decided to disband the Marine Paratroopers. On account of the way the war in the Pacific was going, the military brass had decided that dropping Paratroopers on the Burma Road was no longer necessary, and my pay envelope reflected that decision. Nevertheless, my brother Donald was now also in the Corps, so between us we could still ensure that Momma and Phyllis were getting enough financial assistance.

I hadn't seen Momma for more than two years, so I took a train out to Chicago and then a bus to Ottawa. It was strange being back in Illinois, especially in midwinter. I had become used to the tropics and very tolerant of the sunshine, intense heat, and humidity. Yet here I was trudging through a couple of feet of snow again, just as I had done for years as a kid. But I was now almost twenty-one years old, and I felt so much older, so much more worldly and mature. War and travel do that to you. You grow up quickly.

I was delighted to see that Phyllis had turned into a lovely nineteen-year-old woman. Suitors weren't in abundance, as most young men who might have wooed her were in the service. For the three or four days that I spent at home my favorite meals and pies were served and I spent a lot of time relating war stories around the kitchen table. But a furlough was a furlough, and a guy of my age wanted to spend as much time as possible doing other things, like screwing his brains out. Which I certainly did. I took a bus into Chicago, looked up old friends, and made a lot of new ones. I had a great time, more than making up for sexual abstinence in the military. I partied hard and barely got any sleep. Sometimes I needed an ice pack to soothe my overworked dick in the morning. But, alas, nothing that good lasts forever. Before I knew it I was on board a train bound for California.

By the time I returned to Camp Pendleton the Marine Corps had been considerably expanded, so I became a member of the twenty-eighth Marines of the new Fifth Division. My brother Donald had finished boot camp and was also stationed at Camp Pendleton. He and I were now part of the same outfit and we managed to spend a lot of time together catching up. It was great fun having him around and it wasn't until then that I realized how much I had missed him. Don had recently married, having met a woman named Bonnie Feller in San Francisco, where he had been working in a shipyard. They were madly in love and I was truly pleased for him. He never played the field like I did. He was a loyal, devoted, one-woman man.

In late 1944 my shore leave ended and we shipped out to Hawaii for more practice landings on the beaches, mainly intended as training for new guys like Don. But it was time well spent for all of us because from Hawaii we sailed for a destination that we were all beginning to hear about, Iwo Jima. When we left for that tiny Japanese stronghold situated only a thousand miles away from the Land of the Rising Sun itself we had no idea what we were in for.

My good buddy Bill Nall, who had signed up for the Marines on the same day that I did and who was with me throughout the war, was one of the first to be killed. We were in the thick of a bitter battle, attempting to storm a Japanese machine-gun position when I heard the news. I was devastated. I just fell onto my haunches and wept, with bullets whizzing all around me. Little did I know that a day later I was to receive even worse news.

As the following morning broke through a haze of acrid smoke and dust we were still desperately trying to capture that infernal machine-gun position. Dead and wounded Marines lay all around me. Bullets were zinging everywhere. A couple of our guys who had tried to storm the hideout with hand grenades had just been mown down by gunfire and were screaming in agony. Shells continued to burst. My eardrums hurt so much from the noise that it felt like my head was going to splinter into a thousand pieces. Then, through the cacophony of sounds I could hear my name being called. I looked behind me to see a fellow Marine hiding behind a rock, beckoning me to come over. I don't know how or why I did it but I slithered over to him on my stomach and slumped against the rock, breathless and exhausted. He was also panting, his uniform so wet from sweat that it clung to him as though he had been in a rainstorm.

"Got bad news, Scotty," he gasped.

I waited for it.

"It's Don," he said, his eyes glaring at me through the grime and dust that covered his face.

In fits and starts he told me that he had just seen my brother Don get killed no more than a thousand feet away from where I was. He said a shell had exploded near him and that a flying piece of shrapnel had torn right through him, literally cutting him in half at the stomach. Death was instantaneous. It's hard to believe, but as this young guy crouched there spluttering these gory details to me an even more horrifying thing happened: a shell burst just overhead. It took me a few seconds to recover but as I came out of the shock I looked at the other guy and noticed that his eyes had widened to the size of saucers. And then, almost like a slow motion scene in a movie, he looked down at his waist. At the same moment, he dropped his rifle and, with both hands, grasped his stomach. It was too ghastly to be true, but the exact same thing that he had just been describing about my brother had happened to him!

He slowly keeled over, his eyes still wide, not a sound passing his lips. As his body slumped to the ground I could see that a piece of shrapnel had ripped right through his waist. His guts had spewed all over the black, muddy soil. I was so horrified that I couldn't move. I knew his chances of survival were nil. Then he froze, looked at me, and gasped one more time. His eyes glazed, rolled backward in their sockets, and he was dead. I was too stunned to take this all in and simply crawled away, only to stop and retch violently. I will be forever indebted to that poor guy for finding me and for telling me about Don, and I will always mourn his fate. It is impossible for me to forget him. That incident was the single most harrowing thing I experienced during those gruesome years of fighting.

Don was twenty-three years old when he was killed. That kid who told me about his death and whose name I can no longer remember was a lot younger. Both bodies were eventually shipped back home to the States, but who can be certain they were really them? And what difference does it make? No one ever got to see the actual bodies. Momma attended Don's funeral and was presented with a flag. Hopefully, she experienced some kind of closure that eased her grief. As for the other guy, I have no idea where he was buried.

In APRIL 1945 we headed for home, sailing directly to the naval dockyard in Bremerton, near Seattle. During the entire voyage I could think of little else but the desire to play as hard as I could. Needless to say, that included getting as much sex as possible. I wanted to do anything and everything I could to put the horrors and miseries of battle behind me. Like just about every other soul on board that ship I needed to purge myself of all that had happened. Every single one of us was impatient to go ashore. Life took on a new dimension, becoming more precious than ever. The war had taught me an incalculably valuable lesson. After I had seen all those young guys stacked up dead or blown to pieces in that vicious conflict I realized that one of the most important things of all was to stay alive and to rejoice in the gift of every single day. When we finally docked at Bremerton in May 1945, I was transferred to Bainbridge Island Naval Radio Station to await the official end to hostilities.

Two months later, in June, armed with a weekend pass, I went across Puget Sound to Seattle one Saturday evening, ending up in the bar of the Olympic Hotel, which was a very fashionable place in the center of the city. I was sipping an orange juice when I spotted a very nice looking young lady sitting on the other side of the room. I eyed her for a while, until I was certain that she was alone, and then I went over and asked if I could join her. She agreed, albeit a little reluctantly at first, but as the evening wore on we got into some serious talking. Her name was Betty Keller and she told me that she had been married to a Navy officer who had been killed on the air-craft carrier *Yorktown* that had been sunk during the epic Battle of Midway in 1942. She went on to say that she was presently dating another naval officer. However, he had been called out to Bremer-ton to attend to some serious matter that morning. They originally had a date to meet at the hotel that evening and even though he wouldn't be back until Monday morning she decided to come over to the Olympic anyway. By midnight we were exploring each other's bodies in a big, comfortable bed in a room upstairs.

I screwed around with a few other girls during the next few months but I really liked Betty. She was pretty, and there was some-thing else about her that appealed to me. She had no airs. She was a very plain, ordinary, unspoiled sort of a woman. As for the sex, it was okay, but I knew there would never be any real fireworks with her. However, I felt that this was someone who could very well turn out to be a loyal, dependable, reliable, loving woman and someone I certainly wouldn't mind having around and spending time with. We saw each other seven or eight times during the next six weeks.

In August of 1945 the Japanese unconditionally surrendered and the war was over. I was duly discharged from active service and received what they called my "mustering out" pay. This included funds to cover the cost of second-class rail travel back to Illinois. As far as the military was concerned, that's where they were responsible for sending me because that's where I originally enlisted. But I wasn't sure that I wanted to go there. I was thinking more about Califor-nia. Having spent so much time there in training and then at Camp Pendleton I felt a strong attachment to the place. Needless to say, memories of those crazy days hitting the high life of Hollywood were a draw, too. The military tried to persuade me to join the Marine Re-serves, for which I was offered $20 a month, but I wasn't interested.

Fuck that, I thought. *I'm outta here.* And just as well I made that decision because nearly all of my buddies who did sign up for the Reserves were later killed or wounded in the Korean War.

I managed to get a message through to Momma in Ottawa that I might not be coming home. I told her that my prospects for a job were better in California than in the Midwest, even though I had nothing to back up that claim. In typical style she was understanding and empathetic and said that I should do whatever I thought was best. So I made a decision. I invited Betty Keller to come to California with me and I was overjoyed when she said yes. And so began another new chapter in my life.

WE SET UP HOME in a dilapidated little boarding house in Hollywood. And we were happy. I managed to pick up odd jobs here and there: tree trimming, cleaning stoves, driving a cab, and delivering furniture for a store diagonally across the street from a busy gas station on Hollywood Boulevard. The money I earned just about paid the rent and bought us groceries. What more did we need? Well, it turned out that I actually needed quite a bit more. Betty didn't entirely fulfill my sexual needs so I still played around a lot. She either didn't cotton on to that fact, or she simply didn't mind. I'm not sure which. If I stayed out late at night she never once questioned it. That was the kind of woman she was. She just hung back and let me be. You don't often find women like that, I can tell you, and because of it I cared deeply for her. She just wasn't able to provide the sexual excitement and variety that I craved. What else can I say?

In February 1946 I was walking past the gas station near the furniture store where I worked in Hollywood and noticed a HELP WANTED sign outside. I don't know why but I stopped, stared at the sign, and thought to myself, *Why not?* So I walked into the office behind the driveway where the pumps were located. The owner was a rather stout middle-aged man in his early fifties. He was seated at his desk and looked up as I entered, then sized me up and grinned. I told him I was there to talk about the job.

I liked him right away. His name was Bill Booth and he said he was looking for someone to take care of the station and pump gas from about five o'clock in the afternoon until around midnight. He had to head back home to San Pedro, somewhere down the coast in the Long Beach area, at five in order to get home for dinner with his family. Even in those days it took forever to get anywhere in L.A., especially because there weren't any freeways yet. He said that because of the gas station's proximity to downtown Hollywood and its buzzing nightlife—which encompassed theaters, clubs, restaurants, bars, and dance halls, plus all the thriving movie studios in the surrounding area—there was enough business to keep the station open until at least eleven at night, or later. He needed someone willing and reliable enough to take care of things at least until after the theaters and clubs closed. He told me that he had one other employee, a mechanic by the name of Wilbur McGee, who worked in the service and repair bay during the day. But it was the evening hours that worried him. He was losing business. Was I interested? Was I!

We agreed that I would start work just as soon as I got back from a planned visit to Illinois. I had managed to save up a few bucks for a down payment on a secondhand 1939 Plymouth, and Betty and I took off in it on a road trip across the country via New Orleans, to Chicago and Ottawa. We spent time with Momma, Phyllis, and my stepdad. I also visited Don's grave and then slipped away to have some fun on my own with my old friends—both male and female— in Chicago. Then I went back for Betty and we drove all the way back to California. When we returned I started my new job as a pump jockey at the Hollywood Richfield gas station at 5777 Hollywood Boulevard, at the corner of Van Ness Boulevard. It was March 1946. I wasn't quite twenty-three years old but I was raring to go. The hours were from five in the afternoon to midnight or later, depending on business and on whether I felt like staying open longer, seven days a week. I was kitted out with smart new blue trousers and a nice blue shirt that had "Scotty" stitched on it in yellow letters, as well as an eagle, the logo of the Richfield Gas Company. I looked and felt pretty dapper in that outfit, I have to admit.

10

Firmament of Stars

It always amazed me that Bill Booth, the proprietor of the gas station, never cottoned on to what I was doing. Even though tricks only got underway at night long after he and Mac had left the premises, he had no inkling about what was taking place in the trailer. Or in the washroom, for that matter. He was oblivious to everything. Not once did he think that all those young good-looking guys and pretty girls might be lounging around for reasons other than having nothing else to do. During the daytime when he and Mac manned the station he would receive dozens of telephone calls for me. He never asked why there were so many callers, or what any of them wanted. He simply wrote down their numbers on a notepad for me to call them back. Both Bill and Mac would go about their normal business routine until I arrived at five o'clock and would never question whether any of my buddies and their girlfriends had an ulterior motive for being there. As far as they were concerned I was just a very popular guy with lots of friends, and that was that. If they had suspected anything, I would not have been able to build up my wide circle of contacts and run things the way I did.

* * *

ONE NIGHT AROUND MIDNIGHT after I had locked up the gas station I drove a couple of my friends out to Westwood for a night of sexual fun and games at a private home. We all partook of the shenanigans and I collapsed into bed at home at around six the following morning. When I woke up at about noon I had lunch with Betty and Donna and then, at two or three in the afternoon, I decided to drive out to the station. Along the way I became aware of the fact that I had not had enough sleep. I was still exhausted. I looked at myself in the rearview mirror and thought I needed to stop and rest somewhere. The trailer at the gas station would have been perfect but I didn't want Bill Booth or Mac to know that I was using it. There was only one thing to do. Ferndale Park was a quiet, shaded oasis of lawns and trees out where Los Feliz Boulevard met Western Avenue. I decided to stop off there and take a nap in the grass. I parked the car at the side of the park, strode across the lawns, and found a quiet and secluded spot in the shade. I lay down and instantly fell fast asleep. It wasn't long before I was having a highly erotic dream. In it, a long line of beautiful women were coming up to me and, one by one, they each performed exquisite oral sex on me. It felt so believable that I only slowly emerged from my slumber and opened my eyes. Squinting against beams of sunlight splaying through the branches of the tree above me I saw something. No, not something, but *someone*. This was no dream.

A figure was sitting beside me. The person was in silhouette and I couldn't see who it was. As I traversed that magical realm from the dream world to full consciousness my vision cleared and I could see that the person was a guy. He was sitting on the grass next to me reading a novel. Without even looking at me as he continued to read, holding the book in one hand, he had slipped his other hand through the fly of my Levi denims and was playing with my cock. Though shocked at my discovery, the sensations were so good that I dared not move. As soon as he realized that my eyes were open he lowered the book, turned to me, and smiled.

"Good afternoon," he said very politely, pretending that absolutely nothing was amiss or irregular.

"Hello," I gurgled, not quite believing but thoroughly enjoying what was happening.

I wanted to ask him his name but before I could say anything he gently tightened his grip around my throbbing member and made me come. I lay there as he wiped his hand on a hankie and smiled again. I sat up, took the hankie from him, and, without saying a word, mopped myself up and buttoned my fly. I could still not fully comprehend what had just happened when he thrust out his hand and we shook.

"Name's Alex Tiers," he said.

"Bowers," I replied groggily. "Scotty Bowers."

"Good to meet you, Scotty," he said. "Care to wash up? I don't live too far away."

And so began another friendship that would last for years.

Alex was a naughty devil. An aspiring actor, he lived in a very nice apartment on the corner of Tamarind and Franklin Avenues in Hollywood. He was very wealthy, having inherited a lot of "old money" from his father and family on the East Coast. As I dried off from the shower I had just taken in his bathroom he started telling me about himself and I was surprised to learn that we had a friend in common: George Cukor. It turned out that for a while Alex and George had shared a house in Malibu when George had first come out to California from his native New York. I realized then that even though this was Hollywood, life really revolved around small societal nodes.

One night I got a call from George Cukor inviting me to lunch the following Saturday. As I had seen quite a lot of him by now and was really very fond of him I gladly accepted. In fact, we spoke frequently because whenever I wasn't able to see George for a quick trick myself I had sent other guys over to him.

When I arrived at his mansion at around noon on Saturday he was in a foul mood. I hadn't seen him like that before. When I entered the living room I saw Katharine Hepburn and hairstylist Sydney Guilaroff. I had been tricking Syd regularly and he had become very fond of me. Once again Hepburn looked every bit a man, dressed in slacks with her hair fairly short though not parted. I seem to remember that George had given the maid the day off, because he busied himself with lunch preparations in the kitchen while Hepburn, Syd, and I chatted.

I can't remember exactly what we talked about but I distinctly remember the conversation eventually shifting to the topic of Hepburn's hairstyle on a new picture she was working on with Syd. It was called *Adam's Rib* and was being shot on the MGM lot. George was the director. The movie was about two lawyers who were married to one another but on the opposing sides of the courtroom during the trial of a woman accused of trying to murder her philandering husband. It was being promoted in the trades with the catch line, "It's the hilarious answer to who wears the pants." It was an ironically appropriate proclamation because Hepburn was playing the lead opposite MGM superstar Spencer Tracy. According to the rumor mills Hepburn was said to be having an affair with Tracy. However, as I saw things, nothing could possibly be further from the truth. For one thing, Hepburn was a lesbian and I could not imagine this incontrovertibly butch lady having an affair with a man, *any* man.

I recall Hepburn being adamant about the way she wanted her hair to be styled in the movie, but Syd insisted that it be done differently. They got into an almighty row that only subsided when George himself joined in the fray. Eventually George announced lunch and we all took our places at the dining room table.

Hepburn was still smoldering. She looked at George, dropped her head coyly, and imploringly whined, "Please don't be angry with me, George. I've got to fight for my independence in this town. You know that."

"My dearest Kate," George hissed back condescendingly, "the only thing you have to do in this town is to listen to the good advice of those who know what they're talking about."

"Oh, George, come on," Hepburn retorted. "Be nice to me."

"Why?" he replied.

"Aww," Hepburn responded in a melancholic kind of way. "You know, I've been in this town all these years and other than you and Syd here I really don't have many friends at all."

George took little time in answering. He looked at her and said, "Yeah, that's right, Kate, and you know why? Because you're a real spoiled *bitch.*"

And with that the afternoon drew to an uncomfortable and premature close. Later on, after we had all said our good-byes, I walked Hepburn to her car. On the way she turned to me and asked whether I thought she seemed like a spoiled bitch. I remember laughing aloud when she asked that and said that, no, I really didn't think she was anything like that at all. That seemed to make her feel a little more comfortable. She warmed to me and began to chat. I no longer recall what we talked about but just before we parted she insisted that I call her Kate. And then she asked me to do her a favor.

"I know about your reputation, Scotty. When you get a chance, do you think you can find a nice young dark-haired girl for me? Someone that's not too heavily madeup."

I said of course I would. I liked Kate. I couldn't care less what people said about her. Admittedly, she did have notoriously bad skin, especially when seen up close. Fortunately, makeup and clever lighting took care of that in the movies. But in real life without makeup her complexion was really awful. Nevertheless, I found her captivating. She had an irresistible magnetism. Behind that blemished face lurked a great intelligence.

There were scenes in Martin Scorsese's 2004 movie *The Aviator* that hinted at a love affair between Katharine Hepburn and movie producer, aviation pioneer, and one-time owner of RKO Radio Pictures studios Howard Hughes, but they are entirely implausible. It would have been out of the question, not only because dear old Kate was a lesbian but also because of her poor skin.

I arranged many ladies for Hughes. Any arrangement I made for him had to be treated with the utmost confidentiality. A date for a trick had to be executed in a clandestine, cloak-and-dagger manner, with no one ever knowing anything about it. Howard was as straight as an arrow and really liked women but, ironically, he hardly ever had sex with them. He was so fanatically fussy about his own health as well as the cleanliness and pristine beauty of the young lady that if she ever wore even the slightest hint of makeup that he did not like he would make her take a shower immediately and wash everything off. And if, heaven forbid, she had even the tiniest blemish or a pimple he simply would not touch her.

Over the next fifty years Katharine Hepburn and I would become the very best of friends. In the course of time I would fix her up with over 150 different women. Most of them she would only see once or twice, and then tire of them. But there was one exception. There was a very cute little seventeen-year-old trick that I set Kate up with early in our friendship. The girl's name was Barbara. Kate became infatuated with her, not as a lover or a partner but purely as an occasional trick. Shortly after they started seeing one another Kate bought her a brand-new two-toned Ford Fairlane as a gift. Kate saw Barbara off and on for just over forty-nine years. Kate lived out East most of the time but Barbara remained here in California. Three months before dear Kate passed away in June 2003 Barbara—who had married no less than three times during that period—received a letter from Kate's attorneys. With the letter was a check for $100,000. It was a birthday gift for her from Kate. Kate knew she was dying so it was probably also a parting or farewell present. Barbara and I had kept in touch with one another and when she received the check she told me that she really had me to thank for it. After all, she said, I was the one who introduced her to Kate. But, she added, she really didn't have any need for the check at all. Her third husband had passed away and left her his fortune. Lucky girl.

As far as the media and the public were concerned there was really only one person in Kate Hepburn's life, and that was Spencer Tracy. But as far as I could tell it was a nonexistent fairy-tale romance that the studio publicists and the spin doctors had concocted to conceal her lesbianism. Their fabrications were fed to the press, the gossip columnists, and the public, and everyone swallowed it. As people later knew, Kate romanticized her relationship with Spencer in order to confer with industry standards and ideals. In time, I would eventually get to know Spencer very well, too.

I REALLY DON'T RECALL the details anymore but long before I met Spencer Tracy I got a call one evening at the gas station from someone who said they were contacting me on behalf of a well-known Hollywood personality whose name they were reluctant to provide. I had received calls like that before and I had little patience with them. I preferred to know exactly who I was dealing with. If they wanted me to set up a trick for them I had to know who the person was. I tried to match people carefully. I wasn't a pimp or a dating and escort service. Sex is a very personal thing and I wanted to make sure that I hooked the right kind of people up together, people with mutually attractive attributes, energy, and chemistry.

"Who are you calling for?" I asked.

There was silence on the line for a moment as the caller slapped a hand over the mouthpiece. I could hear muted mumbling in the background. Then there was the sound of the phone being handed from one person to another.

"Scotty Bowers?" I heard a new voice ask.

"That's me," I said. "May I ask who's calling?"

"This is Errol Flynn," the voice said.

There was no doubt about it. It was definitely Flynn. I recognized that distinctive voice immediately.

"That gas station of yours has gained quite a reputation, you know," he laughed.

I got a thrill whenever I heard a comment like that.

"How about lunch on Wednesday?" he asked. "We could talk then."

For the life of me I cannot recall exactly where we arranged to meet but I think it was at the Polo Lounge in the Beverly Hills Hotel. When I arrived on the appointed day Flynn was already seated at a table. A pretty attendant was placing a fresh glass of vodka on the rocks beside one that was almost finished. He was a dashingly handsome man. Though only forty years of age, his best films were already behind him. These included *Adventures of Don Juan; Objective, Burma!; They Died with Their Boots On; The Private Lives of Elizabeth and Essex;* and the one for which he will perhaps always be best known, *The Adventures of Robin Hood.* He stood up as I reached his table, gave me the famous smile that set women's hearts aflutter, and invited me to sit down.

Though born in Australia, Flynn had a beautifully cultivated British accent. He seemed like a very nice guy, a real gentleman. He told me that he was looking for some new talent. By that he meant women. I said that I would do what I could to help him out. I asked him, "What sort of lady are you looking for?"

"Well, let's put it this way," he said. "I like my booze old and my women young. *Very* young. That always makes for a pleasant combination, wouldn't you say?"

He gave me a wickedly teasing smile. This was a man who was a connoisseur in all things delicate and fine, and that included women. He loved them young. In fact, the younger the better. I pointed out that there was a legal age restriction when it came to sex.

"Oh, tut, tut, dear boy," he said, downing the glass of vodka. "I don't care if she has to *be* eighteen, just as long as she *looks* and *behaves* like someone between, well, let's say fourteen and sixteen. All right?"

He told me that he was working on *That Forsyte Woman* over at MGM. His costars were Greer Garson, Robert Young, Janet Leigh, and Walter Pidgeon. He was most intrigued to hear that I knew Pidgeon personally, as well as the gentlemen in charge of set decoration and hairstyles, Edwin B. Willis and Syd Guilaroff. Suddenly I wasn't just a kid from a lowly gas station anymore. I really *knew* people. This impressed him no end. By the time we were on dessert I really liked him and I knew the feeling was mutual.

When I later gave up my job at the gas station and had my evenings free, I would take many pretty and very obliging young ladies over to Errol Flynn's place. He was especially pleased when I brought a girl over and then stayed to have dinner with the two of them. Although he was passionately fond of women, he enjoyed my company. I got the impression that it was a relief for him to be outside the orbit of the rich and famous. He used to cozy up to the woman I had brought over, talking pretty and smooching with her while I mixed drinks for him. He always thought I was crazy to be a teetotaler.

"Life without alcohol is like life without color, without music, without women, without sex," he said to me once.

Unfortunately, Errol had a problem, a very big problem. He could not control his drinking habit. It always got the better of him. I remember a number of occasions when the evening would start out pleasant enough but then he would slowly sink into alcohol-soaked oblivion. It's a shame that he was such a boozer. He drank all the time and ate very little. I always tried to persuade him to enjoy a good meal but the booze always won. By one o'clock in the morning he would have already consumed an entire bottle of vodka. Then he would stagger over to the girl and, slurring every word, he would sweetly whisper to her, "I'm going to fuck you now, baby. I'm going to make love to you like nothing you've ever experienced."

And then he would sway backward and forward once or twice and, in a mighty crash, fall face-first on the floor, out for the count, totally wasted. By then the poor girl was so horny after all the buildup, the sweet talk, and the kissing that she couldn't wait to have sex. She was hot and ready, so I had no choice. I would carefully push Errol aside, get undressed, and oblige the lady myself!

Four or five hours after he had passed out Errol would wake up, crawl over to the bathroom, splash some cold water on his face, maneuver himself into the kitchen, pour a tumbler of vodka, down it in one gulp, and then drive off for his dawn shooting call at the studio. Amazingly, by the time he drove through the studio gates he was cold sober. I seldom knew anyone else who could manage such a feat. He hardly ever had a hangover on the set, or at least not one that anyone could detect. When he got to the studio the makeup people would shave him, then he'd take a shower, have his makeup applied and his hair styled, get into costume, quickly glance through his lines for the scenes scheduled for shooting that day, and nonchalantly strut onto the set as if nothing had happened the night before. Meantime, in his dressing room or his trailer there would always be a bottle of vodka, ready and waiting. He would pour himself shots from it all day long between takes.

When he was sober Errol was really great company. He was a wonderful conversationalist and very witty. But when he and his buddies got together they could drink up a storm. By the time he reached the age of forty-five he started to look awful. The lack of nourishment and the ravaging effect of all that booze turned him into a haggard-looking guy. His face began to get puffy. Blood vessels started to show. His skin started to become withered and wrinkled. It was awful to see his rapid physical decline. He married three times and had four children, but his career and his flamboyant lifestyle came to an untimely end. The alcohol eventually got him and he died of, among other things, sclerosis of the liver in 1959, just a few months after he turned fifty.

*   *   *

SHORTLY AFTER I MET Errol Flynn back in 1949 I met a lovely forty-one-year-old actress whose original name had been Margarita Carmen Cansino. Trained by her father Eduardo Cansino as a dancer, she made a few films under the name Rita Cansino, but when her true talents were discovered in a movie called *Only Angels Have Wings,* she was signed to a contract at Columbia Pictures and her name was changed to Rita Hayworth.

She was a very beautiful woman. She had light brown eyes, a fabulous complexion, classical bone structure, and, although her natural hair color was black, she usually dyed it red. Because she exuded an absolutely irresistible sexuality the world dubbed her the "Love Goddess." She was slender and lovely and always stole the scene away from her costars, even when she played opposite Ol' Blue Eyes himself, Frank Sinatra. When I met her she had just divorced Hollywood wunderkind Orson Welles and had married Prince Aly Khan, grandson of the Aga Khan II, a member of the Persian royal family and imam to more than fifteen million Muslims in the Middle East, Asia, and Africa.

Rita had a brother named Eduardo Jr., whom we all called Eddie. It was he who introduced me to his sister at a party one weekend. But Eddie was not in his sister's league. He drove a beat-up old World War II Jeep and delivered the *Los Angeles Times* to subscribers in the Hollywood Hills. He used to pick up his papers from the printers at four in the morning and then drive up into the residential areas in the mountains to drop them off. He was married to a third-rate actress and they had two or three kids. He really struggled to make ends meet. Through him I also met his Dad, Eduardo Sr. He was a dancer and choreographer from New York and once he moved out to the coast and settled in L.A. he ran a popular dance studio on the corner of Sunset Boulevard and Bronson Avenue, not too far away from the gas station where I worked.

One day Rita and her dad got into a dreadful argument about some family matter or other, and for years after that she wouldn't speak to him. Once I got to know her well enough, I begged her to patch up her differences with her father but no, nothing doing, she'd say. She was a hardheaded woman. Beautiful and talented, yes. Difficult, absolutely. She also had a mean and stingy streak. To put it bluntly, she was very selfish. Perhaps exposure to all that wealth from her marriages spoiled her. Who can tell? She knew her brother Eddie was having a hard time but she turned a blind eye to it, hightailing it from soundstages to glamorous movie premieres to the playgrounds of Europe and the French Riviera. I felt really sorry for Eddie. He didn't deserve to be treated that way by his sister. I cannot recall how many times he got a flat tire while doing his newspaper rounds. The tires on his Jeep had virtually no treads left on them and he never had enough money for a spare. Rita could never find it within herself to give the poor guy a dime. Eddie would remove the punctured wheel from his Jeep and roll it down all those narrow, twisting streets in the Hollywood Hills to Hollywood Boulevard and then into our gas station, where Mac patched it up for him. If Eddie was too far away or if the roads were too steep, he would have to hitch a ride to the station and then have Mac drive up and collect the punctured tire. It was pathetic. I, of course, knew what it was like to have a newspaper beat. But I couldn't imagine how tough it had to be for Eddie to deal with flat tires on top of the hassle of making his rounds. Even though the war had been over for about four years, back in those days it was still difficult to get good tires because of shortages. Besides, new tires were very expensive.

One evening I was at the gas station and a guy I'd never seen before pulled up in a delivery truck and offered me a set of four perfectly good used tires and inner tubes for a giveaway sum of only a hundred bucks. I bought them immediately and wheeled them into the station, hoping that I could sell them to Eddie. But, as usual, he was strapped for cash, even though I said I would sell them to him for exactly the same price I had paid for them. I knew he needed those tires and tubes desperately so I called up Rita and said, "Rita honey, Eddie really needs a new set of wheels and I've got an absolute bargain here. Won't you help him out?"

The phone went silent for a moment and then she said, "You're a sweetheart, Scotty, and I love you for that, but fuck Eddie. Why should I? What has he ever done for me?"

Rita made more than sixty movies, including *The Lady from Shanghai, Separate Tables, Pal Joey, Salome, Gilda,* and the epic Cinerama adventure with John Wayne, *Circus World,* but she wouldn't lift a finger to help her own brother.

11

Vice Squad

The vice squad division of the Los Angeles Police Department was the bane of many people's lives during the forties and fifties. They mercilessly hounded members of the gay and lesbian communities, turning whole sectors of society into criminals. Its members were always in civilian clothes, never in uniform. They resorted to undercover skulduggery to trap, arrest, and condemn their prey, no matter how devious their methods. They would use any ploy to corner their victims. Just about everyone they arrested had money, was well-known, or had a good job. Their prime targets were successful professionals, members of the business world, and, of course, movie people. Many were married. Some were bisexual. What united them was the fact that they often had to come up with exorbitant sums of cash to keep their names out of the papers and to avoid going to court. People were arrested en masse in gay bars, or just as they came out of a bar, or after being followed by cops from a bar. If a guy came out of a bar and suddenly had an urge to pee and innocently went into an alleyway next to the bar to relieve himself he would be asking for trouble. The vice squad would pounce on him. Handcuffs would be slapped on him and he would be accused of exposing himself in public. If he tried to explain that he was only taking a piss the cops would instantly throw another charge at him for resisting arrest. It was ruthless.

When some queens were arrested, especially if they were loaded with booze, they would kid around with the arresting officers by jokingly saying, "Jail? You're going to send me to jail? With all those lovely men in there? Oh, I'd *love* that. *Take* me. Handcuff me. Arrest me. Throw me in there, *please!*"

The arresting officers weren't always amused by this lightheartedness, and the fines would be doubled.

At the conclusion of the war a handful of Los Angeles lawyers made their living exclusively off queens, lesbians, and anyone else who had anything to do with the gay world. It was a lucrative business defending them. All their energies were devoted to arguing their cases in court. Two attorneys in particular handled most of the cases: Harry Weiss and Sheldon Andelson. Weiss's trademark was a large white panama hat that he always wore, no matter where or when. Because he was so effective in getting guys off the hook, he was known by the nickname of "Mr. Fix It." Both Weiss and Andelson were gay and were hardworking champions of the early gay rights movement in the city. In fact, Harry Weiss himself owned about three or four gay bars in town.

I first met Harry just after the war when he was living with his mother just beyond Western Avenue, off Santa Monica Boulevard. He had a lover by the name of Glenn McMann. They eventually moved up to Argyle and Franklin. Harry finally ended up living on Tower Road in Beverly Hills, in a palatial house, replete with an elevator that connected the upstairs rooms with the entertainment area downstairs. It also had an enormous bar, where I worked for him on a number of occasions. Harry was smart. He was cunning. He was determined to never lose a case. He had a bunch of runners working for him: people who ran errands, delivering messages, picking up packages, that sort of thing. He often employed a brilliant gambit. He got his runners to track down the two arresting police officers who were due to appear in court to testify against the defendant (Harry's client). The runners would diligently track the officers down before they went to court and subtly slip each of them an envelope containing a typewritten note asking them to please avoid appearing in court, plus $500 in cash. Police officers didn't earn much in those days, and $500 was an awful lot of money. Harry never signed the note or included his business card with the cash so that if the arresting officers ever thought of pressing charges against him for obstructing justice no one could ever prove that the money or the note came from him. Usually on the day of the trial the officers would simply not show up in court. When the trial got underway and the prosecuting attorney or the judge called for them as witnesses they were nowhere to be seen. When asked where they were the judge would be informed that they were suddenly called out on another important assignment or that they were in the process of apprehending a criminal somewhere. The judge would angrily retort, "Couldn't make it to court, eh? Well, stop wasting my time! Case dismissed!" I was in the public gallery one day when the judge dismissed no less than fourteen separate cases simply because the cops had been paid off by Harry Weiss.

The vice squad continued to hound, victimize, and harass people who dared overstep the line of what society and the law regarded as normal or acceptable behavior. I was by no means immune to their persistent pursuits. During that time of my life, I was still young with a lean, firm, muscular body, so a photographer friend of mine by the name of Lenny Robertson took three sets of pictures of me having sex with three gorgeous young girls. The pictures were shot in Lenny's bedroom. Each set depicted me with a different girl. One set showed me with a dazzling Oriental beauty, one with a stunning black lady, and one with a lovely white girl with blonde hair. It was during the days when nudie pictures were hard to come by and when pornographic images—whether of the soft- or hard-core variety—were virtually unobtainable. Lenny knew there was a healthy market for explicit porn so why not make a few bucks out of it? He photographed the images so that my face was never distinguishable. You could clearly see every other part of my anatomy but never my face. I was photographed having intercourse with the women in various positions, with my head buried in their crotches performing cunnilingus on them, with my face smothered by their boobs, kissing them, in the sixty-nine position, doggie style, you name it. Fortunately I had no tattoos, moles, or bodily markings that could be used to identify me. Lenny sold the pictures to mutual friends and to people we knew for ten dollars a set. I never saw a cent from the sales but it didn't matter. I was happy to oblige.

One day the vice squad dropped in to see me at the gas station and produced the photographs. They were always prowling around, always suspicious. They often drove past the station at night, obviously curious as to why there were so many cars and young people around, especially when other gas stations in the area were much quieter than mine.

"This you?" they asked, showing me the photographs.

"Nope," I said. "Never seen them in my life."

Because my face was not visible, they could not physically identify me and pin anything on me. So, reluctantly, they left. Lenny Robertson, on the other hand, managed to avoid a jail sentence but had to pay a steep fine for taking and selling the pictures. The whole thing was a travesty, a farce, a mockery of what went on in the world. We did no harm. We polluted no minds. We just showed three beautiful females doing what comes naturally with a male; what was criminal about that?

Not all law enforcement officers were the enemy. I had a good customer at the gas station who was a member of the traffic department of the LAPD. His name was Officer Calvin someone-or-other but we all called him Cal. He was a big muscular guy who lived in a rooming house just up the road from the gas station. He was always working out, lifting weights, jogging around the block, getting into shape. He was in his midtwenties, mild-mannered, soft-spoken, and not your typical cop. He used to come down to the station sometimes and hang around with the other young guys. The problem was that he wasn't too bright. He never spotted a gay man in a crowd. Even if one or two of the guys were limp-wristed and lisped, he wouldn't pick up on it. We all liked Cal. He had a pretty Italian girlfriend who lived across the street from him. He had never managed to take her to bed and thought that she was still a virgin. I used to kid him about it.

"When're you going to make love to her, Cal?" I asked.

"Oh, no," he would say. "Not yet. She's still pure, buddy, and I ain't gonna do nothin' until she says she wants it or until we're married."

But I knew otherwise. I had been fixing up tricks for her for a long time; blow jobs, hand jobs, straight intercourse, whatever. She did it all. My trailer in the backyard had seen a lot of her.

Cal rode a nice Harley-Davidson motorcycle for the traffic department and he was very proud of it. Every now and again he would bring it down to the station for some gas or to give it a wash and polish. One night he was in the service bay cleaning and buffing it to a gleaming finish. He was off duty and dressed in casual clothes. All of a sudden three or four guys from the vice squad walked into the office at the station and the head honcho said to me, "Okay, now listen, pal, we've spent the last two nights on the roof of the bowling alley next to the motel across the street watching this joint and we just can't figure out why so many cars pull in here compared to other gas stations in the area. What's going on? You fellas up to somethin'?"

Apparently they had been watching the gas station for a couple of weeks already and could not figure out why the place was so popular.

"This is Monday night," the cop said, "and no other gas station in Hollywood is as busy as this one. They've all got good pump attendants and their prices are the same as yours, yet they get maybe one or two cars every half hour. Here you sometimes get as many ten or fifteen. What's the deal? What's goin' on?"

"Nothing," I said. "I guess we just give good service."

This irritated the cop. He walked right up to me and thrust his face into mine.

"Are you hiding somethin' from us, pal? You up to no good?"

I just shrugged and pointed to Cal cleaning his motorcycle in the service bay.

"Ask him," I said. "He's LAPD. He should know."

So the vice squad marched over and questioned Cal, but he couldn't tell them anything. He was so unobservant and unaware of what was going on that he had absolutely no idea what I was up to, even when I had people slipping in and out of the trailer in the backyard. He merely told them that Richfield Gas was a real fun place to pop into and spend a while. He said there were always a lot of guys with their girlfriends around to talk to, that most of them knew about the latest sports scores and the current music scene and that the place was harmless enough. He said young folks just gathered there because it was convenient, always open till late, and people had got used to meeting and hanging out there. It was all innocent enough, he assured them. I'm not sure what the vice squad made of what he told them but they left. The kid was utterly clueless about what was really going on. And just as well, because I had a lesbian trio in one bedroom of the trailer that night and a gay guy sucking the dick of one of my Marine buddies in the other.

The demise of the vice squad was a long time coming.

To tell the happy ending to the story, we have to briefly fast-forward to 1972. A lawyer friend of mine by the name of Burt Pines was campaigning to become Los Angeles city attorney. Pines was straight, married, and had two kids but he was sympathetic to the gay rights movement.

Another good friend of mine, a very wealthy gay guy by the name of Lloyd Rigler, for whom I had set up innumerable tricks over the years, was very respectful of Burt Pines's efforts to secure better conditions for the gay community.

One day Lloyd approached Burt and said, "Burt, I'll help with the financing of your election campaign on one condition."

"And what's that?" Pines asked.

"That if you're elected into office the first thing you'll do is pull the LAPD's vice squad off the backs of the queens."

"Why?" Pines wanted to know.

"Just to leave the poor goddamned queens alone," Lloyd answered. "They've suffered enough from the squad over the years. Just let 'em be, that's all I ask. Jesus, they're not doing any harm. They just want to live, and love, and *make* love, and lead a life just like everybody else, that's all."

Pines looked at Lloyd, thrust out his hand, and they shook.

"Agreed," said Pines.

The 1972 city election results securely put Burt Pines into office as Los Angeles city attorney and, almost overnight, the nefarious vice squad quietly pulled back from the gay scene, never again to torment the queens. As the great tide of the civil rights movement swept the country it never reared its ugly head in the gay community again, instead concentrating almost exclusively on busting drug and crime rings.

As an aside, Lloyd Rigler had a partner by the name of Lawrence Deutsch. They were extremely happy together but Lawrence was a chain-smoker. Sadly, in 1977 he died of lung cancer. Lloyd became a lost and lonely man. He couldn't stop grieving. On many occasions I tried to pull him out of his depression, simply because I could see he was wasting away. One day I had an idea. I knew a very nice, good-looking guy by the name of Steve Davis. He had hung around the gas station in the early days. He wasn't exactly bright but he was attractive, in good shape, and a decent person. He wasn't ambitious and had never really made anything of himself. He eked out a meager living by mowing lawns, polishing cars, and washing windows. So I took Steve over to Lloyd's home for a drink one evening. And that did it. Lloyd was instantly smitten with Steve.

As Lloyd was much older than Steve he took him under his wing, mothered him, and eventually invited him to move in. Well, it wasn't long before Steve was wearing fancy clothes from chic Beverly Hills boutiques and driving an expensive sports car. Lloyd was so head over heels enamored with Steve that he would do anything he asked of him. It turned out that what Steve really wanted to do was to go to Nashville, Tennessee, and become a country and western singer. So dear old gullible Lloyd threw millions of dollars at the project, encouraging Steve to foster his dreams. Steve eventually built a big recording studio in Nashville but, needless to say, he wasn't that talented at singing. In time, the aging Lloyd Rigler acquired a very fine apartment directly across the road from the Pierre Hotel on Central Park in New York City, the Hotel Royal Tahitien in Tahiti, as well as a big ranch in Central California. When Lloyd died Steve inherited all of it. From then on he simply lived like a king—or a queen, if you like—for the rest of his life. He never had another care in the world.

Over the years it was always interesting to see how many older guys struck up long-term relationships with the younger men I introduced them to. Often, what began as a one-night trick ended up as a long and loving relationship. On the other hand, some queens just got taken for a ride. I've known older gay men who had a young trick for a night and then, before you knew it, the younger guy had moved in with him. The queen would get back to me and say, "You know, Scotty, that kid you sent over really loves me. We've been together for months now. I paid him twenty bucks that first night and now he never even asks me for money. I guess that means he loves me."

I would simply remind him that since he had already spent about $150,000 on the kid by buying him a brand-new Mercedes sports car, a Rolex watch, and a complete new wardrobe, naturally he wasn't going to ask for money! And it certainly didn't mean that the young man loved him. He simply knew where his bread was buttered. There were, of course, many exceptions to this kind of situation, but you'd be surprised at how often it happened.

12

Paternity

A really good-looking woman used to stop by periodically to buy gas. She must have been around forty or forty-five, and she had an absolutely gorgeous, much younger, girlfriend. The girlfriend was a classic all-American beauty. They were in a solid, loving relationship and they desperately wanted a baby. But they didn't want to adopt. They had heard about me, and asked me if I would have intercourse with the young girl. I agreed. As I said before, I liked pleasing people. I would go to any length to help folks out if I could.

I went over to their place in Silver Lake one evening after I locked up the gas station. They had the lights turned down low and soft music playing. A few words passed between us and then the young lady went into the bedroom, got undressed, slid under the covers, and I went in, undressed, and made love to her. Even though she was a lesbian, I was horny as hell because she was a real beauty. She was slim, supple, and had fabulous bone structure. Her long brown hair was soft and smelled fresh. I was aching to kiss her but she didn't let me go that far. I don't know whether she enjoyed the experience as much as I did but she got pregnant and nine months later a healthy little baby girl was born.

They offered to pay me for my services but I declined. I was more than happy to be of assistance. The couple continued to live in Los Angeles until the child was ten and then they moved to Connecticut. I never saw them, or the child, again. I accepted the situation for what it was and that was that. In retrospect, it would have been nice for me to hear how she was doing as she grew up.

A few years after I left the gas station a similar circumstance unfolded, only with a heterosexual couple. A Stanford professor who I met at a party had a very good friend in Denver, Colorado. As it was explained to me, this guy was in his early forties and was an extremely wealthy businessman. I was also told that he was as square and as conservative as they come. After a business meeting in Colorado Springs one weekend he was driving back to Denver and, for whatever reason, the trip took him along the beautiful but treacherous road through Pikes Peak. As he was driving down the highway from the higher regions of the mountain he lost control of his car and it rolled over. The result was that he suffered a crushed spine. The injury caused permanent neural damage. That complication was exacerbated by the fact that aggressive medication had also been prescribed. The effect was that the poor guy became totally impotent. He lost all sensation in his penis and no longer produced semen or sperm. An added tragedy was that he and his wife were desperately anxious to have a baby. Fortunately, his wife was fertile and in the peak of health. Like the lesbian couple in L.A., they, too, did not want to adopt a child.

Eventually the guy heard about me from my Stanford contact, so he came out to Los Angeles to meet me. He wanted to see if I was as presentable as people had said I was. What did I look like? What was my personality like? What kind of a guy was I? Was I worthy enough to be considered as the possible father of his child? If I passed muster he agreed to pay me a tidy sum for my services. Once he had thoroughly checked me out—from the color of my eyes to my temperament to my state of health—he wanted to find out what stock I came from. He insisted on meeting my entire family. Sparing no expense, he flew to Illinois with me and met my mother, my father, my sister, and my grandparents. We never let on why we had come out to see them. The pretense was that I was with him on a business trip and that he had simply come along with me for the brief visits I managed to pay to all the folks back home. But in actual fact he studied every single one of them very carefully. He wanted to know about the health of my family, their lifestyle, their longevity, their demeanor. He questioned my mother about any illnesses I had as a boy. Was I a good kid? Did I ever get into any trouble? Was I a good student? Did I do well at school? What were my physical, mental, and emotional attributes as I grew up? In effect, in his mind he was doing a detailed genetic profile of me. On our return to L.A., he had a series of doctors run more exhaustive tests. They checked out my blood type and heart rate. Were my kidneys and liver okay? Were my lungs clear? I had to ejaculate into a petri dish and they studied my sperm motility under a microscope. There wasn't a thing about me that the guy didn't know when he returned to Denver, with the promise that I would soon be hearing from him.

As the next few weeks went by his wife was subjected to equally intensive physical examinations. When it was determined what dates she would be fertile and most likely to get pregnant I was summoned. With the help of two doctors everything had been carefully prepared. I received a telegram and an airline ticket from him. I arrived in Denver, was met by a chauffeur-driven limousine, and was taken to the very plush and expensive Brown Palace Hotel downtown. At the desk a welcome note and a check awaited me. Also in the envelope was an agreement that I was required to sign. It stipulated that I would never mention our little arrangement to anyone, that I would never give out the name of the family, and, if the pregnancy was successful, that I forego all rights to see the child. In short, if a healthy child was born I was never to see him or her. Ever.

The next day a driver was sent to pick me up and I was taken to the couple's large home on the outskirts of town. There was no sign of the guy or his wife. A maid showed me in and I was offered a drink and a snack. I was asked to wait in the study, where a doctor joined me. Strict instructions were given to me. I was told that nothing should be said when I met the woman, that no words should pass between us. I was instructed to take a shower and put on a robe. I was told that when I was taken into the bedroom I should get into bed and do what I had to do as quickly and as quietly as possible.

At precisely eight o'clock that evening I was led into a dark room where the couple lay naked in bed. As the door closed I could discern that the guy was necking with his wife. An aphrodisiac ambience permeated the room. There was just a trace of soft music in the background and the place was filled with the aromatic scent of either fresh flowers or an expensive perfume, I'm not sure which. The man continued to kiss his wife, fondle her breasts, and manually stimulate her as I crawled under the covers beside her on the other side of the bed. She lay between us. After a few minutes the guy tugged at my arm, indicating that I should mount his wife. By then I was rock hard and had no trouble penetrating her. She was warm, moist, and snug inside and it took only a couple of dozen thrusts before I ejaculated. As arranged, I then got out of the bed, slipped on the robe, and quietly left the room.

I had sex with her four times over a two-day period, just to try to make sure that she would get pregnant. Then I flew back to Los Angeles. Nine months later the woman gave birth to a healthy baby girl. Three months after that I was sent for again and after another two-day session with her she gave birth to a bouncing little baby boy. I never knew the woman's name and I was never told the names of the two children. There has never been any further contact between the husband and me. It may sound like a corny thing to say but, in all honesty, I feel deeply grateful to have been able to help the family out. No one in my circle of friends ever learned about this episode.

I certainly never told anybody about it, including Betty. It was a very personal matter and I respected the Denver family's wishes for complete privacy. Over the years I often longed to know how those two children were doing but I never broke the agreement that I had signed. I only hope the kids grew into healthy, happy adults and are now living prosperous, meaningful lives.

13

Mixing Drinks

One fine spring evening in 1950 a few of my buddies, their girl-friends, and I were sitting around the gas station, shooting the breeze, and making small talk. It was one of those deliciously balmy endings to a lovely Southern California day. We sat on the little raised paved island on which the gas pumps stood in the middle of the driveway. One or two guys stood a safe distance away puffing on cigarettes. A few miles to the west, on Hollywood Boulevard, brilliant white searchlight beams fingered the sky, slowly crisscrossing the heavens to indicate that a movie premiere was taking place, probably at Grauman's Chinese Theatre. Business at the station was quiet. A guy and a girl were at it in the trailer but, other than that, not much was happening.

That was the night the phone rang, opening another chapter in my life. The details are now sketchy and I can no longer recall exactly how the conversation ran but, as I remember it, it was my friend Randolph Scott, Cary Grant's lover, on the phone. He told me that they were having a party the next Saturday evening but that their regular bartender was not going to be able to make it. Could I help out? Would I fill in for him? I protested, reminding Randy that as a teetotaler I knew absolutely nothing at all about mixing drinks. But he was persuasive and said that he and Cary would really appreciate it if I could help out. So, what's a guy to do? Remember, I had been tricking both Cary and Randy for years. I was really fond of them both and so I agreed.

Mac the mechanic stood in for me that Saturday night while I went over to Cary and Randolph's place behind the Chateau Marmont. It was quite a gathering of Hollywood glitterati, both male and female. It was a costume party. There were some gorgeous women there, many of them wearing skimpy see-through veils, body-hugging silks, and little else. And they weren't all dykes. There were lovers, sweethearts, hookers, and maybe even a wife or two among them. Under the muted lighting the crowd looked gorgeous. It was what the paparazzi would have called a gathering of the beautiful people. Of course, Randolph had totally underestimated the demands his guests would make on my less-than-limited bartending skills. People were asking for drinks I had never heard of before. While I could get by meeting requests for beer, scotch, vodka, champagne, and wine I had no clue how to mix a daiquiri, a Manhattan, a Rob Roy, or a caipirinha. I wasn't too good at martinis either. Fortunately, Cary and Randolph had neatly laid out all the necessary liquor and mixers on the long bar counter in their comfortable living room so, with a little bit of help from others, and aided by the low lighting to conceal my lack of expertise, I somehow fumbled through the evening and got away with it. It was a lot of fun. And there was a lot of exposed flesh around to bump into, which made things easier. You get what I mean?

That evening sealed my fate. Or my fortune. Or my future. I'm not sure which. The point is that because people had seen me bartending that evening I would often be invited to bartend at private parties in the months and years to come. In fact, bartending would eventually open up a whole new career for me.

As was typical at events like that particular evening, eventually the public rooms emptied while the party shifted to the bedrooms, where a lot of sucking, fucking, and other activities would go on until dawn. At around midnight I was tidying things up around the bar counter when, through the cigarette smoke and gloomy lighting, I caught sight of a man across the room smiling at me. I recognized him as my pal, movie actor Vincent Price. Someone—I no longer remember who—had introduced me to him as a trick a few months earlier.

Vinny—I always called him that—was thirty-nine years old at the time. He was a suave, debonair, handsome movie star who stood six feet two inches tall. With his smooth, low-pitched voice, thick crop of immaculately groomed dark hair, and his beautifully coordinated, slow movements he was a box-office draw. He had starred in films that included *The House of the Seven Gables, Brigham Young, The Song of Bernadette, Laura, Leave Her to Heaven,* and *The Three Musketeers.* But it was in the horror genre where he would eventually become most famous.

At the time I met him, Vinny had recently married his second wife, Mary Grant. She was a competent costume designer who worked on about a dozen motion picture productions. They had a daughter together but Vinny was decidedly gay and the marriage would not last. However, in 1974 he would marry Australian-born actress, Coral Browne. She worked primarily in England and although she was a dyke—I know because I would fix her up with many tricks with young women in future years—the couple were devoted to one another. They had virtually no sex life together but they cared deeply for each other. I tricked Vinny for years. Sex with him was pleasant, unhurried, gentle. There was what I can only refer to as a kind of refinement about it. It was erotic, tantalizing, fulfilling. High class stuff all the way. What else can I say?

Vinny was an avid art collector, a connoisseur of fine wines, a lover of English and American poetry, and an outstandingly good gourmet chef. Over the years I would enjoy many delicious meals that he personally prepared for guests at his various homes, including one at the top end of Doheny Drive in Beverly Hills, one on Miller Drive, and at his Malibu beach house. In due course I would also bartend for him, meeting his wide circle of influential and fascinating friends, many of whom made up the intelligentsia of Tinseltown.

One of Vincent Price's closest friends was a wealthy member of the British aristocracy by the name of Arthur Brown, though many affectionately referred to him as Albert. Albert lived in England for part of each year, and in the Pacific Palisades in L.A. for the rest. His family were industrialists and worth a fortune. I recall him telling me that his ancestors had amassed vast sums of money when the Industrial Revolution got underway during the nineteenth century. Albert was an extremely articulate, softly spoken, distinguished-looking man in his late thirties or early forties. He wanted for nothing. He spent his years enjoying the fineries of life. Good food, good company, good books, good music, travel, and sex. He took an instant liking to me and I would trick him myself or bring over some of my most dapper and refined-looking young male friends to amuse him. He had the peculiar English habit of seldom referring to me by my real name and preferred calling me "Ducks" or "Ducky." It was a very English thing. I thought it really cute.

Through this new circle of British friends I would often receive requests to bartend at various dinners and parties so, with the approval of Bill Booth—the gas station owner—Mac and I figured out a flexible schedule whereby we could start sharing the night shift at the gas station. Naturally, I had to make sure that all my contacts knew that if I was not at the station no messing around was allowed. Tricking or sex were never to be discussed with Mac. If I wasn't there or didn't personally answer the phone, the trailer was unavailable. My usual group of friends would still come around after five o'clock but if Mac was on duty and I wasn't there they'd drift away within an hour or so. Everyone understood that it was critical that neither Bill nor Mac ever find out what was really going on during my watch. Surprisingly, the new system worked out pretty well and everyone quickly learned that if Scotty Bowers didn't answer the phone at night the subject of tricks, sex, and such-like were strictly taboo.

It was through my newly acquired friend Albert that I met Peter Bull, a British actor who divided his time between London and Los Angeles. Peter was in his late thirties and the son of Sir William Bull, British member of Parliament for the constituency of South Hammersmith. Peter had gone to the esteemed all-boys boarding school, Winchester College, and was the product of a classic English public school education. He took a liking to me and we often had sex together. To say that he was eccentric would be an understatement, but he was an absolutely charming man. At the time I met him he had appeared in films such as *Oliver Twist, Contraband,* and *Saraband for Dead Lovers,* and he was preparing to return to England to shoot scenes for a film that would become a true classic. It was *The African Queen,* to be directed by John Huston. In it Peter would appear as an officer on board the German gunboat *Louisa* that was sunk by a makeshift torpedo cobbled together on board the boat *African Queen* by the story's two leads, played by Humphrey Bogart and my good friend Kate Hepburn. Peter was a lot of fun to be with. He had a marvelously dry sense of humor and the biggest teddy bear collection that I had ever seen. He always traveled with a portion of it. He would ultimately write the definitive book on the subject, *Bear with Me.* Whenever we had sex together we would first have to clear his large double bed of soft, cuddly bears and carefully stash them on shelves and along the skirting board of the floor. He adored those bears as though they were his own children. If you wanted to make Peter happy all you had to do was buy him another teddy bear and he was in heaven.

I was gathering a plethora of really high-class British friends. One Sunday when I was over at George Cukor's home for brunch I was introduced to a writer-director named Brian Desmond Hurst. Brian was about sixty years old at the time and was best known for the 1939 production *The Lion Has Wings.* It was one of the first and finest of the propaganda films that came out of England to boost

British morale as World War II got underway. Brian was a literate and articulate man who was also responsible for directing *Dangerous Exile* and *The Mark of Cain*. In 1951 he would go on to direct *Scrooge,* which starred Peter Bull. It wasn't long before I was tricking Brian, too, and, needless to say, sending other young men from the gas station crowd over to him whenever he requested it. He was a bit conservative but he would never say no to watching two guys having sex together and then gently easing himself into the action.

George Cukor was also responsible for connecting me with one of the most talented and respected people who had ever come over from England to work in Hollywood: the renowned photographer and costume designer Cecil Beaton. When I met him he was one of the top portrait and fashion photographers in the world, dividing his time between *Vogue* magazine's London, Paris, and New York offices. He was originally lured to Hollywood to photograph movie stars, and infused all his portraits with his unique touch. His camera captured not only the beauty and glamour of female stars and the rugged handsomeness of male actors, but also made their personalities shine through. He was brilliant at capturing people and the hidden something behind them that made them tick. He was able to do this with members of the British royal family, too. His images provided a window into their very persona. Beaton loved working in Hollywood but he wasn't always that easy to get along with. He was fastidious, arrogant, and never hesitated to say what he really thought or felt about people. He had an intense dislike of Katharine Hepburn. I was shocked at his forthrightness as we sat around the pool of George Cukor's home late one afternoon. George was going on about Kate's haughty attitude regarding her makeup when Beaton chirped in with his own take on the woman.

"Oh, forget about it, George. I don't know why you bother with someone whose skin is as scaly as a dead crocodile. Nothing could ever enliven it or make her look beautiful."

Although Kate did have poor skin I thought that was a rather cruel remark from Cecil. But his scathing comments extended to British royalty, too. When someone asked him just after the war how Queen Elizabeth, mother of the present Queen Elizabeth II, could influence feminine fashion by setting an example, he dryly commented, "The best thing she should do to influence fashion? Oh, very simple, darling. She should just stay at home and never be seen."

In addition to being one of the world's leading photographers, Cecil was also a consummate costume designer, turning his talents to Broadway and the London stage. He was quite a handful. You could be easily bruised by his searing criticism. Fortunately, he took a shining to me and we saw a lot of one another. He was fairly prudish and shy when it came to sex but he did seem to shed some of his really stiff British inhibitions with me. He would eventually take me into his confidence and sometimes behaved like a spoiled child, telling me how the world didn't understand him. He was often painfully prissy. Whenever he had tea, the tea and milk had to be poured in the correct order. Exactly one lump of sugar had to be dropped into the cup at a precise time and in only a very certain way. He was an absolute stickler for details. He always eyed things from an artistic standpoint. He would get into my car and finger the seats and the upholstery or the dashboard and say, "You really ought to make this brown, you know. This color is all wrong." Or he would look at me very carefully before being seen in public with me, examine my coat or shirt and then pass judgment, saying something like, "This is all wrong, you know. It should really be gray." Or yellow, or blue, or whatever. Nothing was ever right. Before having sex, Cecil would carefully draw back the bed sheets, neatly and tightly fold the overhang under the mattress, tuck in all loose ends, then straighten out any creases. He would have driven some people crazy but I happily tolerated his obsession for detail and, as a result, we got along fine.

The most difficult period that I experienced with Cecil was many years later, in 1964, when he was working as the production designer, art director, and costume designer on the Warner Bros. production of the musical, *My Fair Lady*. George Cukor was the director. Even though George and Cecil had been close friends—and perhaps even lovers—for years, they occasionally got into the most unholy arguments and fights, usually over trivial matters such as how much Audrey Hepburn's hat ought to be tilted on her head in the Ascot race sequence, or whether Rex Harrison's buttonhole was sufficiently visible, or whether Wilfrid Hyde-White should be wearing a smoking jacket or a dinner jacket in a scene. Apparently they even argued about how much makeup needed to be applied to Stanley Holloway to make him appear a little more dirty and street-worn in the scene where Professor Higgins comes to bargain with him about keeping his daughter Eliza at his home in order to train her in the better usage of the English tongue.

The film was a mammoth, expensive, and challenging production. It was shot entirely on the Warner Bros. soundstages in Burbank. It is not surprising that tempers occasionally flared or that the patience and tenacity of the key creative personnel were taxed. But when George and Cecil got into an argument it was usually blown out of all proportion and brought filming to a standstill. Many times it ended with Cecil storming off the set and having his driver take him back to his private bungalow on the grounds of the Hotel Bel-Air to sulk. That's when George would call me.

"Scotty," he would say, "the goddamned queen has walked off the set again. I need her back here by tomorrow but she won't listen to reason. Please go out there, make nice, help her to simmer down, and make sure she makes tomorrow's call time. Okay?"

"Of course, George," I'd say. "Don't worry. I'll see what I can do."

I would have to go through the rigmarole of getting Mac to take over for me while I drove out to the Hotel Bel-Air to try to placate Cecil. I would spend the entire night with him while he ranted and raved about how cruel and uncompromising George was. He would hug me tightly and cry on my shoulder, sniffling for hours. Meanwhile, I would gently undress him, make tea for him, climb into bed with him, give him a massage, soothe his brow, and ease us into a long, slow night of gentle sex until he fell asleep like a baby. In the morning I would wake him up, conjure up a white lie by telling him that George had called and was deeply repentant about hurting his feelings, and then make sure that his driver got him back to the studio lot in time for his call. Sometimes, if he was reluctant to face George, I would drive him out to the studio myself. The conflagrations between those two extremely individual, hardheaded, and obstinate personalities occurred at least a dozen times during the filming of *My Fair Lady,* but having me spend the night with Cecil always seemed to help quell their fighting. What a volatile Madonna he was, but I was very fond of him.

14

A Royal Affair

One day Cecil told me that two very important British royal visitors were due to come to town for a short stay. He said they were none other the Duke and Duchess of Windsor, both close friends of his. He confided in me that he was especially close to the duke. Now you have to remember that this couple were more famous in their day than the so-called Camelot couple, John Fitzgerald Kennedy and his bride Jacqueline Kennedy, were decades later.

In the midthirties the story of the Duke and Duchess of Windsor had taken the entire world by storm. It was the stuff of legend. It was also touted by the international press as the romance of the century. Remember that at that time the British Empire was still at its height. Enormous swathes of the earth were under British rule. Innumerable nations were British colonies within the Empire, but there were dominions and protectorates and independent countries all over the world that also owed allegiance to Britain and who regarded the British monarch as head of state. George V was their emperor and king. His wife was the beloved Queen Mary and the couple had five sons and a daughter. The eldest son would become king when his father died. Edward, the Prince of Wales, was that son.

Edward reputedly had a number of romantic flings but in June 1931, at the age of thirty-six, he attended a party at which he was introduced to a charismatic and sophisticated American socialite by the name of Wallis Simpson. As the legend goes, it was instant chemistry; love at first sight. But there was a problem. She was still married. To a *second* husband, no less. And, to top it off, she was American. This made the royal affair scandalous. Future kings do not have affairs with divorcées, let alone entertain notions of marrying them. His parents, the entire royal family, the government, and a large proportion of the British population were dead set against Edward's love for Mrs. Simpson. For years the press in England, the rest of the Empire, Europe, and America kept the story of the royal romance alive.

When King George V died in 1936 it was Edward the Prince of Wales who automatically took over the duties of king and it was in that capacity that he served his nation for a full year. By then Wallis Simpson had divorced her second husband and the couple planned to marry. This generated an even greater outcry. Although he was acting monarch and referred to by his loyal subjects as Your Majesty, no coronation had yet taken place, and a man is not officially the head of state until he is crowned king. Everything was put on hold until Edward renounced his desire to marry his beloved, twice-divorced commoner and foreigner.

It was a crisis that swept the British nation like wildfire. But Edward was resolute. Said to be heartbroken that he would not be permitted to marry Wallis Simpson, he was left with few options. He reluctantly made the decision to renounce the throne. In short, to abdicate. On December 11, 1936, he broadcast an impassioned speech to the nation and Empire announcing his abdication and marital intentions. Suddenly public sympathy poured out to him but it was too late. His younger brother Albert took his place and was crowned with the name King George VI.

After his younger brother took the throne Edward himself receded into the shadows. He was given the title Duke of Windsor and he married Wallis Simpson in 1937 in a small private ceremony in France. She was bestowed with the title Duchess of Windsor but was never accorded the right to be referred to as Your Royal Highness. That was a form of address strictly reserved for Edward. Relations between the couple and the royal family were strained and difficult. Because Wallis Simpson was denied a royal title and was always regarded as an outsider, the couple moved to Paris. In 1940 Edward's brother, the king, supported by Britain's Prime Minister Winston Churchill, appointed him as Governor of the Bahamas, where he and Wallis spent five years. It was a relatively unimportant and low-ranking position as far as royal duties go, but Edward and his bride were happy there. In time, they also socialized with the upper classes of Paris and the French Riviera, spending their time partying, shopping, dining, and generally enjoying life.

They visited the United States many times. I cannot remember the exact year—it must have been during the late forties or early fifties—but when Cecil Beaton told me that they were going to be visiting Los Angeles and were to stay at our mutual friend Albert Brown's home in the Pacific Palisades I looked forward to meeting the couple. Then Cecil came out with a bombshell. He told me that the Duke's sexual inclinations leaned not only toward his beloved Wallis Simpson, but to men. You could have knocked me over with a feather when I heard that. This was the romance of the century, for crying out loud. And now I'm told that the guy is *gay!*

I could hardly believe it. But Cecil had more to say. He said that Edward—the duke—was a classic example of a bisexual man. He was equally drawn to the delights found in both a heterosexual and a homosexual world. According to him, the whole myth of the great royal romance was a fabrication, a giant cover-up by the royal family and the British government to conceal the truth about Edward's sexual preferences. A king could not possibly get away with living the kind of lifestyle as that favored by Edward. It would have stifled him. Apparently Wallis Simpson shared similar bisexual urges. Because of that she was the ideal candidate to become Edward's wife. Although she was portrayed as the great love of his life and the person behind his reason for abdicating from the British throne she was in actual fact the perfect partner to share his double life with him. He liked boys. She liked girls. Occasionally they even had sex with each other but, essentially, he was gay and she was a dyke. What better way to save face and ensure that they would have the freedom to live their lives in peace and out of the public spotlight than to marry one another?

Frankly, I cared not one iota whether they were gay, straight, or bi. And I cared even less about the controversy surrounding their marriage or, indeed, why they even married at all. What business was it of mine? And who cared a rat's ass whether they preferred men or women outside their marriage? If that's what made them happy, what else mattered?

One day Albert called me and invited me over to his home in the Palisades.

"They're here, Ducks," he said, "and they're dying to meet you."

On the following Saturday my aging Plymouth coughed its way up to the Pacific Palisades. A butler welcomed me at the door and showed me into the library, where Albert and two of my other British friends, actor Peter Bull and director Brian Desmond Hurst, plus a couple of other people I didn't know, were chatting with none other than Edward the Duke of Windsor and Wallis the Duchess of Windsor. It was quite a gathering of the aristocracy. Apart from the duchess I think I was the only American there! But before I could even begin to feel out of place Albert beamed at me and called out, "Ah, here he is! Do come in, Scotty!"

The very first person to grab my hand and shake it warmly was the duke himself. I wasn't sure what to call him. He must have sensed that because he smiled and said, "Please, call me Edward."

"Hi Eddy," I said. I've always had a habit of shortening people's names to catchy nicknames. Why should Edward be different, ex-king or not? Fortunately, he didn't seem the least bit offended by my informality and then introduced me to his wife, who he referred to as Wally. So that's what I called her, too.

With the ice broken we all began to get to know one another. There were no pretentious charades or aloofness in their behavior toward me whatsoever. Edward gently pulled me aside and said, "You know, Scotty, a lot of people have told me about you, long before Wally and I came to California. Albert, Peter, Brian, and Cecil all said that I ought to look you up when we got here."

He was referring of course to our mutual friends, his host Arthur Brown, as well as Peter Bull, Brian Desmond Hurst, and Cecil Beaton. He went on to tell me how highly they had all spoken of me to him in London and how much he had been looking forward to meeting me. It was obvious that his relationship with those four men transcended mere platonic friendship. This became patently clear less than twenty minutes later when he and I slipped into the guesthouse at the bottom end of the large garden, stripped off, and began making out. Eddy was good. *Really* good. He sucked me off like a pro.

I spent about an hour and a half at Albert's place that afternoon and did not leave until Wally explained exactly what sort of young lady she wished me to send over for her. Over the next few days I would send up a nice young guy for Eddy and a pretty, dark-haired girl for Wally. Each time I sent somebody different. The royal couple enjoyed variety and, to be frank, I never told the kids I sent over what their real identities were. Besides, most of the guys and gals were too young to remember the great scandal of the thirties. In all the years when they visited California and I arranged tricks for them no one ever really knew who they were. Even though I became a very busy man in later years, I often tricked Eddy myself. We became good friends and were very attached to one another.

After I'd left the gas station and my bartending days really began in earnest, I would get to know many of the top hotel managers, restaurateurs, and chefs in town. One of them was a guy named Hathaway who, for a time, was the manager of the Beverly Hills Hotel. I once got Hathaway to set aside one of the more plush garden bungalows of the hotel for Eddy and Wally without revealing their true identities to him. While they were there it was easy for me to bring over a bunch of new young people for them. We would have a mixture of half a dozen males and females engage in a display of gay and straight sex in the bungalow and then Eddy, Wally, and I would each pair off with the one we fancied most. Eddy liked a three-way with a girl, too, now and again, and occasionally he wanted a woman only, and there were indeed occasions when he got involved in a three-way with Wally and another woman. But his preference was definitely for the boys.

There was an extremely good-looking, well-groomed fellow who loved to take it in the "back door," meaning, of course, that he was the passive partner, or the bottom, in anal intercourse. Edward was particularly fond of giving it to him that way while slowly sucking on my dick. That invariably ended up in an orgiastic eruption by the three of us at the same time. Eddy was a gentle lover. In fact, he was a gentleman through and through. He was considerate, very thoughtful of all his partners' physical and emotional needs, and he was a damn good lover. He was a well-mannered, kind-hearted, and very decent man.

Eddy and Wally had spent some time in the Greek Islands after they got married. They loved the Aegean and the freedom it offered them. One day while they were in L.A. a rather unusual coincidence occurred. A good friend of mine, a set decorator by the name of John Austin, had been over to Mykonos on location for a movie and had brought back an extremely good-looking nineteen-year-old Greek boy by the name of Damien. John's intention was to have him here for a few months as a boy toy and then send him back home to

Mykonos. He took the guy with him to many parties just to show off his great looks and physique and perhaps to foster a little envy among his friends. He also spread the word around that he would be grateful if anyone could find some part-time photographic modeling or film work for his young Adonis, to help him make a few bucks while he was out here. He called me about this one day and confidentially told me that even though the boy offered him great sex the kid was actually straight. In fact, he had a gorgeous dark-haired, brown-eyed Grecian goddess of a girlfriend back home. I tried to do what I could to help Damien earn a bit of money by arranging tricks for him with various men and women around town. He obliged them all and was grateful for the generous tip each of them provided.

One day while I was driving him from the gas station to a trick at someone's house he was telling me about his life back home in Greece. In his broken, heavily accented English he told me that he had met Edward and Wally during one of their trips to Mykonos. He said he knew that Edward was supposed to have been the king of England but that he had changed his mind in order to run away with the woman that he married. Oddly enough, Damien told me, both Edward and Wally preferred people of their own sex. He admitted that he would bring his girlfriend over to keep Wally happy while he and Eddy got up to mischief together. I told Damien that the couple were in town and asked him if he would like to see them. He was very keen to renew his friendship with them so one evening I surprised Eddy by walking into Albert's guesthouse with Damien at my side. I thought Eddy was going to wet his pants with the sheer joy and excitement of seeing his handsome young Greek lover again. I had seldom seen such unbridled happiness. It was wonderful. However, I don't recall whether they spent anymore time together or whether Eddy and Damien even became sexually involved again.

Wally always behaved like a perfect lady. In public she was consistently sweet, charming, and exceptionally feminine. Unless I was personally involved in a three-way with her I never observed her alone with a woman but from what I could tell she was very much at ease letting her hair down and being completely relaxed. She was not in any way inhibited. She was very fond of dark-haired women, usually those with hair color similar to her own. Often I asked her if there was anything or anyone special that she needed and she would just smile, tilt her head slightly, and, with a twinkle in her eye, say, "Scotty, I totally trust you. You bring along whomever you please. I know she'll be fine."

During threesomes, and certainly when she had sex with Eddy, she was fine with men but, like her husband, she definitely preferred homosexual sex. I brought a slim, trim little number over to her at Albert's guest cottage one evening and when I returned later to take the young lady home she enthusiastically told me that she had never had such incredible sex in all her life. She couldn't even remember how many times she had had an orgasm that night. Wally really knew what she was doing. She did it in style and with intense passion. As I said, I never told any of the girls I fixed her up with who she really was, and none of them ever found out her true identity.

15

At the Crossroads

I was still seeing a lot of George Cukor. One member of his very extensive circle of friends was that great vixen of the silent era, Gloria Swanson. Other than a few exceptions, her career had foundered after the advent of sound, or the "talkies." I think I met her while serving at one of George's Sunday brunches and she and I became buddies. It was 1950, the same year that she was approached by writer-director Billy Wilder to play the lead of a has-been silent movie actress in *Sunset Boulevard*. She invited me to visit her on the set and, although it was great to watch her work, I have to confess that I found the whole experience boring. None of us at the time realized that this was a classic in the making. Perhaps if we did we might have been more respectful of it.

Gloria was a tiny thing, barely five feet tall. She never wanted any of her costars to get too close to her, as that made her look too short. She felt especially intimidated by the height of William Holden, her tall costar in the movie. Whenever the two of them appeared in the same shot together Wilder would have cinematographer John Seitz lower the height of the camera slightly and place Gloria closer to the lens than Holden so that she would not be dwarfed by him. On some of the camera setups when they were alongside one another, Wilder and Seitz would choose a composition and lens that excluded the actors' feet so that Gloria could stand on what was known as a two-by-four or an apple box to make her look a few inches taller. It was fascinating to watch all these cunning devices in use but I cannot help admitting that, to me, the pace of the movie-making process was excruciatingly slow. On one occasion during the filming of *Sunset Boulevard* I spent an entire night on the set on a location near Wilshire Boulevard. Most of the time it was dark, confusing, noisy, cold, and, from my perspective, little happened.

My good friend Alex Tiers, the fellow who had surprised me with a hand job in the park, was infatuated with Gloria. There was nothing physical or sexual about it at all. He was simply obsessed by her star quality, her personality, her character. He would often invite her for dinner at his home. I would come along and prepare the food for them. He would rent a tuxedo for me and I would play the butler, waiter, and bartender, just for the two of them. Due to his substantial inheritance, Alex was never short of money. He gave Gloria expensive gifts: luxury items like diamond earrings, necklaces, bracelets, brooches, rings. During dinner the lights had to be turned down low, and there were candelabras on the table. I had to make sure that there was a nonstop flow of romantic music in the background. Gloria arrived by chauffeur-driven limousine in flowing furs and fancy gowns. She was not a meat eater and was always on a strict diet. She usually toyed with her food, drank little more than a glass of champagne, accepted the gift from Alex, and then, after allowing Alex to kiss her on the hand or subtly on the cheek, she would have me summon her chauffeur. In a flourishing swish of fur, stole, silk, and lace she would laughingly disappear into the night.

AS MY TWENTY-EIGHTH BIRTHDAY neared I decided it was time to take stock of my situation. The moment was right for me to reassess my lot in life. *Where are you heading, Scotty Bowers?*, I asked myself. It was 1950. I'd been in L.A. for just five years since I'd come back from the war. I was receiving more and more offers to bartend, and that was beginning to bring in much better money than I was making at the gas station. Besides, the tricking business was getting totally out of control. The number of calls that I was receiving at the station became too many to handle. It was getting out of proportion and more than I could deal with. And I was increasingly fearful of being busted by the ever-lurking vice squad. Perhaps it was time to move on, to change careers.

My daughter Donna was nearly four years old and it was critical that I start putting money away for her education. Betty and I continued to live together but even though we cared for one another, as I said before, there wasn't much of a sexual relationship left between us. Nevertheless, I didn't want her to have to go out and work; I wanted to be the breadwinner and I was adamant about supporting her and Donna. Bartending would pay better, but even that would have to be augmented by the odd day job painting fences, mending roofs, trimming trees, laying concrete, and the like. I wasn't scared of an honest day's work. The big dilemma was whether I had the balls to hand in my notice to Bill Booth. He had come to rely on me so much and I didn't want to make any waves in his little world. I didn't want him to feel that I was letting him down. I mulled over the situation, carefully examining it from every angle. But whichever way I looked at it the time seemed right for a change. However, I kept putting off my decision. It was driving me crazy and I wasn't sure what to do.

Finally, with much regret and trepidation, I submitted my written resignation to Bill. He reluctantly accepted it, indicating that he understood it was time for a guy of my age to move on in the world, and wished me the best of luck. Meantime, I put out word that I was available for freelance bartending gigs anywhere in town, at any time, day or night. I then informed all my friends and contacts that I was no longer going to be available at the station for arranging tricks.

I received a lot of feedback about that decision, most of it expressing disappointment that Richfield Gas on Hollywood Boulevard was no longer going to be the place to go for a quick trick, or the place where you could arrange to meet pretty people or pick up folks for sex.

Bill soon hired someone to take my place and continued to operate his gas station without ever having even the slightest notion of what had been going on there for the previous five years. He was such a sweetheart, but oh so naive. I loved him dearly and I knew I was going to miss him. I also knew I was going to miss those evenings hanging out with my friends in the driveway. I was going to miss the endless ringing of the telephone at night and the pile of messages waiting for me when I checked in for work at five o'clock the next day. I was going to miss those requests for an hour in the trailer out in the back, or the five titillating minutes peeking through the hole in the wall of the washroom. All of that was now over. History. It was time for the next chapter. When I finally hung up my blue Richfield Oil uniform and walked out of the gas station at the end of 1950, it was in every way the end of an era.

16

Moving On

A lot of the gay guys who had asked me to arrange tricks for them during the gas station days were bitterly disappointed when I decided to move on. Although I was still available to arrange tricks for them, many had preferred the system we had going at the gas station. They liked to be able to drive in, arrange a trick, and quietly disappear into the night with a young man of their choice. Now they would have to resort to calling me up on the phone and, at times, leaving their name and number with Betty. To some of them this eroded the spontaneity and secretive nature of their sexual liaisons. But there were still many places in town where they could go to pick up men.

Hollywood Boulevard itself was full of gay bars at that time. Some of the better known ones were Slim Gordon's, Bradley's, and the Jade Room. In earlier days there was also the famous Streets of Paris, located below street level in a basement near Cherokee Avenue. In its restroom one wall alongside the urinals was set aside for "glory holes." What's a glory hole? Well, it is a commonly known fact that men love fellatio. All men. And in the gay world it is arguably the commonest form of sexual release. Many gay men gain added pleasure by having their dicks sucked by complete strangers. And that's what a glory hole is for. The penis is thrust into a hole in the wall and someone completely unknown sucks it off from the other side. No names, no faces, no identities, no nothing. Just sheer erotic carnal pleasure. The Streets of Paris had a row of about six or seven glory holes. Each one was separated from the one alongside it by a waist-high wall, purely for semiprivacy reasons. But a lot of guys got an added kick by being able to see the guy next to him with his loins thrust up against the wall squirming with pleasure until he reached full sexual release. Then the guy would pull his cock out of the hole, slip his trousers back up, and go back into the bar. The person who had just satisfied him sexually would remain completely incognito. During the fifties and sixties I tended bar at the private parties of many queens who had glory holes in their homes. These were often in fancy, palatial, marble-clad corners just off the pool area or situated in a room alongside the guest bathroom or bedroom.

Gay bars were a dime a dozen along Hollywood Boulevard during the fifties. Just between Highland Avenue and Vine Street, a distance of six or seven short blocks, there were at least ten gay bars, all of them well-patronized.

John Walsh was a singer who appeared at both gay and straight bars and at high-class nightclubs. I had been tricking him regularly for years and we had become good friends. He managed two extremely successful nightclubs. Café Gala, on the Sunset Strip, was owned by a wealthy British-born widow, the Baroness Catherine d'Erlanger. It was a top-class joint, frequented by the Hollywood crowd, and it had a spectacular view overlooking the city from the main dining area. Then there was the Plymouth House, also on Sunset; it was an extremely fashionable and expensive restaurant, also popular with Hollywood movie stars, producers, writers, directors, songwriters, and composers.

Just about the time I left Richfield Gas to go it alone I got a call from Johnny inviting me to join him starting a new upscale club to be located at 881 North La Cienega Boulevard. At that time there were still many private houses in that part of town. Baroness d'Erlanger had bought one of them and wanted Johnny to turn it into one of the best nightclubs in town. The place would take its name from its address and would simply become known as the 881 Club. It was to be a chic, expensive establishment with a fully equipped kitchen specializing in French cuisine. Johnny was very enthusiastic about the project and pleaded with me to join him in the process of converting the 1920s house into one of the classiest places in the city. I was thrilled. I had just resigned from the gas station and here I was being offered this gig. It came at just the right time.

We dove into the project. I cut lumber, laid down bricks, installed windows, built a bar, helped with the plumbing, lent a hand with electrical rewiring, changed the ceilings, laid down new floors, and did whatever I could with a small army of helpers. When the manual labor was over John and I stood back, put our hands on our hips, stared at our handiwork, and slapped each other on the back. We had done it and we were mightily proud of pulling it all off in a matter of only a few months. The 881 Club was ready for business.

Johnny knew that I had been dabbling in bartending at private parties for some time and as he had not yet found a professional bartender he liked he asked me if I would temporarily man the bar for him. I told him that I would happily do it for a couple of weeks but that I really wanted to get on with my life and build up my own party bartending business. Johnny was most grateful that I agreed to help out so, on opening night, armed with a veritable tower of how-to manuals on mixing exotic drinks tucked under the counter, and wearing a brand-new dress shirt and black tie, I proudly took my place behind the bar at the 881.

Things went very well that first week. Spurred on by rave reviews in the press, on the radio, and on TV, and by word of mouth, new clients flocked to the restaurant. Pretty soon we were taking reservations a month ahead of time. After the first couple of weeks I asked Johnny whether he had interviewed any candidates to take my place behind the bar but he said that he hadn't and asked if I could stay on for a few more weeks. I happily agreed; the truth is that I was enjoying myself enormously. With the help of my manuals and a bit of advice from some of our more patient customers, I was doing very well dispensing cocktails, aperitifs, wine, champagne, and after-dinner liqueur.

After our first month in business the Baroness d'Erlanger called a special meeting. She had been coming in for dinner every night and was thrilled with the quality of the food and the service. But she felt there was something missing. She was adamant that John, the maître d', the waiters, the bartender, and all staff who had direct contact with customers learn to speak fluent French.

"This is a French restaurant, bar, and club," she reminded everyone in her high-pitched and perfect British accent. "The menu, the wine list, the ambience, the food is all French. It is important, therefore, that we all speak French. We owe it to our customers. *Oui?*"

Oui indeed. Over the next few weeks the entire staff, myself included, armed ourselves with language courses on vinyl records and with dictionaries and training manuals to master the rudimentary elements of the French language. Whenever the baroness came in for dinner and asked us how things were progressing we all lied through our teeth by telling her that we were doing wonderfully with our studies.

My weeks behind the 881 Club bar slowly turned into months. Every time I broached the subject of my replacement with Johnny he would dismiss it with an excuse like, "I'm really sorry, Scotty, but there's just no one out there who comes even close to your level or expertise. But I'll keep trying."

Trying my foot. I don't think Johnny did anything to attempt to replace me. I knew the guy was fond of me. It's never a good idea to mix business with pleasure but we were still tricking one another periodically and we had a really good personal thing going. Johnny once went as far as saying that my personality and my popularity were good for the restaurant. I had developed a following. Both men and women liked me. Johnny believed that many of them were coming to the restaurant because of me. I guess there was some truth in that. People from the upper ranks of society who used to come around to the gas station to have me arrange tricks for them were now coming to the restaurant for the same reason. In a way, the 881 Club had replaced Richfield Gas as a place for connecting people for sex. I just couldn't escape it. Folks followed me wherever I went.

After a few months in business the restaurant received a visit from a representative of the bartenders' union.

"You work here?" the stocky man in the suit asked me as I served him a beer at the bar.

"No," I replied as innocently as I could. "The management is still negotiating with a few potential bartenders and haven't come to an agreement yet. I'm just helping out in the meantime."

The guy eyed me suspiciously and said that if I had any intention of staying on in the job I could only do so if I joined the union. A few weeks later he was back again.

"You still here?" he asked. "I thought you said you were only helping out."

Trying to keep a straight face, I told him that the restaurant's owners had hired a couple of different guys but that both of them had let them down. And away he went. Until another couple of weeks went by and there he was seated at the bar again.

"I think you're lyin' to me, buddy," he said, ordering his usual single beer.

"Oh, no," I lied again, trying my best to sound serious and quickly making up some cock and bull story to try to put him off.

"Yeah, right," the union man said sarcastically. And left.

This went on for weeks until I started running out of excuses and he ran out of patience. He threatened that he would have the place picketed or closed down if I stayed on without joining the union. I know he brought the matter up with John Walsh, and with the baroness herself, because about a month later my union card arrived in the mail. Johnny just winked at me when I showed it to him.

"You're legal now, Scotty," he joked. "I can't let you go now." So that was it. He had obviously applied for union membership on my behalf and paid my dues for me. He must have figured that that was one way to ensure that he had my loyalty and that I wouldn't leave the job. And the ploy seemed to work because before I knew it I had been at the 881 Club for a whole year.

But it was a year well spent. I had acquired a lot of valuable knowledge about bartending. I learned when to shake and when to stir. About how to mix the right ingredients in precisely the right order and quantities. I became familiar with my tools: the citrus stripper, the reamer, the cocktail muddler, the shaker, the strainer, the blender, the jigger, and the measurer. I learned a great deal about extracts like anise, Worcestershire sauce, coconut, Tabasco, and wormwood. About ciders, syrups, liqueurs, rum, tequila, and schnapps. I got to know most of the local and imported beers and, as the restaurant had built up a very impressive cellar, I grew familiar with the best of local and imported wines, champagnes, and ports.

But the baroness continued to bug me about my French.

"How are you progressing, Monsieur Scotty?" she would ask as I placed her favorite drink, a pink martini, in front of her when she took her usual place in the restaurant for dinner one evening.

"Oh, just swell, ma'am," I lied. "I have a French teacher now and we've already gone beyond basic French."

"That is wonderful, *mon cheri*," she cooed. And then she threw a French sentence at me. I could not understand a single word of it. I had to think quickly. I told her that I wouldn't insult her with my French until I was word perfect. She was impressed. She held out her hand. I reached out, touched the tips of her fingers, and gently kissed her hand. Her face was aglow.

"Such a sweet boy," she sighed as she smiled at me.

Me at the age of nine months.

Me at the age of three, with my brother Donald (five) and sister Phyllis (one).

Photographs courtesy of the author

Walter Pidgeon, a well-known actor in the '40s and the first guy who picked me up at the gas station.

Sadly, I don't have a photo of the Hollywood Boulevard gas station, but it looked much like this one.

Syd Guilaroff, hairstylist to Garbo, Taylor, Monroe, and others, shown here with Lana Turner; and Bill Haines, actor turned interior designer – two of the first guys I tricked in Hollywood.

Cole Porter was a great friend of mine back
in the '40s – and he loved the Marines I used to send
over to his place.

George Cukor with Greta Garbo. Cukor's pool parties
were legendary – anyone who was anyone would be there.
I first tricked him in the '40s and he introduced me to
lots of future friends.

Cary Grant and Randolph Scott – these guys were both married when I got to know them, but that didn't stop the three of us from becoming very closely acquainted.

Cary Grant & Randolph Scott: Paramount/Courtesy Neal Peters Collection

Me when I enlisted for the Marines at age eighteen.

Even though she didn't get along
with everybody, Hepburn and
I enjoyed a great friendship.
The studios claimed she was madly
in love with Spencer Tracy, but
I never saw any evidence of that.
Kate preferred the company of
women, and I always found her
the young brunettes she liked best.

Katharine Hepburn: MGM/Courtesy Neal Peters Collection

Errol Flynn was quite the lothario, but he drank so much he couldn't always satisfy the ladies I set up for him to have sex with – that's where I would step in . . .

Rita Hayworth was such a beautiful lady, but we never had the chance to go to bed together. I knew her brother Eduardo though, and through him I found out that the two of them did not get along at all.

Henry Willson agented all the best beefcake actors – I fixed him up with many guys, mostly in the '50s.

Vinny Price and his second wife Coral Browne – I tricked him for years, and set her up with young women in the '70s, but the two of them nonetheless had a very happy, if sex-free, marriage.

The Duke and Duchess of Windsor came to visit L.A. in the early '50s, and I was so flattered to hear they'd heard of me! Eddy and I had a lot of fun together, and Wally was also not as straight as she seemed.

Spencer Tracy was an incredible actor and a very sensitive guy. I used to help him out at his place in the evenings – and sometimes stayed the night.

Vivien Leigh and I went to bed together while she was shooting *A Streetcar Named Desire* and her husband Larry Olivier was busy working on another film. She was an amazing lover.

Somerset Maugham was bisexual, and heavily into voyeurism.

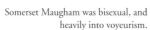

I used to trick Noël Coward when he came to Los Angeles
He was a very sexual person, and—like everyone—had his
likes and his dislikes.

Ex-actress and high-class hooker Barbara Payton.
She was quite the professional in the bedroom!

I was great pals with Desi Arnaz, the
actor husband of *I Love Lucy*'s
Lucille Ball – who was not happy
about me setting up Desi with other
women!

Poor henpecked Paul Novak with his long-term lover Mae West. Mickey Hargitay is on the left.

Steve Reeves, who I once sent over to Cukor as a trick. Like a lot of bodybuilders, he was straight but did things with guys for the cash.

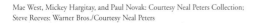

Edith Piaf, who I met when she was singing at the Mocambo – we had sex nearly every night for the four weeks she was in town. I never met Marlene Dietrich, but I sure would have liked to!

Ty Power, an old Marine buddy of mine and famous actor, whose biography was missing some of the juicy details of what he liked to get up to in the bedroom.

Charles Laughton was a brilliant actor, and had a very unusual fetish – but each to his own!

I became good friends with Ramón Novarro when he was in his fifties. He was gay, and had a very healthy sexual appetite.

I first met Rock Hudson at the gas station in '46 or '47, but got to know him better in the '50s, when I bartended at some parties for him. His homosexuality was one of the closest guarded secrets in Hollywood.

Ramón Novarro: MGM/Courtesy Neal Peters Collection;
Rock Hudson: Universal Pictures/Courtesy Neal Peters Collection

Tony Perkins, Tab Hunter's
long-term boyfriend, who
I tricked on several occasions.

James Dean with Tab Hunter.

I first tricked Brian Epstein, manager
of the Beatles, in the early '60s and
helped him out when the Beatles came
to Los Angeles in '64.

Montgomery Clift was a fussy guy when
it came to tricks.

J. Edgar Hoover, who I was very surprised to meet in the late '50s in some unusual circumstances! Here he is on the set of the movie *The Greatest Show on Earth* with Cornel Wilde, Betty Hutton, and Charlton Heston.

I tricked Raymond Burr, star of *Perry Mason,* very often, and set him up with his long-term partner, Bob Benevides.

Tennessee Williams once wrote an account of my life and adventures in Hollywood, but I told him to burn it – it was beautifully written, but made me sound like the mother of all queens!

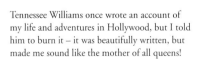

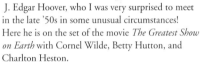

Hoover Cornel Wilde, Betty Hutton, and Charlton Heston on the set of *The Greatest Show on Earth* (1952), source unknown; Raymond Burr: CBS/Courtesy Neal Peters Collection; Tennessee Williams: Courtesy Neal Peters Collection

A photo of me taken in 2010, when I was eighty-seven years old.

Cary Grant. Need I say more?

I believe the baroness fancied me. But I wasn't going to go there. That would be pushing it. Besides, business was business and pleasure was pleasure. I had to keep them apart.

Hollywood heavyweights and studio big shots were patronizing us regularly. I would say that roughly 60 percent of our clients were gay or lesbian, and 40 percent straight. Henry Willson was a powerful and notorious agent who represented people like Rock Hudson, Tab Hunter, Robert Wagner, Chad Everett, Rory Calhoun, Guy Madison, John Derek, John Saxon, Clint Walker, and a host of young male beefcake actors, as well as actresses like Rhonda Fleming, Natalie Wood, and Lana Turner. He became a regular. In fact, he was there just about every night. We had a telephone at each booth and table in the restaurant, and Henry's ear was constantly glued to a phone no matter what time of day or night it was.

I fixed up many tricks for Henry. He was gay and totally into playing the dominant role during sex. No preambles or cock sucking for him. Henry only wanted to fuck and he was always the top.

Johnny Walsh was very good at picking the talent to perform at the club. Phyllis Diller was signed to do stand-up comedy work there for all of ten dollars a night. It was one of her earliest gigs in Hollywood, following her earlier success up in San Francisco. The crowds loved her. John signed the sultry twenty-four-year-old Julie London as a singer. Her signature song was "Cry me a River" and people went crazy when she sang it. At the end of her act they begged her to do it again as an encore, so I heard dear old Julie perform that song four times a night for heaven knows how many months. When you spend so much time close to people in show business you get to know a lot about the skeletons in their closets. Julie was married to the handsome, deep-voiced thirty-one-year-old actor Jack Webb, who had just begun to play the character Sergeant Joe Friday in the TV series that would rocket him to fame, *Dragnet*. But she was having a wild fling with jazz and pop singer Bobby Troup, who sometimes appeared with her at the club. I think Jack knew about it, and they would later divorce. Eight years later Bobby would become Julie's second husband.

Being behind the bar had its occasional challenges. There were men who brought women into the club on dates who expected them to keep up with their drinking habits. A couple of guys actually held to the belief that if a woman was not able to drink as much as her male escort he was wasting time and money on her. I had a regular who was a scotch drinker, and he liked his women to drink scotch, too. They had to keep up with him, drink for drink. In what is known as "the well," the wet area just beneath the countertop level of the bar where the bartender keeps his slices of lemon, jars of maraschino cherries, and the accoutrements of his trade, I kept a bottle of the kind of scotch this particular guy drank. But it was filled with apple juice, the same color as the scotch. As he sat there ordering drinks for himself and his lady friend I would pour her the apple juice and him the scotch. He would slowly get wasted and was never the wiser that his lady friend was not consuming as much alcohol as he was. If she excused herself to go to washroom he would sway on his bar stool and in a drunken drawl ask me, "Scotty, why the fuck am I so canned while this dumb broad behaves as though she hasn't been drinking? Christ, d'you think I can't hold my liquor anymore?"

I would just smile, shrug, and pour him another one. The evening invariably ended with me calling a cab for the lady because the guy was far too loaded to drive her home.

After a thirteen-month stint at the 881 Club I had to move on. I helped John Walsh find a replacement for me and made sure that the thriving bar would be in good hands after I left. It was time for me to embark on my life as a part-time party bartender. I wished the baroness and Johnny well and left the place with only the happiest of memories behind me.

17

Myths

By the midfifties, Los Angeles was changing. Its population had reached two million, making it the fourth largest city in the nation after New York, Chicago, and Detroit. Mike Romanoff had opened his fancy new Romanoff's restaurant on Rodeo Drive. Robinsons had launched its flagship department store at the corner of Wilshire and Santa Monica boulevards. The gigantic new CBS Television City was under construction in Hollywood, intended primarily for the development and production of color television programming. After being temporarily closed down for financial reasons, the Hollywood Bowl reopened and celebrated its thirty-third season of music and entertainment under the stars.

My daughter Donna had grown into a beautiful little girl with sparkling blue eyes and long brown hair. She was a good student, attending a grammar school on the corner of Beachwood Drive and Tamarind Avenue in Hollywood, not too far from our small apartment. Even though I did not see much of her due to my vagabond lifestyle, I adored her.

As for my good friend George Cukor, he had made extensive alterations to his property on Cordell Drive in West Los Angeles.

On the western side of his large home he had built two smaller houses. The interior of his own dwelling had been redecorated by Bill Haines, the art director and designer who had taken me up as his guest to San Simeon, William Randolph Hearst's spectacular residence on the Pacific coast back when I was a kid on a weekend pass during my boot camp days in the Marines. The orange grove around George's house had been replaced by landscaped gardens. One of the two new houses George built was rented out to Martin Pollard, a very successful and high-profile local Chevrolet dealer. The other one, where George's property fronted onto St. Ives Drive, was rented out to famed Metro-Goldwyn-Mayer megastar Spencer Tracy. George and Tracy were the best of friends. They respected one another's talents enormously. The two of them had first worked together at MGM in 1942 on the very successful romantic drama *Keeper of the Flame,* in which Tracy costarred with Katharine Hepburn.

Tracy was still a Hollywood phenomenon. During the forties there was a saying in the film industry that MGM had more stars in its firmament than there were in heaven. Tracy was one of the biggest and brightest. In a career spanning more than four decades he would be nominated for nine Academy Awards. He won two, for Best Actor in *Captains Courageous* in 1937 and for Best Actor in *Boys Town* in 1938.

When George heard that I was no longer working at the 881 Club he invited me over for brunch one Sunday. And that was the first time I met Spencer Tracy. By then I was used to being in the company of big names, but Tracy was different. He was an actor of almost mythical proportions. People felt humbled in his presence. When I arrived at George's place and saw Tracy lounging at the pool my heart skipped a beat. How was I going to react? What could I possibly talk to him about? Would I be intimidated by him? All doubts and fears were cast asunder as soon as George introduced me to him. Tracy was the easiest guy in the world to get along with. Because George didn't drink, and typically didn't have any wine or booze at home, Tracy had brought a large flask of scotch with him. The three of us sat around the pool as these two great talents of the cinema talked shop. George was never one for long, drawn out social gatherings, so by three o'clock Tracy excused himself and trotted up the driveway to the gate and then down the block to the house that he was renting on the west side of George's property. It was the maid's day off, so I decided to linger for a while and help George clear up. As we busied ourselves in the kitchen George told me that Tracy had married his wife, actress Louise Treadwell, back in 1923, the very year I was born. They had a palatial place somewhere in Beverly Hills. But Tracy desperately needed his space and his privacy. He therefore often lived alone in the house he rented from George. His marriage to Louise would last until his death in 1967. They had two children, a son John, born in 1924, and a daughter Susie, born in 1932. Sadly, John was born deaf and there was little doctors could do to help him. News of this unfortunate state of affairs never got into the press. Few people knew about it or about how much Tracy anguished over his son's debilitation. Louise devoted the rest of her life to helping deaf children through the John Tracy Clinic, which she established in Los Angeles in the early forties. Tracy was very supportive of her charitable efforts and funded much of the operating costs of the clinic himself. He was a generous, good-hearted man.

As we stashed away dishes and glassware, George and I also discussed the phony romance between Tracy and Katharine Hepburn that the studio and the publicists had concocted for public consumption. The invented story had been so well managed that the press and public alike accepted it without question. People across the United States and around the world gave it so much credence that both Tracy and Hepburn had little choice but to pretend that it was true. Whenever they worked on a movie together flashbulbs popped. They were hounded by the paparazzi if they were known to be dining out at a restaurant or seen with other members of a film's cast, dancing at the Coconut Grove. On movie productions they were always given trailers, dressing rooms, hotel suites, or bungalows alongside one another to keep the myth alive. And they both played the part. It was as though they were performing in a movie within a movie whenever they did a picture together. Such was the power of the studio publicity machine. It was like the Duke and Duchess of Windsor story all over again. Except in this case *none* of it was true. Hired Hollywood spin doctors even went so far as to say that the reason Tracy never divorced his wife Louise to marry Kate was because of his Catholic upbringing which, according to church decree, forbade divorce. It was all so farcical.

Tracy looked and behaved as masculine as they come. Think Sylvester Stallone, John Wayne, Robert Mitchum, Anthony Quinn. They don't come manlier than that. To the world—on-screen and off—Spencer Tracy was like them. Once I had started bartending more or less full time I saw Tracy a couple of times at small dinner parties, especially at George's place, and progressively began to know him better. As our acquaintanceship developed I began calling him Spence, which he preferred over Spencer. Kate Hepburn called him Spence, too.

One day—I don't remember exactly why—I got a call from Spence. He knew that in addition to working at parties and private dinners I was also available for general handyman chores and, if memory serves me correctly, I think he wanted me to take a look at his hot water cylinder or something like that. When I arrived at about two o'clock in the afternoon he was sitting in his living room listening to classical music, thumbing through a screenplay, and drinking scotch. The rented house was perfect for his needs, especially when he was working. He could spend time alone there relaxing, learning his lines, and developing his characters. And boozing. Lots of boozing. Other than Errol Flynn I seldom saw anyone put away as much alcohol as Spence did. On that particular afternoon he seemed pretty low. Apparently he had been over to his house that morning to see his wife and something had obviously upset him.

He didn't want to talk about it. Perhaps it was something to do with his son John's hearing affliction. Who knows? Anyway, I believe that I messed around with his hot water heater while he kept throwing back scotch after scotch. By sundown he must have finished an entire bottle. I offered to put together a light meal for him, which he agreed to. The next thing I knew another bottle of scotch came out and he was downing the stuff like orange juice.

As evening settled around us I laid out the meal I'd prepared and joined him in the living room. To distract him from his melancholic mood I asked him to talk about the script he had been paging through earlier that day. Flinging it across the table at me, with his words now slurring noticeably, he told me that it was for a picture called *Pat and Mike* that he was going to star in with Kate Hepburn later that year. And that's what pierced a hole in the hornet's nest. The minute he started talking about Kate something deep inside him was unleashed. He launched into a tirade about her. This was not the cool, calm, collected Spencer Tracy we were all familiar with through the characters he played on-screen. This was an angry, bitter, bruised man. He had been hurt by her. Slurring and stumbling over his words he told me that she was always rude to him, that she treated him like dirt, that she was contemptuous of him. Nothing about their great tabloid romance matched up with what Spence was telling me that evening as night fell.

Before I knew it, it was past midnight. Finally, after another empty bottle of scotch stood on the coffee table he began to undress and begged me not to leave him. I did not have the heart to say no. It was clear to me that Spence desperately needed someone to be with him. He was hurting badly. I could only assume that his pseudo-romance with Kate Hepburn was causing him this distress. I turned off the lights, undressed him, then got undressed myself, climbed into bed with him, and held him tightly like a baby. He continued to slobber and curse and complain. By then he had had so much to drink that I hardly understood a word he was saying. I tried to pacify him by saying that by morning all would be well and that we should try to get some sleep, but he wasn't ready for that. Instead, he lay his head down at my groin, took hold of my penis and began nibbling on my foreskin. This was the last guy on earth that I expected an overture like that from, but I was more than happy to oblige him and despite his inebriated state we had an hour or so of pretty good sex.

At about four in the morning I woke up with a start. Spence had got out of bed and was stumbling around the bedroom trying to find the door to the bathroom to take an urgently needed pee. He fumbled for the light switch but couldn't find it, so he just let loose. One moment he was urinating up against the drapes, the next into an open closet, then all over the carpet. Finally he fell back into bed and immediately lapsed into a deep sleep, snoring like an express train.

The next morning there wasn't even the slightest hint of how drunk he'd been, that he'd pissed in the corner of the bedroom, or that we'd had sex together. He didn't say a word about it. It was as though none of it ever happened.

That was the first of many sexual encounters I had with Spence. Sometimes I would go to his place at five in the afternoon and sit around the kitchen table with him until two in the morning as he drank himself into a stupor. Then he would be ready for a little sex. Despite everything, he was a damn good lover. The great Spencer Tracy was another bisexual man, a fact totally concealed by the studio publicity department. That is, if they ever knew about it at all.

I met a lot of influential people through Spence. One of them was screenwriter Leonard Spigelgass, who wrote *So Evil My Love, Because You're Mine, Deep in My Heart,* and *Gypsy.* I fixed Lenny up with many young guys. Lenny in turn introduced me to the very talented writer Dore Schary, who penned the screenplays for pictures like *Broadway Melody of 1940; Young Tom Edison; Edison, the Man; The Battle of Gettysburg;* and *Sunrise at Campobello.* Dore later became a producer, helming *Westward the Women, Plymouth Adventure, Bad*

Day at Black Rock, and *The Swan.* In 1951 he took over from legendary mogul Louis B. Mayer as head of Metro-Goldwyn-Mayer, then regarded as the crème de la crème of Hollywood studios.

GEORGE CUKOR'S HOME on Cordell Drive was a magnet for so many august and talented people. Two of them were a husband and wife who were also two of the most respected actors of their day: Laurence Olivier and Vivien Leigh. When I met them at a small dinner at George's in the early fifties they seemed hopelessly in love (they eventually divorced in 1961 after twenty-one years of marriage).

Olivier was forty-four, sprightly, and had been knighted by King George VI three years earlier. He could quote Shakespeare and remember entire scenes from the Bard's plays as easily as some people remember their home address or telephone number. Despite his title he insisted that everyone, including me, call him Larry, even though the first time I met him at George's I was helping to serve dinner, not seated as a guest at the table. He was witty, articulate, at ease, and never pompous. He didn't need to be. He knew who he was and was deeply aware of how much people respected him. He was the doyen of the British stage and everyone knew it. He was also the life of a party. Whenever he came to dinner he led the conversation, set the mood, and maintained the pace. It was wonderful to see him and George in conversation. I so much wanted to see the two of them make a film together, but that would have to wait for more than two decades, until 1975, when George directed Larry and Kate Hepburn in the made-for-TV movie *Love Among the Ruins.*

Larry often came to town from his native England. Even though he was married he secretly harbored a liking for boys. He never openly admitted it but, to me, it was obvious. When he was here alone he would frequently call me up and ask me to arrange for a busty blonde and a well-hung guy to make up a threesome with him. Each time I sent a couple over to his hotel room—or wherever he was staying—he would ask for a different girl but, quite often, he would request the same guy.

"He was very nice," Larry would say. "Make sure you send him over again next time."

Larry's exquisitely beautiful wife Vivien Leigh had been born in India of British parents, received a British education, and was thirty-eight years old when I met her. When she was twenty-six years old she played Scarlett O'Hara in *Gone with the Wind*, which won her a well-deserved Academy Award for Best Actress. She first met George Cukor on that film, since he was the director before being replaced by Victor Fleming because of creative differences with producer David O. Selznick. Leigh was upset about the change in director and throughout shooting she would often secretly consult George about how to play Scarlett. She once confided in me that she felt she was getting better direction behind the scenes from George than she was getting on the set from Victor Fleming. Rumor once had it that the film's male star, Clarke Gable, had not been happy about being directed by Cukor because he was gay.

"I don't want that fag directing me in a goddamned Civil War movie," Gable was reputed to have said.

But there was no truth in the rumor. Someone had planted the story in the gossip columns of the Hollywood trade papers simply to undermine George's reputation. The real problem had to do with Selznick and George's differing visions for the film. Victor Fleming did a fabulous job of it, but I wonder how George's subtleties and sensitivities would have translated to the screen.

The film Vivien Leigh was about to start shooting at the time I met her was the Tennessee Williams classic, *A Streetcar Named Desire*. She had played the character Blanche DuBois on the stage many times, but a movie is not a play. Filming is a tedious, drawn-out process. Someone once said that being an actor in a movie is like trying to beat the world record for running a mile as quickly as possible but while you have to stop every five seconds to catch your breath. Playing a role out of sequence, repeating your actions over and over again, performing for a camera and not a live audience is totally different than acting on the stage. It's a very tough job indeed. Vivien had come to America with Larry because they both knew that doing the movie of *Streetcar* was going to be a tough assignment and Larry wanted to be near her. The production was going to tax her acting talents to the hilt. Nevertheless, after the film was released she would be honored with an Academy Award as well as a BAFTA Award for her superb performance in it.

Unfortunately, Vivien was a very highly strung person and suffered from what we today know as bipolar disorder, for which in those days there was little treatment besides electric shock therapy. Even at dinner parties I could see her mood swing from one extreme to the other. One thing I did know is that she fancied me, and I had the hots for her. While she was making *Streetcar* Larry signed to do a film called *Carrie,* for director William Wyler, so the couple were not consistently together, and Vivien often came around to George's place for dinner alone. One night he had her and three or four other guests over, and because she was alone, George insisted that she spend the night in the guest room next to the swimming pool. As usual I helped serve dinner. She and I kept eyeing one another throughout the evening, trying our best to avoid being spotted by George and the other guests. For us the whole meal was one long teasing game of foreplay, and by the time we got to dessert and coffee we were both horny as hell for one another. After the other guests left I helped the maid tidy up. On my way out George and Vivien both stood at the front door. George gave me a big bear hug and a quick kiss on the forehead and Vivien gave me a light kiss on my cheek and whispered into my ear "Get your ass back over here in half an hour. I'll leave the gate unlocked."

I just smiled, bid them goodnight, and left.

Thirty minutes later I turned my car back onto Cordell Drive and parked it about a hundred feet away from George's property. The gate had indeed been left unlocked by Vivien and so, quiet as a mouse, I opened it and made my way across the lawn down to the pool level and slipped into the guest room. Vivien was dressed in a robe and looked sexier than I'd ever seen her. We had to be careful. The room directly above the guest suite was called the Suede Room. George had furnished it as a sort of study-cum-sitting room. Bill Haines, the decorator, had plastered the walls with plush suedelike wallpaper. George was very proud of the room and hardly ever used it. The room to the west of that was his bedroom, and George was a very light sleeper. The slightest noise would wake him. Vivien and I looked at one another, sniggered quietly, and tried to make as few sounds as possible as we began to passionately make out. It wasn't long before our clothes were off and we were tumbling around the big double bed engaged in various forms of foreplay. She was a hot, hot lady. She was very sexual and very excitable. Once she got going she required full and complete satisfaction. That night we screwed as though the survival of the world depended on it. Vivien could not control herself. She was loud. She would squeal and holler and laugh. She had orgasm after orgasm and each one was noisier than the last. She yelled and called out louder and louder. I tried to shush her by gently putting my finger on her lips but she wasn't interested.

"I don't care if George hears us," she wailed deliriously. "I just don't care."

And then she hollered in ecstasy some more. This was one of the best fucks I had ever had. I didn't want it to end and I, too, didn't care one iota if we woke George and the entire neighborhood. By the time we were completely spent, a couple of hours later, we collapsed on the bed, thoroughly drained and exhausted.

Vivien eventually got up the next morning, perched herself in front of her dressing table mirror, and began brushing her hair. Suddenly her weird behavior kicked in. We'd just had wonderfully intense sex, and I know we both felt good, but without even turning to face me she continued brushing her hair and said, "Why are we doing this, Scotty? This isn't right, you know."

"What isn't?" I asked.

"This is all wrong. We cannot do this anymore," she uttered. "Please leave. I don't ever want to see you again."

"You sure?" I asked, quite shocked at her 180-degree turnabout.

"Yes. Absolutely," she said emphatically. "We can't ever see each other again."

She got up, disappeared into the bathroom, and refused to come out. Feeling more than a little hurt by being so coldly dismissed I got dressed and made for the door. But just as I was leaving Vivien flew out of the bathroom, threw herself on me and slobbered, "Oh, darling, darling boy. I'm sorry. Can you come around again tonight?"

She was as impossibly unpredictable as they come, but she was quite a gal. I saw her often after that. You seldom get a roll in the hay the way you did with Vivien Leigh.

18

Bar Service

My bartending life was flourishing. I was beginning to work just about every night of the week. I was pouring drinks and serving at dinners at private homes for old friends and new ones: Tyrone Power, Walter Pidgeon, Ed Willis, Syd Guilaroff, Randy Scott, Cary Grant, Errol Flynn, Spencer Tracy, William Holden, Bob Hope, and a host of others.

Bob Hope was a very nice man and always discreet about his extramarital affairs. He liked older women, not the younger ones who were originally part of my gas station brigade. I fixed him up with a lot of hookers, many of them high class, expensive ladies. His favorite was a very well-known ex-actress by the name of Barbara Payton. For many years she was regarded as the number one hooker in town. She had class and she had style. She also had looks and a great body. And she had great technique, and charged accordingly. However, earlier on she had lived quite frugally in one of the apartment buildings where Betty and I lived before we got our house. Barbara and I had sex together a few times and I have to say that a half hour with her was like two hours with someone else. She was electrifyingly sexy and made a man feel totally and wholly satisfied. There were quite a few occasions when Bob Hope came over to see her. Once or twice she let me hide in the closet in her bedroom and peek at them. Bob didn't take his time over anything, including sex. He'd be in and out of her apartment within twenty to thirty minutes. He never wasted any time—or money—on drinks or dinner or gifts or small talk. It was simply a matter of arriving, getting straight to business, and then leaving. He just wanted to get his rocks off, pure and simple.

Bob was totally straight and loved the ladies a lot. He and his wife Dolores lived in Toluca Lake, and I'm not sure whether she knew that he saw hookers periodically. He was a smart, funny, jovial guy. And in the course of his work, especially during the war when he was entertaining the troops, he always had a lot of pretty girls around him. As a result of his wartime experience Bob knew a lot of important people on Capitol Hill, in the Pentagon, and in the military. He would frequently call me up and say, "Scotty, I've got a captain friend coming into town. Do you have a nice girl for him?"

I would arrange things accordingly, often driving the lady myself to wherever the guy was staying, sometimes at a military base, usually at a downtown hotel, but never at Bob's place in Toluca Lake because he didn't want Dolores to find out about these little liaisons.

I USED TO BARTEND and serve dinner regularly for the actor Franklin Pangborn. He was very aloof, prissy, and amusing, and usually cast in the role of a maître d' or a hotel clerk or restaurant manager. He had appeared in a bunch of forgettable movies that included *Stage Door, Topper Takes a Trip, Bachelor Daddy, Two Weeks to Live,* and *My Best Gal,* but he also appeared in *Now, Voyager* and *Hail the Conquering Hero.* Frank saw himself as something of a socialite and was fond of throwing glittering get-togethers at his home in Beverly Hills. One day at about three in the morning, after working at one of his parties, I was leaving his house in my two-door white Chrysler 300 when a cop stopped me. Beverly Hills had its own police force and even though the cops were generally a little friendlier and less threatening than those in the employ of the city of Los Angeles I immediately panicked. Nothing untoward had transpired at Frank's party but most of his guests were gay and in those days the vice squad was always on the prowl for gay people. I pulled over to the side of the road as a large officer came striding up to my side window and tapped on it. I was scared.

"What are you doing here?" he demanded.

"Well, officer," I replied, slightly stuttering, "I'm coming from a party."

"At this time of the morning?" he asked.

"Well, yes," I squeaked.

Cocking his head to one side he asked me what kind of a party it was. I was hesitant to tell him that it was a gay party. By now I was certain that whatever I said would get me into a load of trouble. The cops were generally homophobic. They didn't like anyone who was different, especially folks who were involved with the movies or the arts. I suspected he would be only too keen to find the slightest reason to arrest me for something I hadn't even done. I told him that it was a gathering of friends, just a bunch of guys celebrating the fact that one of their buddies had just got a part in a new movie. Well, that did it.

"Guys?" he asked. "Only guys?"

I couldn't lie, so I nodded. I felt guilt written all over my face.

"Step out of the car, please," he said. "Bring your driver's license and insurance papers with you."

I opened the glove compartment, took out my insurance papers, got out of the car, and pulled my driver's license from my wallet. He eyed my every move. Taking my documents he looked at them under the light of a small flashlight that he had detached from his belt. Without so much as glancing at me he said, "I've seen your car around here quite a bit in recent weeks."

"Yes," I responded, getting more nervous by the second. "I get around a lot and this guy's a good friend of mine."

"You must be pretty popular," the cop said, handing me back my license and insurance papers. "Who's your friend, the party giver?"

"Pangborn," I said, "Franklin Pangborn."

"The movie star?" he asked.

"The very one," I said.

He stared at me for a moment or two, not saying a word. "Get back in your car and follow me," he ordered.

I nervously got back into my car, started it up, and began following him as he drove off. We went about two blocks before he turned down a dark side street. Then he pulled into a driveway of a large unlit mansion and drove around to the back. I obediently followed. He motioned to me to turn off my engine and get into his car.

As I slid into the seat next to him he leaned back, sighed, and, without looking at me he explained that the owners of the house were away and that they had paid him to keep an eye on the place. He said he went to check on it twice every night. Then he looked at me.

"There's not a soul here," he said.

Before I knew it the big cop was all over me. He put one hand on my knee, unbuttoned my fly with the other hand, leaned over, and began sucking on my cock. I couldn't believe this was happening but settled back and let him have his way with me. When it was all over his entire personality changed. He told me he was married, had kids, lived in faraway Covina and that his life was more frustrating than he could bear. In the next half hour he gave me his whole life story, spilled his deepest secrets, bared his soul. I hardly had a chance to say a word, so I just listened. And then listened some more. When he had finished what he had to say he thanked me for listening and said I could leave.

But not before he asked, "Can I see you again?"

I nodded. I felt for the guy. I sensed his pain, his frustration, his difficulty living a life in which he could not reveal his true self. I saw him periodically during the next two to three years. He often stopped me on the streets of Beverly Hills at night. He recognized my license plate, which had no numerals on it, only the word DONNA, after my daughter. After some time he just seemed to disappear. I never heard from him again and never found out what happened to him. I hope he found happiness.

LIFE WENT ON. Parties came and went.

One evening at a function where my friends Peter Bull and Brian Desmond Hurst were guests—it was sometime during the late fifties, I think—I was introduced to one of the most interesting Englishmen I had ever met. He was the highly acclaimed author and playwright Somerset Maugham. He was in his seventies and was in town working on an outline for a screenplay or a television script, I cannot remember which. His best-known novel was *Of Human Bondage,* published in 1915, yet he'd also written *The Moon and Sixpence, The Trembling of a Leaf, East of Suez, The Constant Wife,* and the brilliant antiwar play, *For Services Rendered,* by the time I met him. His later writings included *The Razor's Edge, Catalina,* and *Quartet.* He was utterly charming, suave, and dignified. He was seldom dressed in anything but the finest, tailored double-breasted suit and tie but there were occasions when he was informally attired in a cashmere sweater, shirt, and cravat. The studio or production company that had been responsible for bringing him over from England for the writing assignment had put him up at the Beverly Hills Hotel. It wasn't a suite but a regular-sized room and he was sharing it with his boyfriend-cum-secretary, Alan Searle. Because I was tricking the manager of the Beverly Hills Hotel, I was able to persuade him to arrange a nice larger bungalow for Maugham and Searle, where they would be more comfortable and private. Maugham's full name was William Somerset Maugham so, once you got to know him well enough, you called him Willie. Already too old to serve in World War II he had spent the war years in Hollywood and the Deep South. Because he was bisexual he had quite a few affairs with women and was married from 1917 to 1928. An extramarital affair with the woman who became his wife produced a daughter, Liza.

Willie's great love had been a man named Gerald Haxton. They spent many years together before Gerald died in 1944. I don't think Willie ever got over his death. Nevertheless, once he met Alan Searle, a good-looking but rather opinionated and scandal-mongering fellow quite a lot younger than Willie, he took him under his wing and they became inseparable.

I found Willie and Alan to be delightful, and the three of us got along splendidly. They were also avid sexual voyeurs, seldom if ever getting involved in the action themselves. They had interesting and varied tastes and I would often fix up tricks for them in their bungalow at the Beverly Hills Hotel. Sometimes they wanted to watch two men who were lovers. Occasionally they wanted to see a guy and a girl together. At other times they wanted only two girls. Now and then I would bring three or four young couples to their bungalow and each pair would do something entirely different. One couple would be in the sixty-nine position, two gay males would take turns sucking one another off, two lesbians would perform cunnilingus on each other, a straight duet would be having sex in the missionary position, and so on. Willie would sit in an armchair fully dressed in jacket and tie, his legs elegantly crossed, sipping wine, and watching while Alan sat close by, observing everything with a deadpan expression on his face. Alan seldom showed his emotions. He was always as stiff-upper-lipped as an eccentric Englishman could possibly be. The lights were always turned down very low during these little sessions. I would cover all the lamp shades and reading lights with pillowcases or towels to keep the room very dim. Willie was generous to the young performers. The shows would go on for an hour or two and then conclude with him giving each of the performers a substantial tip.

Another fine talent from across the pond whom I got to know extremely well was Britain's master of mirth, myth, and music, Noël

Coward. In fact, he was often referred to by his nickname, the "Master." During conversation, his fellow Brits and many of his American friends would easily switch between calling him Noël and Master. I cannot recall where I met him, though it must certainly have been at a private Hollywood dinner party where I was working.

I remember his engaging British accent as he removed his long cigarette holder from his mouth, flashed his white teeth at me, firmly shook my hand, and said, "How utterly splendid it is to meet you, Mr. Bowers. I have heard so much about you."

I knew he meant it. I was proud of the fact that my reputation was preceding me. Just as things used to be at the gas station a few years back, if any kind of tricking was involved, people knew that all they had to do was call me.

I must have been introduced to Noël sometime around the mid-fifties because I clearly remember him talking to the dinner guests about his upcoming cabaret debut in Las Vegas and about a series of planned CBS television shows with Mary Martin, fresh from her role as Ensign Nellie Forbush in Rodgers and Hammerstein's smash hit Broadway musical, *South Pacific*. Noël was in town often, usually staying at the Beverly Hills Hotel. He was always jotting down notes and scribbling things on pieces of paper. Like so many other talented and successful British artists and performers at the time, Noël had left his native England to avoid the country's excessively high taxation rates. He first settled in Bermuda and later bought homes in Jamaica and Switzerland. He was highly critical of Prince Edward, the Duke of Windsor, for abdicating in order to marry Wallis Simpson. He thought it "irresponsible." Oddly, he never mentioned anything in my presence about Edward's homosexuality. I'm certain he must have known about it.

Noël had many lovers in his day, including Prince George, the Duke of Kent; actors Alan Webb and Louis Hayward; and playwright Keith Winter. His longest relationship was with the South African actor Graham Payn, who featured in a few of his

London stage productions. But he was usually alone when he was in Los Angeles. We were attracted to one another and so I tricked him often. However, for the Master, penetrative sex was out. It was strictly oral, with lots of bodily touching, caressing, and kneading in between. We had many long steamy sessions together. I knew exactly what he liked and he always commended me on my skills. When it comes to sex every single person is different, but those differences are usually so slight, so subtle, that unless you're really tuned in you can overlook them or not even be aware that they exist. Good sex is all about how much is too much, how little is too little, about that thin dividing line between consistency and variety, between meeting the expected and surprising with the unexpected. It is about that delicate moment of touch in exactly the right place at the right moment to heighten the experience, to create a sizzling electrical charge that permeates the full body from head to toe. Noël had distinct likes, dislikes, and preferences and I quickly learned which of his buttons to press. On one of his visits to town he tried to get me to return to his home in the Caribbean with him. He even handed me a first-class return steamer ticket but I had to turn down the enticing offer. There was just too much going on in L.A., which prevented me from being away for that long. On another occasion Noël asked me to spend a vacation in Tahiti with him but, again, I had to refuse. Instead, I sent quite a few young guys down to the Caribbean for him. They would stay at his home with him for a few weeks, keeping him happily distracted as he continued to write. He paid all their expenses and fares, no questions asked.

Noël had an incredible intellect. He was witty, wise, and had an infectious sense of humor. When he was in stimulating company he always had something new to say. He *never* repeated himself. His command of the English language was astonishing. One night Noël and the actress Tallulah Bankhead were at a party where

I was working. Tallulah was a very bright lady who had once been a member of the famed Algonquin Round Table. The guests at this particular party were having a lively competition to determine who could come up with the cleverest, wittiest, most incisive statement about a subject that everyone had agreed upon. Try as she might, Tallulah could not beat Noël at the game. He would always top whatever she said.

One evening Noël was a guest at yet another party where I was bartending and Maxene Andrews walked in, arm in arm with a girlfriend. Maxene was one of the three famous Andrews sisters who had boogie-woogied their way to the top of the hit parade and sang to the troops during World War II. Maxene was a lesbian, and quite open about it.

As they swished past the chair where Noël was sitting he closed his eyes, raised his eyebrows, flicked the ash off the end of the cigarette in his long cigarette holder, and uttered quite loudly, "Good gracious me. How odd of God to waste three cunts on the Andrews sisters. He could have done well enough with two."

And then he turned to his companion and continued whatever conversation they had been having. Everyone in the room exploded with laughter. Fortunately, Maxene and her companion were out of earshot.

As time went by my circle of friends continued to grow. My services as a host and bartender at private dinners, cocktail parties, birthdays, and all sorts of social gatherings were in ever greater demand. I became well-known for a special little trick that I started performing. I can't remember when I first did it but people began demanding that I do it, especially at gay parties. This was my "Swizzle Stick Trick." Since nature endowed me with a cock of which I have always been proud I would often whip it out and stir drinks with it. Folks loved that. At mixed parties where the women knew me well enough I would also do it. People loved to order cocktails and watch me stir them with my flaccid penis. Needless to say, I would always add ice to the drink only after I'd stirred it!

Those were wild and wonderful days. Often just before I drifted off into sleep I would stare up at the ceiling and simply count my blessings, feeling overwhelmingly grateful for my lot in life. There was no doubt about it, Hollywood was simply the most marvelous place in the world for anyone to be.

19

Finding Out

I was working at a party in the Hollywood Hills in the early fifties when I first met him; few people knew who he was. Yet he was to make an indelible impression on the science of human sexual research and become a household name. He was biologist and professor of entomology and zoology, Dr. Alfred Charles Kinsey, then in his late fifties. He had shaken the very foundations of science, sociology, and medicine in 1948 with the publication of his first book, *Sexual Behavior in the Human Male*. At the time we met he was writing his second ground-breaking tome, *Sexual Behavior in the Human Female*. He was discussing it with a group of friends and medical associates at a party and was complaining about how difficult it was to gain access to young women who were prepared to freely share stories of their sexual experiences with him.

Toward the end of the evening when the conversation around the table had grown louder, and as groups of diners broke off into different discussions, I leaned over his shoulder to remove his dessert plate and whispered into his ear, "I think I might be able to help you in your research, sir."

Later in the evening he took me aside and told me all about the Institute for Sex Research, known as the ISR, which he had established as a nonprofit organization on the campus of Indiana University in Bloomington, Indiana. His research associates were Clyde Martin, Wardwell Pomeroy, and Paul Gebhard. Nothing like the ISR had ever existed before. However, Kinsey said he was getting frustrated over the difficulties he was having gaining access to young women to interview because there was a longstanding social stigma against open discussion of female sexual behavior. He wanted to investigate the subject as deeply as possible, just as he had done a few years earlier with his report on males. He wanted to know what I meant when I said I might be able to help him. I told him that I thought I might be able to introduce him to some of my female friends who may want to share their stories with him. To discuss it further we arranged to meet a couple of days later. That was when my close and utterly fascinating relationship with Alfred Kinsey began.

At our next meeting I told Kinsey all about what I had been doing ever since I got out of the Marines. He was intrigued. No, he was more than that. He was utterly fascinated. Because of the new book he was working on he was particularly interested in what I knew about the female of the species, most specifically with regard to lesbianism. His aim was to focus on numerous aspects of female sexuality: marital sex, extramarital sex, homosexuality, bisexuality, oral sex, masturbation, and prostitution. He was fascinated but not surprised when I told him how prevalent I had found lesbianism to be in society. Up until then researchers were much more aware of gay sexual activities among men but not much was known about lesbian behavior. Kinsey wanted to break through those barriers. He wanted to prove that there was just as much homosexual activity going on among women as there was among men and that it ought to be classified as a normal part of human sexual behavior. He explained to me what he was looking for and I expressed an interest in showing him not only how much lesbianism there was but also the degree of variation there was in the many forms of lesbian sexual activities. After our meeting he made enquiries around town about my credentials and within a week he enthusiastically embraced me as a member of his team. But everything would take place in confidence. I would never be credited for any assistance I might bring to the project and all the young ladies I recruited to help his institute in its research would remain nameless. Their identities would not be revealed.

And so began a number of trips to Bloomington, Indiana. Over a period of about two months Kinsey flew me and a group of young women whom I had handpicked, from Los Angeles on United Airlines to Chicago and then from there on Lake Central Airlines to Bloomington. To remain within the boundaries of the law the girls I had chosen were always eighteen or older, but we were especially keen to recruit those who looked about seventeen, simply because that is the average age at which females became sexually active, especially those commencing college. To accurately reflect that group we wanted them to look like typical bobby-soxers of the time, replete with pom-poms, ribbons, saddle shoes, white socks, and short skirts.

We shot hours of 16mm and 8mm film of them on the Indiana University campus, portraying them as typical college students. We followed them around in groups of two or three, observing them in class, coming out of class, chewing gum, giggling, and wiggling as boys made passes at them, and then eavesdropping over their shoulders as they retired to their rooms and dormitories. There, behind locked doors, prevailing myths were shattered as the girls undressed, made out with one another, and engaged in various forms of sex. They practiced cunnilingus, played with dildos, masturbated, and did everything that college-aged kids did in real life in the big wide world. There was nothing abnormal in any of this. That's what young ladies did, even back in the fifties. The people we had chosen for these scenes were not necessarily lesbian but they were more than happy to experiment, discover, and explore their sexuality for the cameras. And that was the point of it all. We wanted to show the sexual variety expressed among young females. At that time most doctors, psychologists, psychiatrists, sociologists, anthropologists, educationists, academics, and certainly religious leaders and parents refused to accept the idea that young college girls engaged in sexual experimentation of any kind, let alone—heaven forbid!—lesbian activities. Kinsey wanted to pull off people's blindfolds, provide them with the truth, and open their minds to reality.

Because of strict antipornography laws in Indiana we had to take extra precautions when processing the film that we had shot. Kinsey and I made contact with a guy who I will simply refer to as Bob because he asked me never to reveal his name to anyone. Of course, it would be safe to do so now, but a promise is a promise. Bob worked as an industrial chemist for the Eastman Kodak Company in Rochester, New York. Once filming was completed Kinsey used to fly Bob to Bloomington, together with big metal cases full of processing and laboratory equipment, and Bob set it all up in a darkened warehouse beside a local film processing laboratory where we had established discreet local contacts. There the motion picture film was processed and printed and then brought over in unmarked cans to the institute.

Behind the bolted doors of meeting rooms and lecture halls we showed the material to groups of researchers and counselors. Middle-aged women were always the most resistant. They were especially doubtful about our work or simply wanted to deny that lesbianism existed on American college campuses. But Kinsey quickly managed to dispel their myopic thinking. When *Sexual Behavior in the Human Female* came out in book form in 1953 it caused an outcry. However, people gradually simmered down and began to grasp the validity and extensive range of Kinsey and his team's research. Women's clubs and other organizations were the last barriers to fall as they reluctantly came to accept the fact that lesbianism indeed existed and was practiced in American society, from college age upward. Prior to that, as I said earlier, the thinking was that only men engaged in homosexuality. Some hard-liners still clung to the belief that lesbianism was only to be found in prisons, where women were alone, or in places where they were deprived of heterosexual relationships. Kinsey and his team overturned all that thinking. Lesbianism was as prevalent as gay sex. It was part of human life. Amazingly, once the book came out the sluice gates opened. Counselors at colleges and universities all over the country began to be inundated by questions from female students who admitted that they were confused about their sexual orientation or who came out of the closet and openly stated that they were lesbian.

I got to know Kinsey and his partners Martin, Pomeroy, and Gebhard really well. But the better I knew them the more I realized that they were actually surprisingly square and out of touch with things. They didn't really have the full picture of what was going on in the alternative and counterculture tiers of society. Despite all of Kinsey's work he was still rather naive in some ways. I wanted to help him. I wanted to expose him to what he was trying to find out. I wanted to contribute to the database of knowledge of what really went on in the big wide world.

I brought the subject up with Willie Somerset Maugham one day and was thrilled when Willie said, "Well, dear boy, arrange a little soirée of a mixed bag of, say, half a dozen at my bungalow on Saturday night and bring this Kinsey fellow along with you. I'd love to meet him."

So I did. I arranged for a straight couple, plus two gays and two lesbians to give us a little performance at Willie's bungalow at the Beverly Hills Hotel. I dragged Kinsey along with me. Actually, dragged is the wrong term. He was only too happy to be there. He was also thrilled to meet Willie and Alan. As Kinsey stared at the young people getting up to their antics I watched him. He was mesmerized. I don't think he expected anything like what he saw that night. It was raw, open, unfettered, uninhibited, totally indulgent sex. At times I wanted to laugh out loud as I watched the expressions on his face, but I managed to stifle the urge by convincing myself that this little spectacle wasn't meant for fun but, for want of a better term, "wholesome scientific research."

Over the years, Kinsey continued to conduct extensive interviews for the ISR. He often told me that some of the most revealing information came from prisoners. Inmates at state and local penitentiaries were only too happy to spend a day in the prison library talking to him about their sex lives. Prisoners would delve into the minutest detail about their personal histories and sexual experiences, often spending hours at a time with him. Kinsey found their help invaluable. They provided a captivating window into the sexual mores of society.

Kinsey also wanted to research pornography. But that was a totally taboo topic in those days. Unlike current times, pornography was extremely hard to come by during the fifties. It was illegal in every single state of the union. Certainly it existed, but it was always underground, always behind locked doors, always in back alleys, always in hushed and whispered tones in secret places. God help you if you were caught with explicitly sexual pictures. People used to come back from Europe with dirty postcards sewn into the linings of their suitcases or hidden in their unwashed laundry. Pornography was a passport to trouble. Over the years I was at a number of parties where pornographic photographs were being passed around among the guests and suddenly the vice squad appeared at the front door. They would interrogate everyone present and search the place. It didn't matter if you were rich or famous, a pauper or a movie star. No one was above the law. If you were discovered to be in possession of pornographic material you were in deep trouble. Some people had clandestine screenings of 16mm or 8mm porno films at home. If the vice squad was tipped off they would raid the house and immediately seize the projector and films and any other equipment. Those present would be arrested without question and would have to explain themselves to the judge the next morning. Oddly enough, if you were found with photographs of a male and female engaging in normal heterosexual sex—usually a guy having intercourse with a girl in the missionary position—you might be able to get away with just a stern warning. The cops would most likely hand images like that back to their owners.

However, if the photos depicted a woman performing fellatio on a man or a guy going down on a woman or, heaven forbid, two members of the same sex together, that would count as flagrant pornography.

I have no idea how he came to the information but Kinsey always maintained that the biggest collection of pornography in the world was in the possession of the Roman Catholic Church in the Vatican. I found that hard to believe but he was convinced of it. According to him, the second largest selection was owned by ex-King Farouk of Egypt. When he told me that my interest was immediately piqued. The reason was because I had a direct connection to the Egyptian royal family.

"Is that true, Alfred?" I asked him. "Because if it is I might be able to find out more for you."

"How?" he queried.

"Well," I said, "I know Farouk's sister. She lives right here in Los Angeles and I occasionally work at parties and dinners for her."

Kinsey could hardly believe it and I said I would see what I could do.

Princess Faiza Fouad Rauf was a sultry looking Beverly Hills socialite in her thirties who threw extravagant parties and lived the luxurious life of an Egyptian princess. Which is exactly what she was. She was one of the three sisters of King Farouk, monarch of Egypt. His full title was the very fancy sounding His Majesty Farouk I, by the grace of God, King of Egypt and of Sudan, Sovereign of Nubia, of Kordofan, and of Darfur. It doesn't get more grand than that. The problem was that King Farouk was forced to abdicate in 1952 following allegations of corruption, an overly excessive lifestyle, pilfering valuable objects and artifacts from his hosts while on state visits abroad, a lack of empathy for his people, and, worst of all, the ramifications resulting from Egypt's defeat during the 1948 Arab-Israeli War. He was deposed in a military coup led by Gamal Abdel Nasser and forced into exile. After he left Egypt he settled in Italy and Monaco but much of his wealth and treasures went with him. Twice divorced and now single, Farouk fancied himself a playboy, womanized wherever he went, continued to live the high life, spent a fortune on himself, and indulged in his passion for fine cuisine. The result was that he became chronically obese, weighing in at around three hundred pounds. He traveled extensively and occasionally visited his sister Princess Faiza in Beverly Hills. The story of how she came to settle on the west coast of America was fascinating and, I might add, not without tragedy.

While still in Egypt, unlike her two sisters, she refused to marry into a Middle Eastern royal family or become a spouse to a ruler of the Arab world. Her sister Princess Fawzia did the opposite. She became the first wife of Mohammad Reza Shah Pahlavi, the last Shah of Iran. Princess Faiza yearned for something simpler than that, though not necessarily less luxuriant. She settled on her cousin, Mehmet Ali Rauf, a Western-educated scholar and grandson of the Khedive, Ishmael Pasha. Ishmael Pasha was the Turkish viceroy to Egypt during the time of the Ottoman Empire, but Mehmet Ali Rauf's station in life was more that of a common man. No royal blood flowed in his veins. Princess Faiza's brother, King Farouk, was never enchanted with the marriage but reluctantly accepted it. The couple made their home in the Zohria Palace in Cairo but their relationship was not a happy one. When Princess Faiza's brother was forced to abdicate from the Egyptian throne she, too, became a victim of Nasser's revolution and the banishment of the entire royal family. Much of her property was confiscated and the couple moved to Paris where they eventually divorced. Though she had lost much she still had sufficient funds and other resources to begin her life all over again. So she moved to California. She instantly fell in love with the place. She enjoyed the easy, relaxed lifestyle of Los Angeles and felt liberated to be able to mix with whomever she chose.

I began working for her pretty soon after her arrival in town. She was a very beautiful woman and extremely popular among the Hollywood crowd. Honoring my pledge to Dr. Kinsey, while I was over at her home one evening I mentioned to her that I would like to talk to her brother, the former King Farouk, about an important medical research matter. She said that should pose little problem as her brother was due on the east coast of the United States in a couple of weeks and was then planning on visiting her in Beverly Hills.

"In fact," she added, "I'm planning on having a party for him here and would be delighted if you took care of the dinner and bar arrangements for me."

I was at her home a day or two before Farouk arrived. Because he had abdicated from the throne, the title of king had been dropped from his name. However, as an important VIP with past diplomatic connections to the State Department he was accorded the full protective treatment of the Secret Service. I was present when they came out ahead of him to check everything out. They went over the house with a fine-tooth comb, looking underneath tables, beds, and chairs, opening closets and wardrobes, checking telephone and electrical cables, searching behind paintings and wall hangings to look for bugs, and making absolutely certain that his security would not be compromised. I myself was questioned extensively and they insisted on knowing what would be served at the dinner, where the food would be coming from, and what the seating arrangements around the table would be.

When the evening of the party finally arrived I found Farouk to be very easy to talk to. He enjoyed everything we served—mainly rich French cuisine—and ate enough for half a dozen men. He kept up a conversation with the princess's guests and was most appreciative of the trouble we had taken to prepare a meal to his liking. He was stay-ing in Princess Faiza's guest suite during his visit to L.A. and when the party concluded that evening he and I sat for a nice, long, private chat. When I brought up the subject of Kinsey and his research work in Indiana, Farouk broke into a roaring belly laugh and told me that he had heard all about Kinsey and his sexual investigations. Being as fond of the ladies as Farouk was he wanted to know more about the Institute of Sex Research so we talked about it until the early hours of the morning. Farouk made no attempt to hide the fact that he liked sex just as much as the next person. Somewhere during the course of our discussions I jokingly mentioned that Kinsey was very interested in pornography. I told him that there was a rumor that he, Farouk, had quite a collection of his own.

When he heard that he leaned over to me and whispered, "I've got warehouses full of the stuff, so much that I'll never be able to look at all of it."

And then he winked at me. Apparently his collection of pornog-raphy was so extensive that it was kept in storage in warehouses in Rome, Monaco, and, unbeknownst to Egypt's new president, Nasser, even in secret locations in Cairo.

I implored him to send some of it over to Kinsey for study at the ISR in Bloomington. By the time the dawn light began to creep across the landscaped lawns of Princess Faiza's estate Farouk had agreed to have his associates in Europe pack up several crates of his collection and ship them out to Kinsey in Indiana.

Kinsey was thrilled when I told him this, but when the con-signment arrived in the United States a few months later he called me in a panic from Bloomington. He said the U.S. Customs in New York had impounded it. After lengthy enquiries I eventually learned that a lot of the material was one-of-a-kind sophisticated artwork. There were oil paintings, brasses, ivory carvings, and leather-bound drawings. Much of it was antique and of inestimable value. The prob-lem was that a lot of the images depicted Arab men having sex with young boys. There was a lot of homosexuality in the collection and that's why the customs people were holding it.

I immediately called Princess Faiza and begged her to please ask her brother to send a signed letter from his home in France to Kinsey, informing him that the material was strictly on loan to Indiana University for a limited period and was intended for research purposes only. Farouk obligingly did as he was asked, Kinsey submitted the letter to customs, and that did the trick. Because the authorities now viewed it as academic research destined for a university, within weeks the entire shipment was released and arrived safely in Indiana. Kinsey got his porn and everyone was happy. The results of this little episode provided invaluable data for the institute's future findings on the role of pornography in society, from ancient to modern times.

20

Close Encounters of Every Kind

Edith Piaf was forty years old when she first came to American shores in an attempt to repeat her phenomenal success in Europe as a cultural icon singing French ballads. Her songs had an earthiness, a sandpaperlike edge to them because they were rendered in her wonderfully raspy, tobacco-hardened voice. I loved the gravely way she spoke and how she rolled those *r*'s off the back of her tongue and throat. She spent the war years singing in nightclubs in German-occupied France. In 1946 she made the haunting "La Vie en Rose" her signature number, but she is also remembered for other marvelous titles that include "Non, Je ne Regrette Rien," "Hymne à l'amour," and "La Foule." Many still regard her as France's greatest popular singer.

The way I met her was quite interesting. My friend Alex Tiers—the guy who jerked me off in the park while I was sleeping—had a wealthy cousin by the name of Cornelius "Neil" Tiers. Neil's hometown was New York. He had inherited a family fortune and spent his life playing and partying. When war broke out, just for the hell of it he bought his way into the French Foreign Legion and traveled with them in North Africa. When he had had enough of war he simply bought his way out of the Legion. However, while he was serving with them in Paris he met Edith Piaf at a nightclub and was smitten by her, though it never developed into anything more than a platonic friendship. Neil had a house on Coldwater Canyon in Beverly Hills and I often stayed there when he went to New York, usually with someone I was tricking. When Edith was signed to come out to California and sing at the exclusive Mocambo Night Club it was arranged that she would stay at Neil's home. Because Neil was away I spent a lot of time there, and so Edith and I met, immediately hit it off, and began a nice sexual relationship.

The Mocambo was a Hollywood landmark. It was a wildly popular Brazilian-themed venue located at 8588 Sunset Boulevard. Owners Charlie Morrison and Felix Young had lavished a lot of time, money, and attention on it. They created a unique interior at the club that included glassed-in aviaries holding live macaws and cockatoos. It was a perfect venue for Edith and she was signed to play there for a month. Edith was a sweet, dark-eyed, dark-haired short little thing who wasn't exactly pretty but she had an interesting face. I thought she was sexy as hell but she was a sad person who seemed to be on the verge of tears all the time. During sex she would say sing-songy things in French, purring in a low, sugary kind of way. We had sex nearly every night for the four weeks she was out here.

I used to drive her down to the Mocambo, where she performed twice nightly. During the first two weeks of her Los Angeles engagement she played to packed houses. Then the audiences started shrinking. Finally, no one came. Edith was shattered. She felt rejected, alienated, scorned. She believed that because she was so different, her songs so mournfully reflective of Parisian life, she could not reach out and touch Americans. In her dressing room after the show she would chain-smoke strong, foul smelling imported French cigarettes such as Gitanes and Gauloises and weep. I tried my best to keep her spirits up and bring a little joy into her life. After the show I would take her home, brew her strong black coffee laced with a little liqueur and keep her company all night long. And that meant only one thing, making long, slow love to her until she dozed off as dawn broke. She was an acutely vigorous sexual being with a very big heart and she loved the time she spent with me before returning to Paris. In the years following she would send me gifts of little Lalique ashtrays and other objects like that.

MANY WONDERFUL WOMEN came into my life during the fabulous fifties. One of the liveliest and most incorrigible was Mae West. She was never boring, never banal, and always managed to stir up controversy whatever she did and wherever she went. At the age of thirty-three in 1926, Mae was jailed for appearing in a play in Manhattan called *Sex*. A couple of years later she hit the boards on Broadway with *Diamond Lil.* In 1932 she made her first movie in Hollywood. Entitled *Night After Night* it costarred George Raft. Mae was already pushing the envelope in that one, performing in risqué scenes and delivering dialogue using words that audiences had never heard before. She wasn't afraid of cussing or of nudity or of subject matter that spoke of real people in real situations in a way never before seen on-screen. She was witty and charming and she oozed sexuality. Mae became an instant box-office draw, going on to make a film she wrote herself, *She Done Him Wrong,* costarring Cary Grant. The film was nominated for an Academy Award and allowed Mae to go on immediately to make her next movie, *I'm No Angel.* Conservative audiences around the country were in uproar about the raunchy style and tone of her work. Theater owners were taken aback. Critics had no idea what to say. The result of the brouhaha was the birth of what was known as the Motion Picture Production Code. Introduced in 1930, it was more commonly called the Hays Code, deriving its name from its primary author, Will H. Hays.

The code was endorsed and implemented by the Motion Picture Producers and Distributors Association of America. It strictly regulated what could and could not be seen and heard in movies. It stipulated that, among other things, "no motion picture shall lower the moral standards of those who see it. The sympathy of the audience should never be thrown to the side of crime, wrongdoing, evil, or sin." With regard to sex, the code stated that "the sanctity of the institution of marriage had to be rigidly upheld." Motion pictures were not allowed to imply that "low forms of sexual relationships" are an acceptable or common form of behavior. Adultery could not be explicitly treated, justified, or presented. Scenes of passion should be avoided if they were not directly essential to the plot. Excessive and lustful kissing and embracing, suggestive postures and gestures were not to be shown. Passion was not to be treated in a way that "stimulated the lower and baser element." Sexual perversion of any type or inference was forbidden. Miscegenation, or sexual relationships between whites and blacks, was condemned. Venereal diseases were not to be considered as subjects for motion pictures. Scenes of childbirth—even if depicted in silhouette—were forbidden. Sex organs were never to be seen. Obscenities in word, gesture, reference, song, joke, or by suggestion were outlawed. Complete nudity of males or females, whether in shadow or observed at a great distance, was not permitted. Dancing that suggested or represented sexual actions or "indecent passions" was taboo. Husbands and wives could only be depicted fully clothed and in separate beds. The list went on and on.

Everything the Hays Code demanded was contrary to what Mae believed in but the Code didn't stop her. She continued to push the envelope. In scenes in her movies she simply introduced a whole new set of words and phrases that carried double meanings, thereby bypassing the rigid limitations imposed by the code. Mae made many movies during her career, then eventually moved on to star in her own live variety shows in Las Vegas during the fifties. It was the time when smooth-skinned, hormone-filled musclemen were all the rage. As long as they wore even the skimpiest of black or white briefs or a posing pouch, and as long as they pumped iron, they were considered "athletes" and not pornographic models. So as far as the law was concerned, people could watch them, and collect pictures of them. And many did, both male and female. Mae knew the erotic value of a handsome muscleman, so she always had a few of them appear with her in her Las Vegas shows.

Now remember, most muscle boys were straight. One of the better known bodybuilders at the time was Steve Reeves, but there were many others. I once sent Steve Reeves over to George Cukor as a trick. Steve was a little hard up at the time and did it purely for the cash.

Gay guys would congregate around Muscle Beach in Venice Beach, just to watch the musclemen pump iron and work out. Many queens would also hang around gymnasiums in town. Lurking in the shadows or sitting close to the workout areas, they would have their hands in their pockets playing with themselves as they ogled the bodybuilders showing off their muscles. As they watched they would jerk off in their pants.

In 1955, at the age of sixty-seven, about the time I met her, Mae West had fallen in love with one of these muscled guys. He was more than thirty years younger than she was, a veritable Adonis, and a former "Mr. California" wrestling champion. He went by the name of Paul Novak. She was thrilled when she found him and immediately invited me over to meet him. She was infatuated with him. When he was around she behaved like a kid. She was constantly all over the guy, stroking his hair, kissing his forehead, showing him off. She told me how adept he was at sending her to the heights of ecstasy in bed. She boasted about his incredible stamina, about his ability to stay hard all night long. She simply worshiped her beloved Paul and spoiled him rotten. It wasn't long before he moved in with her. I worked at parties for them often and saw them at many get-togethers around town. As her performing career began to wind down she moved from her luxurious Ravenswood apartment building penthouse to a smaller and less expensive apartment in a fine old building called the El Royale on Rossmore Street, which was a southerly extension of Vine Street, near Hancock Park.

As the effects of age began to redefine her life, Mae began to change. It was disturbing to watch it happen. Slowly, she began to control Paul's every move, watching him like a hawk. Eventually poor Paul was absolutely miserable. He was always eager to get out and be social. He enjoyed meeting friends his own age, chatting up girls, or having a beer with the guys, but God help him if he stayed out ten minutes longer than he promised. Then, without fail, my phone would ring at home.

"Where's that man of mine?" Mae would demand of me, or of Betty, if I wasn't there. "Is he there? What's he doing?"

If Betty or I denied knowing where he was Mae would merely spit back, "I know he's out there somewhere. I'm here alone and he's foolin' around. I know it and I just can't stand it. If you see him send him home right away, y'hear?" And then she'd hang up.

Poor Paul. We all felt so sorry for the guy. He was totally denied his freedom. Mae was so much older than he was and there was no more sex between them and yet he had to go home to Momma like a dog with its tail between its legs. He was still a virile, healthy, horny guy, but he had to spend most of his evenings with Mae at home eating TV dinners on a tray while watching boring sitcoms. He became a pathetic, fat slob, and simply wasted away. When dear old Mae died in November 1980 it was too late for Paul to start his own life all over again. By then he was a broken, beaten man.

DURING THE FIFTIES one of the biggest shows on television was the much-beloved *I Love Lucy,* starring the nation's sweetheart, Lucille Ball. She played the character Lucy Ricardo, wife of Ricky Ricardo, portrayed by Desi Arnaz. Desi was also the executive producer of the series as well as the real-life husband of Lucille. America adored them. Once the show went into foreign syndication the world grew to love them, too. They were iconic figures, embraced in every living room with a TV set. It became the most successful and instantly recognizable sitcom of all time. Under an initial contract with CBS, the couple started their own production company, Desilu Productions, owning a piece of their show. They also pioneered a new multiple motion picture camera system for shooting the shows on film that became a standard industry practice for sitcoms.

Desi was a hot-blooded Cuban, born Desiderio Alberto Arnaz y de Acha III. He was six years younger than his pretty, redheaded, all-American New York–born wife. I hardly knew Lucille, but Desi and I became great pals. He was a sweetheart of a guy, with a healthy heterosexual appetite. He often called me up for girls, tipping them more generously than anyone else I knew. Instead of handing over the typical $20, which was the going gratuity at that time for a trick, he would often slip a girl as much as $200 or $300. I don't know where he found the time for all that philandering because he was a very busy man, responsible for churning out a lot of television airtime every week. But Desi saw at least two or three girls every few days. He was a lusty fellow, to say the least. And the girls were crazy for him.

One night at a party where I was bartending, Lucille came striding over to me in a beautiful long evening gown, stopped in front of the bar, glared at me for a second or two, and then . . . *Wham!* She slapped me in the face and yelled "*You!* You stop pimping for my husband, y'hear!"

I tried to profess innocence but apparently Lucille was fully aware of Desi's sexual flings. She claimed that she had been monitoring all of his calls to me and that she was in possession of my phone number.

"I know exactly who you are, mister!," she yelled. "You're the infamous Scotty Bowers. Get out and *stay* out of my husband's life!"

Desi and the other guests were in shock. No one said a word as Lucille stood there glaring at me, her chin thrust out, her eyes on fire.

It was obvious that Lucille knew full well that Desi was heavily into hookers as well as many of my girls from the old gas station crowd. But to this day I'm still not exactly sure why she chose that particular night, and that very awkward moment, to bare her fury with me in full public view. The incident didn't leave me with any anger toward her. She was right. Nobody ever messed around with Lucille. Her temper equaled her charm.

WHILE I PREFERRED the sexual company of women, my "other" life continued to remain robustly alive and well. A guy I saw a lot of during the fifties was a motion picture, theatrical, and musical publicist in his late forties named Rupert Allan. A brilliant Rhodes scholar and a lieutenant commander in the Navy during the war, Rupert had risen to the top of his profession, representing major movie stars like Marilyn Monroe, Bette Davis, Marlene Dietrich, Gina Lollobrigida, Catherine Deneuve, Rock Hudson, Melina Mercouri, Steve McQueen, and one of the most beautiful and popular actresses of all time, Grace Kelly. After Grace was transformed into a fairy-tale princess by marrying Prince Rainier of Monaco in 1956, Rupert was appointed Monaco's consul general in Los Angeles.

Even though I tricked him often, the real love of Rupert's life was a guy of his own age, a motion picture producer by the name of Frank McCarthy. Both men behaved in a totally masculine manner. It was virtually impossible to pick up on the fact that they were gay. Frank was a retired brigadier general who had served as an aide to General George C. Marshall during World War II. Frank and Rupert were lovers, but they respected one another's space and wanted to maintain their own homes. The best way to do this was to have houses next door to one another, so they each bought a property above Beverly Estates Drive up in the mountains of Beverly Hills. Rupert's house was a fine single-story place, whereas Frank's was a more spacious and luxurious two-story home. Through his association with Rupert, Frank knew Princess Grace of Monaco very well. She often visited L.A., especially after she became a mother. She would come over from Monaco with her son, daughter, and a small retinue of aides and they would all stay at Frank's place. There was a large sparkling pool between the two houses so it was an ideal vacation venue for the Monaco royal family. The fact that the two men had separate homes also made it impossible for the press or the gossip columnists to label them as gay lovers. I tricked each of them, but always separately, never together. Rupert became a bit of a drinker. Eventually, it didn't take much to get him loaded. Sometimes I would leave after a session of sex with him and quietly sneak past the pool and across the garden to Frank's house next door for a quickie. During all the years that I did that, the two of them never knew that I was tricking them both.

21

To Each His Own

Living in Hollywood meant that you were never far away from a world of fantasy and make-believe. Whatever else it was, above all this was a town that was built on the solid bedrock of the movie industry. Reality and fiction often blurred, even in the way people lived their lives. There was a wonderful duality about it all, a kind of mixing of personalities, times, eras, events. I found it all very magical. And as I accumulated friends and fellow tricksters who were immersed in the utterly engrossing medium of film I felt especially grateful for their friendship. Many of the people I knew had fascinating stories to tell. If they were actors their lives sometimes mimicked the characters they played on-screen. But most thespians had to dig into the deep recesses of their talents to take on completely new personas when the cameras rolled. It was all rather interesting, especially for a farm boy like me from the Midwest. I found that those who made movies, both in front of and behind the camera, were a pretty fascinating bunch. One of them was my good friend Ramon Novarro.

Born José Ramón Gil Samaniego in 1899, he was the son of a dentist in Durango, Mexico. When he was twelve years old the

Mexican Revolution broke out, and five years later it became impossible for the family to safely continue living in the country. Leaving everything behind they fled to the United States as refugees. Starting life all over again they settled in Los Angeles. It was tough for the dark, lanky, good-looking, five foot eight teenager. He had to support himself and tried his hand as a piano teacher and a ballet dancer, but neither worked. He was obliged to turn to waiting tables at a downtown cafeteria. But it wasn't easy because he wasn't fluent in English. Ramon was gay, and, because of his good looks, he was spotted by an old queen who took him home and introduced him to the gay world of Hollywood. That totally changed his life.

In 1917 he landed a gig as an extra in the fledgling movie industry. He struggled along for five years until 1922 when he was spotted by the director Rex Ingram and cast in the role of Rupert in *The Prisoner of Zenda*. Suddenly, new opportunities opened up for him. Audiences loved him. Ingram was the one who recommended that he change his name to Ramon Novarro as his career as a leading man began to blossom. By 1925 female audiences were swooning over him. Audiences went crazy for him in silent films like *The Red Lily, A Lover's Oath,* and *The Arab.* In 1925 Ramon landed the most coveted role in Hollywood as Judah Ben-Hur in the silent version of *Ben-Hur.* Following that plum role Ramon went on to star in many popular pictures that included *The Student Prince in Old Heidelberg, The Road to Romance,* and *Forbidden Hours.* When Rudolph Valentino died at the age of thirty-one in 1926, Ramon immediately took his place. After the arrival of the talkies he appeared in movies such as *Call of the Flesh, Daybreak, Son of India, Mata Hari, The Barbarian,* and *The Night is Young.* At the peak of his career in the early thirties he was earning upwards of $100,000 per film. He invested his money wisely, especially in property and real estate. The result was that he became a very wealthy man.

Somehow or other our paths crossed during the fifties when Ramon was primarily appearing in episodic television shows. He was a really nice guy, very friendly and outgoing. Though in his fifties, he had not lost his good looks, but he had developed an unfortunate habit of drinking too much. At parties he was always loaded. He would throw back glass after glass of gin and then fall face-first on the floor, Errol Flynn–style. Though still sexually active and very popular in the gay community the heavy drinking caused him to suffer from impotence. Fear of the inability to have an erection is the bane of every man's life. Just about all males I have ever known have been worried about it happening to them at some time or another. It was a regular affliction with Ramon. Nevertheless, he still loved sex. There was nothing that gave him more pleasure than to perform oral sex on a virile, handsome young man. He could easily suck fifteen guys off, one after the other. He referred to semen as "honey." He revered it more than anything else. He believed that by swallowing it he would retain his vigor, his strength, his good looks.

"Scotty," he would call me up and say, "I need some honey. Urgently. Tonight. Help me out and find me a few guys. *Please.*"

So I would bring five or six young guys over to his house. He was usually so drunk that even if he had seen any of them on a previous occasion he wasn't able to recognize them. I would sit in his living room reading a magazine or watching television while the young fellows sat around, waiting to be called into Ramon's bedroom. Summoning them in one by one, behind his closed door he would suck each of them off. Within the space of half an hour he would go through them all and then stumble out and call the first one in again. But young and potent though the young stud may have been, because he had already ejaculated he could not do it again so soon.

Then Ramon would call me in and in a hushed but slurred voice say, "Shit, Scotty, what's the problem? What's wrong with that kid? He doesn't come. Why'd you bring him over?"

"No, Ramon," I would explain. "There's nothing wrong with him. The guy can't come because you've already sucked him off, half an hour ago. Remember?"

"Oh, really? Did I?" he would say, staring at me through a dazed and puzzled fog.

It was sad to see Ramon crumble under the destructive effects of alcoholism. Even sadder was his final demise. On the morning of October 30, 1968, his body was discovered by his servant in his North Hollywood home. The police eventually found out that he had been savagely beaten to death by two young male hustlers who had erroneously been informed that he had thousands of dollars in cash stashed away somewhere in the house. He didn't. There was no money on the property so poor Ramon was murdered in vain. What made it even more tragic was the fact that for months he had been tricking those two guys who murdered him. And—in case you're wondering—no, I didn't know them.

ANOTHER FASCINATING MAN that I met during the fifties was that wonderful British actor, Charles Laughton. I think we were introduced at a party where I was working, and I soon began tricking him regularly, as well as arranging for him to see other guys. I also introduced him to my old pal Tyrone Power. Charles became very enamored with Ty and saw him often. Charles was married to the actress Elsa Lanchester who, in addition to many other roles, had played the bride in the campy horror film, *The Bride of Frankenstein*, in 1935. They had already been married for many years when I met him. I doubt the relationship could ever have been categorized as conventional. Charles, or Chuck as some people called him (much to his dislike), was openly gay. Elsa once told me that although the marriage began with the two of them having sex now and again, things changed as the years rolled by. Gradually, those encounters became more infrequent, so much so that eventually Charles's sex life was exclusively gay. Yet she never held that against him. I always admired Elsa for her unstinting loyalty toward him. In fact, it was far more than loyalty. I do believe that Elsa loved Charles deeply. She stood by him for more than thirty-three years, from the time of their marriage in 1929 right up until Charles's death in 1962. She went beyond the call of duty, tolerating his double life without ever questioning it. She was a remarkable lady. She knew full well that I was tricking her husband and arranging liaisons with other young men for him, but whenever she saw me she was always courteous and friendly. She never bore any animosity or ill feeling toward me or anyone else who was having a relationship with Charles. She unflinchingly accepted her husband's infidelities and double standards. You don't see that very often in either a wife or a husband.

Perhaps because of Charles's sexual rejection of her, Elsa had developed a rather odd but quaint predilection. She had a passion for young gay men. She would seduce them by whatever means possible and then call upon her substantial talents to coerce them into having sex with her. The younger ones, who were often more experimental than their older counterparts, were the easiest to win over, and still willing to dabble in heterosexual behavior. She once told me that she loved nothing better than to "conquer" men who had never had sex with a woman before. Even though she knew it was a futile exercise she fantasized about changing them.

Charles was one of the most talented actors of his time. He appeared in his first film, *The Tonic*, opposite Elsa, in England in 1928. He went on to star in many movies including *The Sign of the Cross, The Barretts of Wimpole Street, The Private Life of Henry VIII, Rembrandt, The Canterville Ghost, Witness for the Prosecution,* and classics like *Hobson's Choice, Mutiny on the Bounty, The Hunchback of Notre Dame,* and *Young Bess.* He won an Oscar in 1934 for his performance in *The Private Life of Henry VIII.* Charles emigrated from England and became an American citizen in 1950. But there was one prickly thing that I always had to be very careful about in front of him. I was never permitted to mention the name of my good friend Laurence Olivier. There was no love lost between those two talented, strong-willed natives from the Sceptered Isle. It wasn't only professional competition and creative jealousy but also a very deeply rooted personal antagonism stemming from heaven knows where. Larry would never mention Charles, even when others in his company talked about him. Charles, on the other hand, would fly into a rage or withdraw into a deep, dark mood and spout unending cynical remarks about Larry when he heard others talking about him. This clash of personalities would come to a furious peak when the two actors worked together in the 1960 production of *Spartacus*. That film has gone down in history as one of the finest and most intelligent of the great Hollywood epics about ancient Rome. It was written by the blacklisted screenwriter Dalton Trumbo and directed by the much-lauded Stanley Kubrick.

In their scenes together Charles and Larry often locked horns. They constantly tried to upstage and out-act one another. At many cocktail parties and dinners during and after filming, the subject of their contest of wills would often be brought up. When Larry was present at these gatherings he would merely shrug, wave his hand in disgust, and dismiss the whole affair as though it did not warrant discussion. Charles, on the other hand, would seize upon the opportunity to belittle Larry whenever he could. If someone brought up the subject around a dinner table he would visibly change expressions, his color would take on a distinctly purple hue, his eyes would glaze over, and he would lean back, take a sip of wine, and hiss like a viper.

Apparently their clashes on the set were extremely volatile, with neither giving in to the other. I heard that Kubrick and producer-actor Kirk Douglas often had to call for a five-minute break in filming as they tried to calm them down.

When it came to sex Charles had some decidedly odd habits. They may seem crude and disgusting but, to me, the dividing line between what many regarded as normal and abnormal had long since disappeared. Who can understand what turns some people on and some off? I had come to realize that I had no right to judge the tastes and preferences of others, no matter how excessive, unusual, or unappetizing they may appear. However, one thing I really had a hard time understanding about Charles was his reticence to wash. He seemed to enjoy being dirty. I distinctly remember him coming to a cocktail party from a shoot one day where he was heavily made up for a character part. He had not bothered to remove his makeup and, when I saw him again four days later at another function, he had still not washed the makeup off.

"Charles," I said, "are you still shooting on that movie?"

"No, dear boy, why?" he replied.

"Well," I said, trying to be as diplomatic as I could, "you still have your makeup on."

"Most observant of you, dear boy," he said, then turned around and swished off toward the bar. He hadn't washed for almost a week!

Like the Midwestern farm boy that I was and, as with so many of his British counterparts, Charles was not circumcised or, as it is more commonly referred to, "uncut." In fact, he had one of the largest foreskins I had ever seen. He had, in the nomenclature of the gay world at that time, a "BLC." That stood for "big lace curtain." Because Charles seldom washed, there was often a buildup of smegma, or a secretion of the sebaceous glands, under the foreskin. Uncircumcised guys have to retract their foreskins in the shower or the bathtub every day to wash this substance away or it accumulates, causing a slightly sour smell to build up. Charles, on the other hand, relished it. Many men—*and* women, I might add—who performed oral sex had developed a liking for the slightly pungent taste of smegma. It was, like oysters I suppose, a carefully honed or acquired taste! Some people referred to it as "cheese." And it really is akin to an aged Gorgonzola or Roquefort.

Allow me to digress here for a moment. A very good friend of mine by the name of Bob Edelmann was heavily into giving head to uncut guys. Bob came from a wealthy Chicago family that had made their fortune producing brass fittings and other parts for the automobile industry. Bob hardly worked a day in his life. He had enough money to spend his time being a playboy, so he often came out to California to "play." Bob was Jewish, which meant that he was circumcised. For some reason or another he had developed an obsession for guys with foreskins, and he loved it when those uncircumcised penises had a bit of cheese under the foreskin. I did him a favor by hooking him up with Charles Laughton one day and the two of them never looked back. Every time Bob was in town I would take him up to Charles's house and the two of them would go at it for half an hour or more. This may all seem a little repulsive but I assure you that dear Bob was one of the sweetest, nicest men I ever knew. And so was Charles.

Charles had yet another rather odd habit. One day, at his request and while his wife Elsa was away on a shoot, I took a nice-looking young man over to his house. I really don't remember his name so I'll simply refer to him as Ted. The only thing I recall is that he was about nineteen or twenty years old, was blessed with a great body, and was very well endowed. When we arrived at Charles's home on Curson Avenue in West Hollywood it was about two or three o'clock in the afternoon. Charles welcomed us, put a hand underneath Ted's chin, squeezed his cheeks, and muttered, "Hmmm. Nice. Very nice."

He said that he hadn't had any lunch yet and asked if we would mind if he had a quick snack. He showed us into the kitchen where he darted from place to place making an awful lot of noise as he opened bread bins, drawers, and closets. He laid out a breadboard, plates, knives, and a napkin on a table and started slicing up a loaf of sourdough bread. He asked Ted to strip completely and perch up on a countertop where he could see him. I sat on a chair at the table. All three of us chatted while Charles placed the bread slices on a plate, buttered them, then removed some crisp lettuce leaves and tomatoes from the refrigerator. These he carefully washed under a faucet of running water at the sink. Every now and again he looked up at Ted, studied his groin and his large penis, which by now had grown fully erect. He kept commenting on how much he approved of his lean, well-formed torso and his muscular, hairy legs. Once he had finished washing the lettuce and tomatoes he sliced them, laid them out on the buttered bread slices, squeezed a couple of drops of lemon juice on them, and then sprinkled on a little salt and coarse, ground pepper.

Glancing up at Ted he smiled and said, "Almost ready."

Ted and I looked at each other, wondering what the devil that remark implied but, no matter. Then Charles thoughtfully studied a shelf full of pans, pots, and skillets. He reached out for one of the smaller pots. Holding the pot with one hand he picked up the plate containing the bread slices with the other. Then he looked at Ted, and, in a very polite way, asked, "Could you follow me please, young man. This'll only take a minute."

Ted stared at me momentarily, a puzzled look written all over his face, and then he hopped off the counter and followed Charles a short way down the hall, his erect penis bobbing proudly as it preceded him. I watched Charles take Ted into a bathroom and close the door. How odd, I thought. Why the bathroom and not the bedroom?

They were gone for about fifteen or twenty minutes and in their absence I whiled away the time by rummaging through a collection of Elsa's cookbooks. Charles was the first to return. He put the plate with the bread slices on the kitchen table. I could see that the lettuce and tomatoes had been lightly smeared with a light brown substance. It looked like gravy or peanut butter or some sort of sandwich spread. Seconds later Ted appeared in the kitchen. His erection was gone and he was looking decidedly sheepish, perhaps even a trifle embarrassed. I stared at him curiously and he pulled a face, hoping that Charles wouldn't notice. He pointed at the bread slices on the plate and then lightly patted his backside. Was this true? Had Charles asked Ted to defecate into the pot? Is *that* what he had smeared on his sandwich? Well, apparently it was.

Charles sat down, carefully placed one slice of bread on top of the other, neatly cut the stack in two, and then, without saying a word or even giving us a cursory glance, bit into it. After he had downed the entire sandwich, he got up and went to the sink to rinse off the plate.

As soon as Charles's back was turned Ted quietly padded over to me and whispered, "Jesus, why did he even take the trouble to wash the fucking lettuce and tomatoes?"

Seconds later Charles turned around and gave Ted an enticing "come hither" sign with his index finger. As the poor fellow meekly followed Charles out of the kitchen and into one of the bedrooms down the hall, Charles called out to me, "Back in a jiff, Scotty. Make yourself comfortable."

And then I heard the bedroom door close. Half an hour later Charles appeared in a dressing gown, followed by my young friend. They both looked a little sweaty but decidedly satisfied. Ted also looked noticeably happy as he clutched a couple of ten-dollar bills. Charles came up and stood beside me with his hand on my shoulder as we watched Ted pull on his jeans and T-shirt.

And then Charles whispered into my ear, "Great lay, Scotty. Wonderful trick. Thanks, old boy, and thanks for waiting."

CHARLES LAUGHTON WASN'T the only person I knew who thrived on unusual fetishes. Tyrone Power had his, too. He liked what is commonly known as "water sports" or a "golden shower." This entails being urinated on by a sexual partner. I eventually got to know quite a few people who derived infinite pleasure from lying in a bathtub, a shower cubicle, or beside a swimming pool, while a bunch of handsome young studs stood over them and urinated. Taking what Charles Laughton liked to an even more provocative level, Tyrone occasionally enjoyed it when his sexual partners—especially young ladies—"dropped a deuce" or defecated on him. In the gay world, people with that inclination were usually referred to as "doo-doo queens." That kind of behavior may seem disgusting but, you know, it's surprising how much of it goes on. Every now and again someone would call me and request a sex partner who was happy to indulge in that sort of thing.

"Got a nice young doo-doo queen—or dyke or girl—for me tonight, Scotty?" I was occasionally asked.

The practice certainly didn't turn me on but it was patently clear that it was regarded as a normal and acceptable part of sexual activity by its devotees, with Charles Laughton being one of them, and Ty Power another. So who was I to judge? To each his own.

THE AUTHOR HECTOR ARCE used to cover the Hollywood celebrity scene for various magazines and also wrote rather good biographies of Groucho Marx and Gary Cooper. In the late seventies he wrote a very revealing biography of Tyrone Power. Ty died in 1958, so Hector never met him personally. He had interviewed many who did know him and was relying on hearsay and other source material for his book. He knew that Ty and I had been close pals so he asked me to look over the manuscript when it was finished. In it were references to Ty's passion for piss and poop. When I came across those paragraphs I immediately flagged them and discussed them with Hector.

"Where'd you get that information, Hector?" I asked.

"Aw, c'mon, Scotty," he said. "It's common knowledge. Everyone knows about the weird stuff Power was into."

"Who told you about it?" I wanted to know.

"Oh, jeez," he said. "I know at least fifteen guys who've told me everything. They all did that to him."

"Well," I said adamantly, "it's lies. All lies. They're just feeding you that nonsense for its sensational value. I can't believe you're accepting it like it was all true."

This put Hector's fenders up. No author wants to provoke arguments that may lead to accusations of inaccuracy, libel, or character defamation. He wasn't sure what to do so he asked me what I thought. I told him to take all those sections out.

Reluctantly, Hector rethought the matter and finally deleted all the potentially contentious passages. Although he exercised caution about what he had said about the people who knew Ty personally he included a couple of paragraphs in the book about me. But he had cunningly changed my name from Scotty to Smitty, just in case. I laughed out loud when I read those sections. When *The Secret Life of Tyrone Power* was published by William Morrow in May 1979 it got good reviews and almost instantly became a coast-to-coast best seller. Needless to say, people who knew me well enough instantly recognized me as the "Smitty" character in the book. But I didn't mind. I had nothing to hide, nor anything to feel ashamed about. To celebrate its publication I went over to Hector's place one evening.

As we toasted the book—he with champagne, me with soda water—I said to him, "You remember those parts you took out about Ty, the ones about the pee and the poop?"

"Yes," he said. "What about them?"

"Well," I said, clinking my glass against his, "they were absolutely true."

At first he was so angry that I thought he was going to tear me apart, limb from limb. Eventually he simmered down and agreed that I had made him do the right thing. It was still too soon after Ty's death to be shattering the myth of one of Hollywood's golden boys. Twenty years after his death Ty was still looked upon as an idol. It was right for us to protect his fans from any disappointment or disgust they may have felt after reading about his odd sexual habits. Today I have no compunction about exposing them. Much time has passed and, as we know, time heals everything. Perhaps Ty's followers are more ready for the truth now than they were thirty years ago when the book was first published. Hector Arce himself is also long dead. The truth is that I never cared one iota about how people got their rocks off in private, just as long as they weren't hurting anybody. We all have our secret preferences and weaknesses, call them whatever you will. So, bless Ty, my old friend. What he did cannot and will not diminish my fondness for him, his greatness as an actor, or his reputation as one of the nicest people who ever inhabited this crazy place called Hollywood.

22

The Young and the Restless

As the fifties drew to a close I decided it was time that Betty and Donna should have a nice, comfortable, quiet house to live in. Up until then we had been moving around town from one rented property to the next, mainly shoebox-size apartments. Betty deserved better than that. The fire may have gone out of our relationship but I still cared for her. I wanted her to be happy. Also, I figured that my beautiful little daughter Donna had a right to a nice room of her own and a garden in which to play. It was time for me to invest what little I had saved up in a property of my own. I told Betty to keep a lookout for something affordable.

One day she excitedly told me that she had found out about a little property from a local realtor that sounded perfect. It was a charming little three-bedroom place with a small garden, on a side street called North St. Andrews Place, surprisingly just up the road from the gas station where I used to work. It sounded ideal. We went over to look at it and fell in love with it right away. According to the realtor the owner had died without leaving a will and there were no known survivors or descendants. As a result, the place was in probate. If I wanted it I would have to go down to city hall and discuss it with someone in the judiciary service.

I was informed that the asking price would be in the region of $20,000. I dug into my savings and stuffed everything I had, $22,000, into a large manila envelope. With this in my jacket pocket I marched into the judge's office. To my dismay I was told that another buyer was also after the property. He was called into the room with me so that the judge could decide who to favor.

Shuffling in his chair the judge put his elbows on his desk, gently tapped his fingers together, looked at both of us, and said, "Well, gentleman, if you want to purchase the property the price is $22,000."

My heart leaped within my breast. It was exactly how much I had on me!

"That's too much," the other buyer objected. "I just can't afford that."

The judge looked at him and then turned to me.

"And you, Mr. Bowers," he said, "what about you?"

I felt my pulse racing as I pulled out the envelope with the money and handed it over to the judge.

"I'll take it, Your Honor," I panted.

The judge took the envelope, tore it open, pulled out the cash, counted it, and smiled. "Sold, to Mr. Bowers," he said. "Congratulations."

He handed me a receipt, a deed of sale, and all the necessary legal papers and I walked out of his office into a clear California day, now a man of property and substance. It sure felt good to be alive. That evening Betty and I had dinner together and then made love for the first time in more than a year. It was wonderful. I knew she was happy and I knew Donna was going to like it in her new home. A couple of weeks later we moved in.

Fortunately, my bartending talents were as much in demand as ever. And I was still Hollywood's go-to guy for setting up tricks. Some folks around town even began calling me "Mr. Sex."

"Whatever you need," they would say, "just call up Mr. Sex, Scotty Bowers. He has whatever you want."

And that was true. If I couldn't satisfy the request personally, I had access to literally scores of men and women of all types, persuasions, ages, and talents who could. Unless I was performing the sex myself—be it straight, gay, or bi—I still was not making any money off arrangements I made for other people. All financial transactions between them were strictly their own affair. I just wanted to see folks happy. I was simply reacting to the ancient ritual of supply and demand. The only difference between me and, say, a farmer, a carpenter, or a storekeeper, was that I specialized in sex. Sex was what I offered, pure and simple. And what better way to calm the soul, heal the body, and make the spirit soar than sex?

As time went by I met a lot of people who dabbled in offbeat, unusual practices in their search for physical gratification. I learned not to question them, especially those who were into the bondage, domination, and sadomasochism or BDSM scene. What people did in private was entirely their own affair, not mine. As long as nobody was getting hurt I had no objection to what folks did. If it helped them get their rocks off, cemented a relationship more closely, offered them some fun, or just made them feel good why not do it? Of course, whenever people called me up to arrange unusual tricks for them I had to make sure that whoever I sent over was also happy to engage in any planned bondage and domination activities. I didn't want to get any of the young people in my little black book hurt.

The baritone-voiced actor John Carradine, who appeared in almost 350 movies, including John Ford's original 1939-version of *Stagecoach,* was another person who asked me to arrange tricks for him. John also liked it rough. In fact, the rougher the better. Unlike a lot of my friends and acquaintances, John was one hundred percent straight. He loved women. He adored them. Actually, he just about worshipped them. He occasionally invited me over to his place "for some fun" and when I arrived he was always with some young lady or other. The kinky stuff was usually well under way by the time I got there. John was invariably tied up, bound hand and foot, sometimes gagged and submitting himself totally to the lady's whims and will.

"Join in, Scotty!" he would yell as the girl—usually wearing high-heeled patent leather boots and a studded leather belt—pulled roughly on the ropes with which John was tied up, or flogged him with a stick or a fly whisk. John had an immeasurable capacity for having a good time and always leaned toward something in the S&M field. His son David had similar tastes. I knew him well, too. Like his father, David Carradine was a very accomplished and busy actor. David indulged in many different sexual practices, some of which were downright dangerous. One of his favorites is clinically referred to as autoerotic asphyxia. It entails inducing borderline unconsciousness to increase excitement and heighten the effect of the sex act. But games like that can be deadly. On June 3, 2009, David's naked body was discovered in the closet of a Bangkok hotel room. He had been bound with a rope slung around the clothes rail in the closet, with one end tied around his neck and the other around his genitals. To this day it is not clear whether he committed suicide or suffered the consequences of extremely unsafe sexual activities. Whatever the case, something horrible had occurred. Dave's death was a sad and tragic loss. He was a fine actor and a good friend of mine.

BDSM always makes me think of my old buddy Jack Ryan. In 1975, Jack became the sixth of Hungarian celebrity and movie star Zsa Zsa Gabor's nine husbands. I had known Zsa Zsa for years, witnessing her weave her way in and out of countless relationships and marriages. Jack was one of her more interesting catches. It was sex that brought him and me together in the late fifties. Jack was totally addicted to carnal pleasures with women. I had arranged innumerable tricks with young ladies for him. When we first met he struck me as being the sort of guy who really wasn't wired for sex, but I was dead wrong about that. Jack, a graduate of Yale University, held over a thousand engineering and design patents around the world. As an engineer with the Raytheon Corporation he worked on the design of missile defense systems, including the Hawk and Sparrow programs. He was brilliant at coming up with new ideas and was eventually recruited as head of research and development with the Mattel toy company in Los Angeles. There he designed over thirty best-selling toys, including perennial favorites like the Chatty Cathy talking doll, Hot Wheels, and the ever-popular and beloved toy of all toys, the Barbie doll.

Shattering my original perception of Jack as a sexual wimp, Barbie was the product of Jack's rich and fertile mind, a mind that was often preoccupied with sex and the mystique of the female form. As time went by I learned that Jack was addicted to women. He loved to tease them, surprise them, excite them, get them all aquiver. And then he would strike. Once the actual sexual activity began Jack would treat his ladies to an experience unlike anything they had ever known. He knew how to pamper and please in ways that most men cannot even imagine.

Jack had a magnificent home in Bel Air. He liked his ladies young, slim, and attractive, and he preferred them to be endowed with really big boobs. He often called me up to arrange a hot date for him, usually at his home. I used to send a young lady over to him by cab or take her to his mansion myself. One evening I took an absolutely gorgeous young large-bosomed brunette over to his place for dinner. I can no longer recall her name but I think it was either Faye or Felicité or something like that. She was a very sweet, good-natured young thing. We pulled into the courtyard outside his property and I waited in the car while she sexily swayed her behind as she walked up to the front door. Without ringing the bell she just stood there, staring at something attached to the door. About thirty seconds later she turned around and gazed at me. What was amiss? I immediately got out of the car and joined her on the porch.

"What's wrong?" I asked.

"This," she said, pointing to a little handwritten note taped to the door.

"Come right in," it said. "Follow the candles."

We looked at each other. I motioned to her to open the door and go inside but she shook her head. She was nervous, so I turned the door handle myself. The door immediately swung open while somewhere overhead a speaker relayed, "Come right in."

It was John's recorded voice. He delivered the message in a deep, sexy, singsong manner. As an inventor John was always rigging up things like that. He was a wizard when it came to electronics and gadgets.

The young lady and I entered the hallway. Immediately we were overcome by the overwhelming aroma of burning incense. As we rounded the corner from the dimly lit hallway into a long passage that led to the far side of the house we were greeted by a strange sight. Dozens of little votive glass jars with candles burning inside them were set along the floor on either side of the passageway. It was like a fairyland. We quizzically looked at each other, shrugged, and continued down the passage. Whatever was going on, someone had to be here. We slowly walked all the way down toward the first bedroom, from which emanated soft, romantic music. *Okay,* I thought. This is where I leave. Obviously, Jack has planned all this and is waiting for his date in the bedroom, possibly even in his large, king-sized bed. I motioned to my young charge that I was going to leave but she shook her head. She was adamant that I stay with her.

The door to the bedroom led to a small entry hall. We silently inched our way into it and stopped. Sure enough, the music was coming from within the bedroom itself. We continued into the room and there, at the foot of the bed, was a very ornate burial casket with the lid wide open. It was perched on top of a metal gurney. This was surrounded by an array of bouquets of roses and a burning candelabra. It was a magnificent, eerie sight. The music was coming from a speaker in the ceiling. Heavy drapes shielded the room from the last light of day outside. My companion seemed to have shed her fear and was intrigued. She had never seen a coffin before. Gingerly she made her way over to the casket and peered inside. Stretched out on the soft silk padding lay John, completely nude and sporting a very healthy looking hard-on.

As soon as the girl bent over to take in this apparition John's eyes flashed wide open, he roared with laughter, and then quickly jerked himself off. That's what John was into . . . surprising women and then jerking off while in a casket. He was so hot and ready when the girl walked into the room that he came right away.

Of course, this odd little performance was always followed by John placating the lady, then fixing her a drink. As the shock of her experience wore off John got dressed and then took her out to a fancy restaurant for dinner. The night always ended with John bringing her back home and screwing the daylights out of her.

The day after I had taken Faye or Felicité or whatever the young damsel's name was up there she reported back and told me that, as far as she was concerned, it was one of the most thrilling evenings she had ever experienced. Apparently they had had wild sex in bed, on the floor, and even in the open casket. She begged me to arrange another date for her with John, but for some odd reason he didn't request her again. I never found out why. Over the years he asked me for many more women and he always greeted them in the same devilishly surprising way. But he never saw the same woman more than two or three times. John liked variety almost as much as he liked scare tactics.

IN THE MIDFIFTIES I began to do gigs at parties at the home of one of Hollywood's hottest male stars, Rock Hudson. I had first met him in 1946 or 1947 at the gas station where he became a regular customer. He was an incredibly handsome actor who came from a humble background. Under the protective guidance and tutelage of his gay agent Henry Willson, he became the quintessential Hollywood superstar. After leaving school Rock had no idea what he was going to do with his life. He started out working for the postal service and then served as an airplane mechanic during the war. After moving to Hollywood from his native Illinois he was discovered by Henry, who I knew from my days bartending at the 881 Club. Henry got the young unknown Roy Harold Scherer to get his teeth capped, take acting lessons, and change his name to Rock Hudson.

In 1955, at about the time I began to do parties for him, Rock starred in George Stevens's epic *Giant,* playing opposite Elizabeth Taylor and the youngest golden boy of Hollywood, James Dean. Rock's tall height, dark good looks, and refined deep voice allowed him to play not only romantic leads but also characters who represented the very essence of strong, virile masculinity. Yet Rock was one hundred percent gay, a fact that Henry Willson, aided by sophisticated studio publicity machinery and an army of gatekeepers, managed to conceal from the media and from his adoring fans right up until the time he died from AIDS in 1985. Rock's homosexuality was one of the longest and most closely guarded secrets in Hollywood, helped along by his three-year marriage, starting in 1955, to Phyllis Gates. Phyllis was a very nice person and one hundred percent lesbian. I knew her well. Over the years I arranged many tricks for her. She liked her female sex partners slim, dark-haired, and young.

Phyllis had been Henry Willson's secretary and her marriage to Rock was conjured up to create the illusion of a happy heterosexual marriage. When they went away on "honeymoon" the media was fed an endless supply of photographs of the young couple holding hands, dining in restaurants, cuddling on the dance floor, swimming in pools, and appearing head over heels in love with one another, whereas in actual fact nothing was further from the truth. They slept in separate beds in separate rooms and never had anything remotely close to a physical relationship. They couldn't help being who they were, of course. The phony marriage must have been hell for them both. Rock had a voracious, almost uncontrollable sexual appetite. Over the years he engaged in extremely promiscuous behavior, and at a certain point he started becoming a little reckless. As time went by, he drank more and more. Depending on who his lover was at the time, Rock and his partner could each polish off a bottle of scotch in an evening. He once asked me, "Scotty, how do you do it? How do you manage to resist booze the way you do? What the hell's wrong with you?"

I would always answer by saying that I valued my life too much to take unnecessary risks with it. Rock would simply pooh-pooh my remarks and laughingly dismiss them.

He also began to smoke heavily, finishing a couple of packs of cigarettes in a day. In later years he cruised the streets every night, picking up vagabonds, strangers, and young men all over town at two or three o'clock in the morning and taking them home for sex. What's more, he tried everything, engaging in potentially danger-ous activities without adequate protection long after AIDS broke out. It was heartbreaking to see him literally destroy himself the way he did.

Rock had a beautiful home on Beverly Crest, just off Coldwater Canyon in Beverly Hills. After he wrapped production on *Giant* with director George Stevens back in 1955 he threw a big party, attended by both cast and crew. I was bartending. Everyone from the movie was there with the exception of James Dean, who had been killed in an automobile accident just before production was completed.

"Pity Jimmy Dean's not here," I said to Rock.

"Fuck him!" Rock replied. "I wouldn't have wanted that little prick near my house."

And then it all came out. Rock and James Dean became bitter enemies on the set of *Giant*. They didn't care for one another at all.

I had already learned that Dean was a difficult young man, not at all pleasant to be around. Granted, he was a very pretty boy and he had a lot of sex appeal. There was also an air of mystery about him and when he walked into a room conversation instantly ceased and all heads turned. People were mesmerized by him. However, beneath the facade he was a prissy little queen, moody and unpredictable. Although he had a few romantic flings with women he was essentially gay. On one occasion he was at a party where I was bartending at the home of businessman Ozz Francesca in Larchmont, near Hancock Park. Ozzie was a terrific guy, originally from Brazil. Though gay he had a wife and daughter. His parties were always opulent, expensive affairs. Through his gay connections Ozzie knew Jimmy Dean well. I saw Jimmy saunter into the party that evening, mope around the room puffing on a cigarette, looking decidedly bored and gloomy. Then, for no apparent reason, he dropped his cigarette on the floor and stubbed it out on a very fancy carpet. I immediately dashed out of the room, grabbed a brush, pan, and vacuum cleaner and made a big fuss of cleaning up the damage. I had no idea why he did that and he just glared at me. Later that same evening he snapped his fingers and demanded some champagne. Ozzie always served only the best and so I opened a bottle of Dom Perignon, poured out a glass, and brought it over to Jimmy. He snatched the glass from me without saying a word, took one sip, pulled a face, and poured it out on the floor.

"Ugh! Don't like it," he sneered. "Bring me something else."

As you can tell, he was a very unpleasant young man and he didn't do much to hide that fact. His devil-may-care recklessness, his attitude of defiance, and his antisocial behavior were well known. He was notorious among his peers, friends, and female and male lovers. Frankly, I wasn't surprised when he slammed into an oncoming vehicle while speeding in his Porsche on a quiet regional Californian road in September 1955. He was only twenty-four years old and we were all deeply saddened by his death but, frankly speaking, it was only a matter of time before Jimmy did himself in. He was his own worst enemy.

Someone else who was in many ways like Jimmy Dean was the actor Montgomery Clift. Monty was a temperamental, moody queen with a surprisingly vicious tongue. He wouldn't hesitate to hurt or offend anyone. He was hard to please and was very dismissive of people. Like Jimmy, Monty always acted a little superior—"grand" is a better word—and hard to get. He was unbearably snobbish. Both he and Jimmy looked down their noses at people, no matter who they were. To them I'm sure I was nothing more than a simpleton bartender and, therefore, worthy of scorn. The difference between the two of them was that Monty relied on me for many of his tricks, whereas Jimmy always had a bevy of boys and girls chasing after him. I guess it would be accurate to say that Jimmy was bisexual whereas Monty was completely gay. Monty was painfully fussy about his lovers. He was extremely fastidious about who he took to bed with him, often for the strangest reason.

"His prick was an inch too long," he once said to me after I had gone out of my way to find the perfect trick for him.

On other occasions if it wasn't that a prick was too long then it was an inch too short, or the guy's hair was not parted properly, or his feet were too small, or his toes too bony. There was always something wrong. Monty was never satisfied. I continued to provide him with tricks until he finished filming *Judgment at Nuremberg* with director Stanley Kramer, in 1961, after which he left L.A. to settle in New York. I cannot say that I regretted seeing him leave town.

After my days at the gas station were over I fixed up a lot of tricks for Anthony Perkins. Tony was an intense, sensitive, complex man. I was extremely fond of him. He projected an air of nervous vulnerability and was extremely popular as an actor. Although Tony was married with two kids he was gay. His longest gay relationship was with Tab Hunter but he saw many men. I tricked him myself on numerous occasions. Like Monty, Tony was very fussy about who he saw. He always wanted "someone different."

"Who've you got who's *different*, Scotty?" he would ask. "Who do you have for me for tomorrow night that will surprise me? Anything really *new*?"

Tony lived up in Laurel Canyon and always insisted that his wife of nineteen years, Berry Berenson, a photographer and the actress Marisa Berenson's sister, never knew about his philandering and his double life.

Roddy McDowall was another guy I came to know well and who, like Jimmy and Monty, usually went around with his nose up in the air. He often used to stay at the Chateau Marmont Hotel simply because it was one of *the* places to be seen in those days. Roddy was born in Britain in 1928 and became a child star at the age of ten. He became known to American audiences as the tender young boy in the classic 1941 film *How Green Was My Valley*, playing opposite Walter Pidgeon, Maureen O'Hara, Anna Lee, and Donald Crisp. I often fixed up tricks for Roddy. Like Montgomery Clift he always wanted someone new, someone different, someone he hadn't had sex with before. And, like Monty, he was excessively fussy and hard to please.

Whenever I arranged what I believed was a perfect trick for him he would always come back and say, "You know, Scotty, he was fine but . . ."

And then he would recite a long list of what he didn't like about the guy.

"Too thin, too fat, too young, too old, too tanned, too smooth, too hairy."

Roddy was addicted to amyl nitrate, a concoction better known as "poppers." Back in the fifties and sixties amyl nitrate came in little glass ampoules, packaged in a box with a yellow wrapping. It was available at any pharmacy because it was originally developed as a vasodilator to treat angina by lowering blood pressure. A user broke open the ampoule and snorted the contents. Roddy used to sniff the contents to get high in order to increase neural—or sexual— sensation. I tricked Roddy regularly and before we had sex he always wanted to snort his beloved popper. But he never wanted to be seen buying the stuff, so he often sent me over to the drugstore to purchase it for him. I had many great nights of intense sex with him at the Chateau Marmont.

Eventually Roddy left town, spending time in New York City and England, working as an actor in movies and onstage. I didn't see or hear from him for about a year or two, until, one night, I was bartending at a boisterous gay party in Hollywood. Roddy walked in and the host immediately went over to him, welcomed him, and walked him around the room, introducing him to all the guests.

Eventually they came over to me at the bar and the host said, "And of course you *must* know Scotty Bowers, don't you?"

Although there was an unmistakable sign that he recognized me right away Roddy thrust his hand out and, in the most pretentious and obnoxious way, said, "No, I don't believe I do. How do you do? My name's Roddy."

And then he sauntered off. I couldn't believe it. After I'd bedded him at least a couple of dozen times and spent long nights with him, he pretended that he didn't know me!

23

In High Places

By the late fifties and early sixties, I had friends all over town. Four of them were the administrative heads of one of the top hotels in Hollywood, the famous Roosevelt, located directly across the street from Grauman's Chinese Theatre on Hollywood Boulevard. Tommy Hull was the owner of the hotel, Deb Nelson was the manager, John Kirsch was the assistant manager, and a guy whose name I can only recall as Pat was the house detective. Those four men were essential to my activities in organizing tricks for the rich and famous. The Roosevelt was a great venue for a weekend of tricking. It was chic, exclusive, and very private. The fact that Deb and John were gay made it all the easier for me to bring gays and dykes there. Even though Tommy and Pat were straight they, too, happily cooperated. They were very discrete and respected their guests without question or hesitation. All I had to do was pick up the phone and tell them that I had a special guest coming. This was the coded term we used for any VIP I was going to be checking into the hotel. One of my regulars, who I always put up at the Roosevelt whenever he came into town, was the sixty-something heir to the famous banking empire, Albert Rothschild. He had homes in New York City, Sicily, and in Ojai, California. Whenever he came to L.A. he would call me up ahead of time and I'd have Deb, Tommy, and John arrange a large secluded suite on the top floor of the hotel for him. Pat, the house detective, would be alerted and it was his job to ensure that adequate security arrangements were in place. Everything was done very quickly, very efficiently, and very hush-hush. Once Albert had been brought into the hotel through a side door and ensconced in his suite I would pay him a visit and he would give me his list of requirements.

Unbeknownst to his family Albert was a closeted gay man. His visits to Hollywood were rare opportunities for him to engage in the kind of sexual behavior that he had to avoid in so many other parts of the world. His favorite indulgence was to have me arrange for anywhere from ten to twelve young men to show up at his door. He would then invite them into his suite and tell them to engage in casual conversation with one another. Albert would sit and watch them, observing their mannerisms, body language, and demeanor. One by one, Albert would eliminate the guys until he was left with only three or four of them. Those were the ones he would choose for sex. One of them would be taken to bed by him personally while the rest were told to engage in group activities in the same room where he could watch them.

Another guy I regularly put up at the Roosevelt Hotel was Malcolm Forbes, the publisher of *Forbes* magazine. Because he was so well known and so wealthy I would never reveal his real name to anyone so, when he was visiting L.A., I made sure that most people knew him only as "Mike Ford." After serving in World War II and being given a Bronze Star and a Purple Heart for bravery, Malcolm had entered his father's publishing business and turned it into one of the most lucrative enterprises in the world. His lifestyle was beyond extravagant. It was of mythic proportions. In addition to his New York home, Mike owned three châteaus in France and a palace in Morocco. He had his own private jets, yachts, an extensive art collection, jewelry, and collectibles that included Fabergé eggs, fleets of expensive custom-built cars, a collection of Harley-Davidson motorcycles, hot air balloons, historical documents, and other priceless artifacts. Although he married Roberta Remsen Laidlaw in 1946 and had five children with her Mike lived what I suppose you could call a very limited and totally closeted gay life. He was bisexual and only occasionally indulged in gay sexual activities. Whenever he came into town he would stay at the Roosevelt Hotel for one night and have sex with six or seven different guys, one after the other. Months or even a year would go by before he came back to L.A. again to have another sexual encounter with men. However, through my extensive list of contacts, now and again I also fixed him up with young male tricks in New York.

Another major name in the world of publishing whom I got to know very well was Alfred A. Knopf. He and his wife Blanche had set up the distinguished Alfred A. Knopf publishing house in 1915, bringing many outstanding foreign and local authors to the American reading public. I was introduced to him by my old friend Clifford Mortimer Crist who used to teach English at Princeton and who subsequently went on to sell college text books under the Knopf imprint for Alfred.

Cliff made his home in New York—where the Knopf publishing house was based—and sometime during the sixties when he was out here on business he asked me to do him a favor. As he didn't drive he wanted me to take him out to the airport to meet his boss Alfred Knopf who was due in from New York for a series of important meetings. So, in my trusty old Chrysler, I drove Cliff to LAX where we met Alfred and then took him over to the Beverly Hills Hotel where he had reserved accommodation. I don't remember the exact details of how and why it came about but just before Alfred followed the bellhop with his bags up to his suite it was arranged that I send up a nice young lady to keep him company.

Alfred was in his early to midsixties and clearly a very cultured and successful businessman so I went to special lengths to ensure that the woman I sent to him that evening was imbued with the kind of maturity and personality more or less commensurate with his own interests and outlook. I knew he wouldn't be satisfied—if you'll pardon the expression—with a dumb blonde who wouldn't have much to say after the sex was over. The long and the short of it is that whoever I sent pleased Alfred very much. Over the ensuing years, every time he was in town he would contact me and I would arrange suitable female company for him. On one of his trips he spent over a week in town and I fixed him up with three or four different women.

On one occasion he was out here with his wife Blanche and so I met her, too, never letting on that I was fixing up tricks for her husband, of course. She and I also struck up a nice friendship and a few months later, when she flew out alone to attend a party at the home of an old school friend of hers in Brentwood, we discovered that we were sexually attracted to one another. She was a pleasant enough looking woman and the chemistry between us was good. So much so, in fact, that she occasionally made special trips out here from New York under the pretext that she was seeing friends, but it was really only to spend time with me.

A CAVALCADE OF COLORFUL and interesting personalities were perpetually passing through my life. I got to know the actor Clifton Webb when he was already in his late sixties or early seventies. Nevertheless, he led an amazingly active though extremely shielded homosexual life. He made his name in movies quite late in his career. He was already fifty-five years old when he played the role of Waldo Lydecker in *Laura* in 1944, for which he was nominated for an Academy Award for Best Supporting Actor. Clifton was an obsessively proper, correct, and well-mannered man. He was polite to the point of being irritating, and he used his extensive and witty vocabulary to ruthlessly cut down an opponent in an argument. I was at many dinner parties where he would sail through a verbal exchange, choosing precisely the right phrase at the right time. He'd learned a lot from his good friend and confidant, Noël Coward. Cliff—as I sometimes called him—was always impeccably dressed. Nothing was ever out of place. He sported a neatly trimmed little moustache a lot of the time and he never had a hair out of place.

Cliff lived with his mother his entire life. She was a pleasant but rather overbearing woman by the name of Maybelle. She looked after, guarded, shielded, and protected her son with an intensity I have seldom seen. Even though she knew he was gay she would never discuss the fact with anyone. If someone mentioned it she would lash out at them unmercifully. Cliff took his mother everywhere: to motion picture sets where he was working, to dinner parties, and even on vacation. They were inseparable. He often had me bring young men over to his house but he was always careful that Maybelle should not see or hear them, even though his homosexuality was no secret between him and his mother. Cliff was especially cautious of being seen with me. Naturally, he knew of my reputation as a hustler and a trickster, so he never wanted our friendship to be on view in public.

"Just keep your distance from me, Scotty," he often whispered to me at cocktail parties and dinners. "I don't want people to think that I'm gay."

That was a good one: Cliff was so outlandishly camp that he advertised his sexuality to all and sundry merely by walking into a room! Despite his phobia of being labeled gay I occasionally arranged tricks for him at parties. These liaisons took place in the open, with Cliff and his trick for the evening strolling from the party area hand in hand, headed for the nearest bedroom.

Whenever this happened his mother would start behaving like a brooding, clucking hen and say, "Now, now, boys, don't misbehave, you hear?"

Then she would call me over and have me serve her another cocktail while "the boys" spent their fifteen or twenty minutes in private.

Maybelle liked me. She often scurried over to me and whispered in my ear, "Oh, Scotty, thank heavens for you, darling. You make my Clifton so happy, you know."

Then she would plant a quick wet kiss on my cheek and chuckle into her glass.

ONE OF MY CLOSE FRIENDS during the early sixties was a fun-loving queen by the name of Dave Damon, a very talented ceramics artist who had a gallery and store on Santa Monica Boulevard. His thriving business also sold garden fountains and statues. Dave was about thirty-five or thereabouts and liked nothing better than to cruise the boulevards at night and pick up young guys. If he liked them he would always refer them to me and they would become part of my on-call cast of male tricksters. One day Dave got me a gig working as a bartender at a well-known doctor's home. I can't recall his name but if memory serves me correctly he was a general practitioner with a large medical group in town. I distinctly remember that he was straight, had a beautiful girlfriend, and knew many influential people. His house was just behind a tall building known as the Sierra Towers, close to Sunset Boulevard and Doheny Drive in Beverly Hills. He subsequently called me back for more dinner parties and social events and on one of those occasions I met a very wealthy doctor from La Jolla who was among his guests. As I can no longer remember his name either; I'll just refer to him as Fred.

Fred was obviously gay and had come to the party alone. However, many of the guests knew him and he seemed to be very popular. He took a shining to me and at the end of the evening he took me aside and invited me to come to his La Jolla home down the coast near San Diego, where he was going to be giving a party for some friends. The pretense was that he wanted me to take care of the food and bar arrangements. The date was two weeks away and he suggested that I should drive down on the Friday and stay over until Monday morning. I was flattered at the offer and took him up on it.

On the appointed Friday I drove down the coast from L.A., getting to his place at about four o'clock in the afternoon. He had told me that the party would take place on the Saturday night, so I was expecting to discuss the dinner menu and bar requirements with him on Friday evening. Instead, I found that his modern, beach-front home was already well stocked with everything, from alcohol to all sorts of exotic food. There was virtually nothing for me to do, and it quickly became obvious that my role was going to be more of a guest than a bartender. Which was fine by me.

Fred suggested that I take a shower, relax, and then change into something smart yet casual for dinner, as he was expecting another couple of guests that evening. A few hours later, from my bedroom window, I saw a sedan pull up outside the house. The driver was a good-looking young guy, probably in his late twenties or early thirties. He rushed out of the car, opened the front passenger door, and a stocky man in his midsixties with thinning black hair stepped out. I thought I recognized him from either the newspapers or the TV news but I wasn't sure. He wasn't a movie actor, that much I knew. Minutes later the doorbell rang. I heard Fred welcome the two men. Obviously the three of them were close friends. I decided it was time for me to join the party so I went downstairs. Fred was in his den, hovering around the bar.

The minute he saw me he beamed and called out, "Oh, Scotty, there you are. Come and join us."

I went into the room and Fred introduced me to the middle-aged guy.

"Meet John," he said. "He's out here from Washington for the weekend."

"John" grabbed my hand and pumped it firmly.

"Good to meet you," he said.

I could swear that I knew him but I just couldn't place him. It was most frustrating but, of course, I didn't let it show.

I was then introduced to the younger man, whose name I no longer remember. Their bags were still in the hallway and the young guy said that he would take them upstairs, so I offered to help. He was a very pleasant fellow and together we carried the luggage upstairs. I was surprised to hear Fred say that the two of them would be staying in one of the extra bedrooms upstairs. It seemed a bit odd to me that they were going to be sharing a room, especially as there was only one bed in it. As I put down the bag that I was carrying I glanced at the name tag attached to the handle. It listed only a name but no street address and no telephone number. But the name alone was enough to give me the biggest surprise of the evening. In bold face it read JOHN EDGAR HOOVER. Then it hit me. Of course! Now I recognized the face. The older man was none other than J. Edgar Hoover, director of the Federal Bureau of Investigations, in Washington D.C.

As soon the young guy put his bag down on the other side of the bed he removed his jacket and tossed it on the bed, revealing a shoulder holster and revolver strapped to his body. *Jesus,* I thought. This guy isn't only Hoover's chauffeur and bodyguard, he's also his lover! They were going to share the bed. So the rumors were true. I had often heard that Hoover might be gay. He was an extremely powerful figure in Washington, as well as on the broad political and law enforcement landscape of the United States. He had founded the FBI in 1935, molding it into the largest and most efficient crime-fighting agency in the nation. It was also the most feared. The FBI investigated not only criminals but political dissenters, activists in many fields, those suspected of being communists and spies, and, yes, even those involved in the burgeoning civil rights and gay rights movements. Yet, here he was, under the same roof where I was staying, for a weekend with his young gay lover. I could hardly believe it. Nevertheless, it was time to go back downstairs and get acquainted with this iconic figure.

It was an interesting weekend, to say the least. The sex began immediately after dinner that night. Fred and I paired off while Hoover and his young bodyguard made out together.

Hoover was a very pleasant and polite man. He was also not shy. He certainly did not behave like the imposing and nasty power monger he was reputed to be. But then a lot of people can be like that. They are very different in a sexual context than a professional one. Sex definitely changes people's behavior—even their identity.

Adding spice to the weekend, Fred kept a very extensive wardrobe of women's clothing locked up in one of the spare bedrooms. On Saturday and Sunday evening he and Hoover got dressed up in drag. A lot of fun was had by all, I can tell you.

On Monday morning I bid everyone good-bye and drove off toward the main road north to Los Angeles. In my rearview mirror I watched Hoover, Fred, and the tall, lanky young guy waving good-bye to me. Though Fred and I remained friends for years, I never saw J. Edgar Hoover again.

24

Drag Queens and Music

Another fascinating person I met in the sixties was a guy by the name of Sascha Brastoff. When we were first introduced he was probably in his midforties. He had originally come out to Hollywood from the East Coast. Not long after his arrival Darryl Zanuck signed him to a seven-year contract as a costume designer at Twentieth Century Fox. Sascha was an ambitious, highly energetic, and talented individual. He had an eclectic background as a ballet dancer in Cleveland, Ohio, a window dresser for Macy's department store in New York, and a very gifted ceramicist. In his spare time Sascha was often throwing clay, firing up kilns, and designing plates, pots, ashtrays, vases, platters, jars, and other ceramic ware. The hobby rapidly became a passion and soon movie stars and studio executives were enthusiastically buying up his beautifully crafted wares. As a result, two years after starting work on the sprawling Twentieth Century Fox lot in Beverly Hills he wangled his way out of his contract with the studio and set up shop as an independent ceramics artist.

Millionaire industrialist Winthrop Rockefeller discovered Sascha's work, took an interest in it, fell head over heels in love with Sascha, and joined his fledgling enterprise as a financial backer. With that kind of support Sascha moved into larger premises, surrounded himself with a large staff, and was soon regarded as one of the top ceramic artists in the country. Each piece that came out of his workshops carried his name and signature, commanded a very high market price, and became a valuable collector's item. He threw a party at his premises whenever he launched a new product line and it was something of an honor to be on his guest list. Apart from his beloved ceramics, Sascha revered two other things above all else: he enjoyed dressing up as a drag queen and he relished giving blow jobs to his many boyfriends. With his witty sense of humor he was the life of any party as he whirled and twirled around the room bedecked in exotic gowns, high-heeled shoes, and Carmen Miranda–style fruity headgear. Dressed in drag Sascha frequently went to parties where there were a lot of straight young single men. He would go around and grab each one of them individually, take them into a closet, a bedroom, a storeroom, a restroom, or anywhere suitable, and suck them off. Nobody ever cottoned on to the fact that the shapely, leggy, big-bosomed bombshell with the velvet tongue and soft, silky lips was a man and not a woman. When Sascha was in drag he looked, walked, talked, and behaved exactly like a woman. You simply could not tell that he was a man. He was so good at cock sucking that every straight guy he ever serviced swore that it was a woman who had just given him a blow job. He was gentle, he took his time, and, with his artificial long fingernails there was no way you could guess that he was a man in drag.

One Saturday night Sascha was invited to a big fund-raising party for the Santa Monica Police Department. It was a gala black tie affair. The event was sponsored by the mayor's office of the City of Santa Monica. The venue was a large hall on the second floor above a swanky store at the corner of Broadway and Fourth Street. I had been invited to the function and turned up at the appointed hour with my date, a pretty hooker friend by the name of Betsy. An hour later I noticed that Sascha had still not arrived and I began to wonder whether he was going to make it to the party.

Just after nine o'clock—fashionably late—a big black limousine pulled up downstairs and out stepped a dazzling woman, swathed in furs, feathers, and pearls. Oddly enough she was unaccompanied and so she was escorted upstairs to the party by two security guards and a bouncer. As she floated into the main room everybody stared at her. She was bewitchingly beautiful and she moved so sexily that every red-blooded male in the room could not take his eyes off her. Half a dozen men, a mix of young and middle-aged, broke away from little groups around the room and surrounded her like vultures descending upon a kill. Each of them nervously shuffled around her, vying for the honor of fetching her a drink or offering her a cigarette or accompanying her onto the dance floor. One of them finally edged out the others and the lady threw back her head, pursed her lips, accepted his hand, and they casually minced their way toward the hors d'oeuvres table on the far side of the room. As they glided past Betsy and me the gorgeous damsel turned and winked. Oh, my God! Why hadn't I realized it earlier? Despite the heavy makeup, lipstick, eyeliner, and unbelievably long, artificial, felinelike lashes it was unmistakable. I knew that wink anywhere. The "lady" was none other than Sascha Brastoff, playing the part better than I had ever seen him do it before. He and his chaperone sailed past us and disappeared into the throngs of people.

About a half hour later the guest of honor for the evening arrived. It was the Santa Monica chief of police and his wife. As soon as they entered the room they began to mingle among the crowd. The cop's wife was known to be a bit of a boozer and she headed straight for the bar. Half an hour later she was well oiled and giggling away amid a crowd of her usual friends. Betsy and I helped ourselves to some food and maneuvered our way through the room. It was getting hot and stuffy inside. We reached a French-style glass doorway that opened onto a narrow balcony and stepped outside into the cool, fresh air. I leaned over the side and then looked across to the next balcony. At first I wasn't sure what I was seeing but as my eyes adjusted to the shadows and the ambient splash of neon light from the building across the street I could clearly make out the form of the chief of police leaning with his back against the railing of the balcony. His legs were spread apart, his head was turned skyward, and he was moaning in agonized ecstasy. Kneeling in front of him with his faced buried in his crotch was Sascha. I could clearly see the wig on Sascha's head bob up and down as he sucked on the big, burly cop. Clearly, the Santa Monica police chief had no idea whatsoever that this ravishing woman with the deft fingers, ruby red lips, and magical tongue was a man. If he did, I shudder to think what would have happened. He probably would have hurled Sascha over the balcony and then tossed the splattered leftovers into the Pacific. Fortunately, by the time the little balcony escapade had played itself out the cop's wife was far too loaded to notice the dazzled look of satisfaction on her husband's face as he happily stumbled back into the room, fumbling with his fly.

A BRITISH GUY in his late twenties by the name of Brian Epstein came into my life during the early sixties. He came from a wealthy Liverpool family and made a few trips across the pond to Los Angeles. Brian was gay, although he did his best to conceal the fact from his rather conservative Jewish family. Before his first visit to California a friend suggested that he contact me when he arrived in town so that I could set up a trick for him. He was a pleasant enough, unassuming sort of guy and, as things turned out, I tricked him myself. We became good friends. Brian was dark-haired, good-looking, and slightly stocky. He had a very pleasant disposition, was fairly quiet, and had a good ear for music. He started out as a salesman in a music store that was owned by his father in Liverpool. Keen to become acquainted with new bands, he visited clubs, bars, and dives around the city, writing about them in the local *Mersey Beat* magazine. It was then that he first came across the name of a little known rock group called the Beatles.

Brian loved their music. Ironically, he seemed to be the only one who did. Most of the critics and experts in Liverpool dismissed the "Fab Four" as "just another band." But Brian was persistent. After attending many of their performances he signed a contract with the lads in early 1962, becoming their manager. He inspired them, coaxed them, pushed them, and encouraged them to write more songs. He made them change their image. He was responsible for their first recording session in London, and their first commercially released LPs. The rest, as they say, is history.

In 1964 Brian arranged the Beatles' first visit to America. On February 9 of that year they appeared on the *The Ed Sullivan Show*. The night they appeared on TV, seventy-three million people in nearly twenty-four million households watched them, at that time the largest audience in American television history. "Beatlemania" began sweeping the world. Groupies—swarms of young girls who religiously followed the group, trying whatever means they could to get into bed with them—began harassing and prowling around after the foursome. By August of 1964 Brian had arranged a multicity North American tour for the group. On August 23, the boys arrived in Los Angeles from Vancouver. The moment their aircraft touched down Brian called me.

"We're in deep trouble, Scotty," he wailed. "We're due to stay at the Beverly Hills Hotel and the groupies have already found out about it. They've completely encircled the place. I can't risk putting the boys up there. They've got to get some rest and peace and quiet. They've got a performance tonight. Is there anywhere you know where we could put them up where they'll be safe?"

Brian was clearly desperate. I had to think fast.

I wracked my brain and thought of my old pal, Charles Cooper, a very wealthy and successful couturier, whose clothes were very much in vogue on both coasts. Charley had a home in Manhattan and a luxurious one here in L.A., on Curson Terrace up above Sunset Boulevard, not too far away from the Chateau Marmont Hotel. The house commanded a stunning view of the city, and had an ambling secluded garden and a large pool. It was gated, surrounded by high walls, and perched on a steep parcel of land that made it virtually impenetrable. Anyone trying to access the house from the side or back would need mountaineering gear to scale the cliffside hill and reach the tall fence. I immediately called Charles in New York.

"You coming back into town soon, Charley?" I asked.

"No, Scotty," he replied. "I'm out east for at least another month. Why? Need anything?"

"As a matter of fact I do," I said.

"What?" he said. "I'll do whatever I can to help, you know that."

I told him that I needed his house for the Beatles and their manager. At first he didn't believe me but finally he bought my story and said that it would be his pleasure to accommodate the boys. Not only that, but by midafternoon a constant stream of delivery vehicles arrived bearing flowers, fresh fruit, champagne, and mountains of food.

I took a cab to the Beverly Hills Hotel to meet Brian. I knew he had a limo for the boys, plus a minibus for their luggage, gear, and musical instruments. I planned to ride to Charley's N. Curson Avenue property with them. Although I had some trouble getting through security and fighting my way through an army of young girls intent on breaking into the hotel I eventually got to the suite where Brian was staying. He was more than relieved to see me and immediately took me over to another suite where the boys were holed up, patiently waiting to be moved to their new digs. I didn't know what to expect as the security guard let us in. I was half expecting to see four stoned young men surrounded by clouds of pot smoke. Instead, I found the four of them just sitting around trying to stave off boredom. They were the sweetest, nicest young men I had met in a long time. Spiriting them out via a back entrance, we bundled them into the limo and drove them to Charley's house, the minibus following close behind us. By late afternoon they were happily splashing in the pool. The next morning the private security company I hired to keep an eye on things told me that at least a dozen young women, using flashlights in the dead of night, had actually managed to scale the cliff and reach the perimeter fence around the house. Fortunately, they were all apprehended before they could enter the house itself. If I had my way, I would happily have let them in. Why shouldn't those four talented young men have had some fun? Don't you agree?

BY THE MIDSIXTIES I had become very good friends with one of the most charismatic and feisty ladies in town, the singer and actress Carol Channing. I had first met Carol at a private dinner party and subsequently worked for her, too. She was a bombshell of a woman and her personality was dynamite. She was a devout member of the Christian Science movement and was committed to living a healthy lifestyle. Whenever she was invited to a cocktail party or a dinner she always brought her own bottled water with her. Many of her friends and associates found the habit funny, as this was long before bottled water became as trendy and as widely used as it is today. She would arrive at a function with her distilled water in special glass containers that had been designed for storing blood plasma. They were completely airtight. Carol was terrified of viruses, bacteria, and germs. When she was seated at a dinner table she would ask me to bring over one of the containers that she had brought with her and that I had earlier stowed in the refrigerator. Heaven forbid if I or anyone else dared try to open it for her. She also brought her own food to parties and wouldn't touch anything else.

I met Carol while she was still married to her second husband, Alexander Carson, with whom she had a son named Channing. She absolutely adored and worshipped that boy. In the early fifties I introduced her to a producer and publicist friend of mine, a guy by the name of Charles Lowe. Charley was the original producer of the long-running TV comedy series *The George Burns and Gracie Allen Show*.

I remember his offices, which were in the old Carnation Building on Wilshire Boulevard. Charley was gay and I often fixed up tricks for him. He was an efficient and respected professional, much admired by everyone in the business. One day, at a friend of mine's party at the Chateau Marmont, I suggested to Charley that he manage Carol because she really needed someone reliable, responsible, and honest to take care of her business affairs and to book gigs for her. I thought Charley was the ideal person to represent her. Further coaxing got Charley and Carol together, and within a short while she appointed him as her business manager and publicist. I was thrilled. They saw a lot of each other, often dining out and frequenting popular nightspots and supper clubs together. But Carol had lots on her mind. She had recently separated from her husband, Alexander Carson, and began to worry about losing custody of her son Channing. One evening after she bared her soul to me I pondered how I might be able to help her. I got an idea. I called my old friend Frank McNamee, a judge in Nevada. At the time he was the second highest judge in the state. I explained Carol's problems to him. Frank was immediately sympathetic and asked me to get Carol to contact him. I did so and within days Carol was on her way to Nevada to meet with Frank. He turned out to be an absolute angel. He put her up for three days in the guest suite of his apartment in Las Vegas and gave her advice. Later on he helped her out further by signing an affidavit stating that Carol had spent thirty days staying with him in his home. In Nevada that was usually construed as being evidence that two people were having a relationship, and, according to state law, it entitled Carol to a divorce from Carson. It also gave her custody of her son.

When Carol offered to pay Frank for doing all this for her he simply smiled and said, "You're a friend of Scotty Bowers, aren't you? That makes you a friend of mine. You don't owe me a dime, my dear."

Although Carol's custody battle ended happily, other aspects of her life remained problematic. In 1956, to the surprise of many—myself included—Carol and Charley Lowe got married. As I said,

Charley was openly gay. I immediately saw the writing on the wall. I felt guilty about it; after all, I was the one who had introduced them. Although they remained married for over forty years it was a marriage in name only. Throughout it Charley continued to play the field in the gay world. In 1998, shortly before Charley died, Carol filed for divorce. I heard that after divorcing Charles she said indignantly that they'd been married for forty-two years and in all that time he'd only had sex with her once.

ON THE HOME FRONT, Betty continued to man the fort in our little house on North St. Andrews Place and my daughter Donna had become a lovely young teenager. She was studious, popular among her friends, and was attending Hollywood High School. I saw her whenever I could but, to be truthful, that wasn't nearly as much as I should have. I probably missed out on some of the best years of her life. Nevertheless, whenever we spent time together she was always overjoyed to see me. As, indeed, was Betty. Bless them both.

25

True Love

Of the many women that have come into my life, two alone stand out above the rest. They brought me not only pleasure, carnal delight, and intense satisfaction, but taught me what real love was. When Betty and I first met after the war I thought I was in love with her but, as I pointed out earlier, the passion didn't last. We continued to care for one another. She was the mother of my daughter. We had a home together—even though I didn't spend much time there. So although we cared for one another, love had long ago gone out of the relationship.

I screwed many women. In fact, I probably screwed more women than men. But love, per se, was never part of any of those short encounters. And then something extraordinary happened.

The year was 1965. My friend Jerry Herman, the guy who wrote the music for the hit Broadway musicals *Hello, Dolly!, Mame,* and *La Cage aux Folles,* and who was nominated for five Tony Awards, winning twice, called me up from New York. He told me he was coming out to the coast with his secretary to negotiate the screen rights for one of his shows with a local studio. I had met Jerry back in 1961 and we had remained friends ever since.

The day after Jerry arrived I went over to the Beverly Hills Hotel where he was staying with his secretary. I went in, waited in the lobby, and Jerry came down to meet me. Then he introduced me to his secretary, whom he had asked to come down and join us for dinner. Her name was Sheila Mack. She was twenty-seven years old and a little on the heavy side, but she had a lovely, open, friendly face. She had light brown hair, gorgeous brown eyes, was about five feet eight, and wore very little makeup. Her complexion was like the proverbial peaches and cream. She seemed extremely calm, content, and peaceful. She radiated an indefinable warmth. As she softly shook my hand, my heart melted. I have no idea why, but I instantly fell head over heels in love with her.

After dinner that night Sheila and I went to her room. It was a wonderful night. It wasn't just sexy, it was *romantic*. As we coupled it wasn't merely a matter of having sex, but of making love. Oh, if only more people could realize the difference. If only more of us could discern the subtle dividing line between lust and love. That night, more than ever before, I learned what love was. Our passion was intense. But our feelings for one another, on some kind of mysterious, esoteric, indefinable level far exceeded the raw beauty of the physical experience. The next morning when I awoke next to her, sensing the softness and feminine magic of her body next to mine, I knew that I had never really, fully, deeply known a woman before. It was a revelation. We were totally, inexorably in love.

Sheila was originally from California. She came from a very wealthy and closely knit family that owned a department store outside San Francisco. The business was run by her brother, apparently a very smart and pleasant guy. As for Sheila, when she left home she went to a finishing school in New York. She remained there and got married quite young. Alas, the marriage lasted less than six months. She divorced and got a job as Jerry Herman's secretary, which consumed just about all of her time.

Jerry was a very busy man, much in demand, and he relied totally on Sheila to keep his professional and business affairs on track. They weren't here in town very long before they had to fly back east but I spent every single moment that I could with Sheila. Those nights with her in the Beverly Hills Hotel were bliss. Unforgettable. But, as so often happens, all good things eventually come to an end. It was very wrenching for both of us to say good-bye. By now Jerry had picked up on our intense relationship and when he bid me farewell he said that if ever I got out to New York I was welcome to stay at his place. With that, he and Sheila glided out of the Beverly Hills Hotel driveway in a limo en route to the airport.

As the car joined the traffic I caught sight of Sheila's hand sticking out of the side window frantically waving to me. As the vehicle disappeared I felt a terrible sense of loss. I was devastated to see her go. But I was overjoyed when, two weeks later, a telegram arrived from Sheila inviting me to spend a weekend with her in New York. I responded with an immediate "Yes!" Within a few days a first-class air ticket turned up in my mailbox. To Betty's credit—bless her soul—when these items were delivered to the house she never even queried me about them. I have to admit that I probably never really gave her the recognition and respect she deserved.

When I got to New York, Sheila met me at the airport and we took a cab to Jerry Herman's place at 50 West Tenth Street in Greenwich Village. Sheila was staying there because Jerry was traveling out of town. His home was remarkable. It had once been a fire station but had been converted into a very fancy place by its previous owner, an old queen and a good friend of mine by the name of Maurice Evans. Maurice was a Shakespearean actor on the Broadway and London stages but I guess his real claim to fame was the role he played as the character Samantha's father in the hit comedy TV series, *Bewitched*. When Maurice bought the building from the New York Fire Department he wanted to maintain the integrity and style of the place. He didn't even remove the original brass pole that extended down from the upper two floors to the ground level where the fire trucks used to be parked. It was down that pole that the firemen used to slide from their sleeping quarters to the engines whenever there was an alarm call. The building had great charm with immense spaces everywhere. The ground floor area could easily accommodate six or eight cars.

Sheila and I spent most of that wonderful weekend oblivious to the world, happily, intoxicatingly, crazily in love and entwined in Jerry's large double bed. I adored her. Unreservedly.

Not long after I returned to L.A. from New York I got a note from Sheila telling me that she was pregnant. Neither of us were certain how to deal with the situation. Then I got another note. She told me that she would be moving out to California within a couple of months. Apparently she had talked Jerry into relocating to Hollywood, where new opportunities in film and television were opening up for his musical talents. I could hardly contain my excitement.

As soon as she arrived back in town she took an apartment at 1125 North Kings Road, between Fountain and Santa Monica Boulevard. The day after she moved in she told me that she had undergone an abortion before leaving New York. In a way we were relieved, but then again, to be truthful, I know that she deeply regretted terminating the pregnancy. Long after we had separated, for years and years afterward, she used to call me up on the approximate date that the baby would have been born and remind me that it would have been time to celebrate the birthday. This went on for fifteen or twenty years. She would call up and say, "Our kid would have been ten years old today, Scotty." Or twelve or fifteen or eighteen or whatever. The abortion broke her heart. She never got over it. And I never really knew how to deal with it, either. The pain was intense. In fact, it probably played a role in our eventual separation.

Sheila and I shacked up together for almost four years. I hardly ever slept at home anymore. If I wasn't out all night bartending or tricking somebody I would sleep over at Sheila's place. She was quite a gal. Apart from being great in bed, she had a heart of gold. She was utterly giving and forgiving. She was not in the least bit possessive, jealous, or controlling. She was so generous, open-minded, and considerate that on Christmas Eve or on my birthday I would come home to her and she would tiptoe me toward the bedroom, slowly open the door, and then show me a gorgeous young girl that she had in bed for me as a gift for the night. She believed in variety. She was convinced that surprises and the odd adventurous foray with other people kept a relationship alive, sizzling, and at its peak. She was determined to keep boredom at bay, no matter what.

There was only one impediment to our relationship. And the name of that problem was Judith Moore.

HERE'S HOW IT HAPPENED. At the time that I was living with Sheila I had a good friend by the name of Al Grossman. Al was a sweet man who was immeasurably wealthy. He came from a highly successful family of industrialists and had inherited a fortune. He never had to work. He socialized a lot and moved in the most elite circles. For years he had been fixing me up with beautiful, moneyed women, many of whom had tipped me generously for sexual services. But he also found me a lot of really good personal dates.

One day in 1968 he left me a message at home and insisted that I call him urgently. In fact, it was Betty who took the call. When I popped in to see her and Donna she gave me the message. I called Al Grossman immediately.

"Get over here tonight, Scotty," he said.

"Where?" I asked.

"My place. Seven o'clock."

"Okay," I answered, thinking he was having a party that evening and wanted a bartender. "How many are you expecting?"

"Just you," he replied.

This made no sense to me.

"What are you talking about, Al?" I asked.

"I met this broad at a dinner last night," he answered. "I want you to meet her."

What could I say?

At seven that evening I knocked on the door of Al's West Hollywood home. He showed me into the library and standing in the middle of the room like an object on display in a museum of fine art was one of the most magnificent creatures I had ever laid eyes on.

"Judith, Scotty. Scotty, Judith," said Al.

I studied her, dumbstruck by her beauty.

"I see you two are gonna get along just fine," Al chuckled.

I hardly remember anything else about that evening. Judith was exactly the same age as Sheila. She was also the same height. But she was a beauty beyond description. She had long, soft, dark hair, brown eyes, magnificent facial features. Her prominent cheekbones made her look like a portrait created by some classical Italian master. Her skin texture was so perfect that she wore only the tiniest hint of makeup. She was thin and trim, yet had just enough bulges in the right places to give her the figure of a fashion model. As she sat down and crossed her legs I was struck by her dainty, sensitive body language. This woman was all sex, a goddess from a far-off, mythical place. I could not take my eyes off her. She was the most captivating and magnificent woman I had ever seen, and that included Sheila plus all the hundreds of others who had preceded her. For once in my life I was speechless. She was perfect in every way.

The next night I took her out to dinner. Judith Moore was her name. She was a divorcée and had been single for a couple of years. She had two young kids. They were both at boarding school. Judith came from a wealthy Wisconsin family. It wasn't dysfunctional in the contemporary sense of the word but its members were fragmented, detached, out of touch with one another. Her mother had divorced her father and moved to Switzerland. Her father lived in Chicago. She didn't see much of either of them. She had a brother who lived in

Portland, Oregon, and another brother who lived in Hawaii. There were years when they didn't even send so much as a Christmas card to one another.

Judith had money. Lots of it. Her grandfather had invented, patented, manufactured, and sold machines that produced paper from pulpwood. The family had become one of the wealthiest in all of the Midwest. She told me she had an apartment here in town, but she also owned homes in Wisconsin, Rome, and London. She made it very clear from the get-go that there were indeed many men in her life and that marriage was remote from her mind. She enjoyed her freedom and she loved to play hard. But, despite her aversion to settling down, she said she also had the capacity to love hard. And it was not long before I began to experience precisely what she meant by that.

I quickly discovered that Judith was the most original person I had ever known. She exuded passion. Her heart was fathomless. She could love with an intensity that eclipsed even that of my dear Sheila. She was kind. She was sweet. She was gentle. She was funny. She was intelligent. She was worldly. She was unique in every way.

But she was never truly mine.

There were times when she went off to be with other men for weeks or months at a time. I never questioned that. She had warned me about it and so I accepted it. I had a key to her apartment and whenever she was back in town all she had to do was snap her fingers and I would be there. When I crawled into bed beside her it was like there was absolutely no one else in her life. She loved unconditionally and intensely. When I entered her it was like I had never known another woman in my entire life. Every time we made love it was like the first time I had ever experienced the sheer wonderment of woman.

Not once did I know her to be moody or downbeat. She never chided me for anything. She didn't know the meaning of cynicism or criticism. She had no clue what malice meant. She sparkled with life.

She welcomed every day, every hour, every minute. She celebrated the mere act of being alive.

I loved her so. There was a strange vacuum in my life every time I spent more than an hour away from her.

But I still had to work. One night I was bartending at a party and the hostess was in a foul mood because she had caught her husband having an affair with his secretary.

"That son of a bitch," she said after the party, "I told him to fuck off."

And then she threw herself at me and whispered, "Scotty, stay with me tonight."

Which I did.

The next morning, long after dawn, I went back to Judith. She opened the door, smiled, welcomed me into the apartment, hugged and kissed me, ran a hot bath for me, and asked me what I would like for breakfast. She never asked where I was or what I had been doing. She accepted everything without question. And she was always game to try new things. She, like Sheila, believed that a little adventurous sexual play involving others now and again didn't weaken a relationship but strengthened it.

She enjoyed the swinging scene. We would go to a restaurant, meet another couple, strike up a rapport, and then go home with them. Judith would happily spend the night with the guy while I was with his wife. Foursomes were okay with her, too. No questions were ever asked. There were no hassles, no hang-ups. Anything was all right, just as long as she knew that whatever we did made me happy.

I was a lucky guy. The years between 1965 and 1973, the years that I was seeing Sheila and Judith, were the happiest and most complete of my life. When I was staying over at Sheila's place I spun a little white lie by telling Judith that I was out with some trick or other. The same applied the other way around. When I was with Judith she knew nothing of Sheila. As far as she was concerned, I was out working somewhere. Fortunately, neither of them prodded or probed.

They accepted everything. So there I was, occasionally at home with Betty at North St. Andrew's Place, but spending most of my time with either Sheila or Judith. Plus, of course, one or two other ladies tucked away here and there and, on top of that, there was my very busy tricking life, involving both men and women. I was a busy man. And I was totally happy.

But I have learned that, for me anyway, few things in this world last forever. Both Sheila and Judith eventually drifted out of my life. But life—and my way of living it—went on.

26

Friends

One of my dearest friends during the sixties was the playwright Tennessee Williams. We were introduced at a party and became very good buddies. In fact, we took an immediate shining to one another and I began tricking him. Tennessee was already into his fifties and was a heavy smoker and drinker, but he was still in good health and proved himself to be a horny devil once we got to know one another. He wasn't exactly good-looking. In fact, he often looked quite disheveled. When I met him he was still grieving over the loss of his long-time companion Frank Merlo, a sailor he had met in 1947 and who passed away from cancer in 1963. That loss, compounded by Tennessee's unhappy childhood, his sister Rose's mental illness and institutionalization, his fractured relationship with his younger brother Dakin, his own battle with depression and alcoholism, and his eventual addiction to prescription drugs, all took a heavy toll on him. Tennessee was a brilliant writer but an insecure, complex man. He suffered many failures and rejections during his career as one of America's most famous playwrights but, despite the disappointments, he was the creator of some of the most extraordinary works ever written for the American theater.

Whenever he came to L.A. he and I would always get together. He loved the Beverly Hills Hotel and the management always made sure that he got his favorite room in the east wing when he stayed there.

One afternoon I got a call from him. He invited me over, saying that he had something to show me that evening. To be honest, Tenny was quite a time-consuming guy. He was smart and he loved to talk. And talk. And talk some more. He was like Spencer Tracy in some ways. He'd consume a lot of alcohol and hours would pass before we'd get down to business. Anyway, I didn't know what he meant by wanting to "show" me anything that particular evening. I guessed it was just another term for a night of sex with him. That evening I arrived at his room. He invited me in, told me to sit down, and then tossed a manuscript in my lap.

"That's for you," he said. "Take a look at it while I go downstairs for a drink."

I settled back and began to read.

I was shocked at what he had written. In his most beautiful, sensitive, and intelligent Tennessee Williams style he had penned a biography of me. But, in effect, the piece was little more than a revealing exposé of my role in arranging tricks for the homosexual community of Los Angeles. He had painted a vivid picture of me as the fairy godmother of the entire gay world in the City of Angels. The piece made it look like I was flying over Hollywood Boulevard directing all the queens in town. It made it seem that if I didn't exist there would be no gay life at all in Hollywood. He had turned me into a maverick, a renegade, a star, a hero. The article was meant to flatter me, to celebrate what I had done, but what it really did was make me look like the mother of all queens. It was way over the top.

When he returned an hour or so later he asked me what I thought and I just said, "Tenny, I know you're a sweetheart, baby, and I know you meant well but, *please*, tear that up."

At first he was disappointed at my reaction but he soon realized how unhappy I was about it and we just hugged and laughed about it. As for the manuscript, it never did see the light of day and I have no idea what he did with it.

A REALLY GOOD FRIEND of mine during the midsixties was Raymond Burr, the lead in the long-running TV crime series, *Perry Mason*. Born in New Westminster, British Columbia, Canada, Ray was one of the nicest guys around. He was a pleasant person as well as one of the most generous and kindhearted human beings I have ever known. He always dug deep into his pocket and his wallet to share with those less privileged than himself.

Ray was gay and I tricked him very often. He behaved in a very masculine manner. There wasn't anything about him that made it obvious he was gay. In fact, he attracted women like moths to a flame. Because Ray played a lawyer on TV he was once invited up to Seattle to address a group of big-shot attorneys at a fund-raising dinner. Because we were really very fond of one another he invited me along on the trip with him. Oddly, we stayed at the same Olympic Hotel in downtown Seattle where I first met Betty after I had completed service as a Marine, only this time we stayed in one of the hotel's luxury penthouse suites.

One evening over dinner we met two gorgeous airline cabin attendants. One was blonde and the other a dark-haired beauty. Both were blessed with great boobs. I invited them up to the penthouse I was sharing with Ray but I had to fuck them both because Ray, bless his soul, wasn't up to it. He just couldn't do anything. He could only get it up with men.

When working on movies or on his TV shows in Los Angeles Ray and I often got together for a meal at night and then retired to his dressing room in the studio. Ray frequently slept over at whichever studio he was shooting. Sometimes, after a heavy bout of sex, I would spend the night in his dressing room with him. Annoyingly, at five o'clock in the morning, the unit production manager or assistant director would burst in on us, turn on all the lights, clap his hands, wake us up, and get Ray going with rehearsals for the day's shooting. By then we would probably have been asleep for only an hour or two at most. Those early-morning disruptions were really awful but Ray was a true professional and dealt with it like a pro. Within an hour he was in character and within two hours he would be in costume, made up, and on set, fresh as a daisy.

Years ago I arranged a quick trick for Ray. I introduced him to a very nice, good-looking but totally down-and-out young man thirteen years his junior. The guy's name was Bob Benevides. He was living in a hole above a store on La Brea Avenue with no job to speak of and only a mattress on the floor for furniture. He also owned an ancient clapped-out car that seldom ran. The next thing I knew, Ray had fixed Bob up with a small role in one of the *Perry Mason* episodes. Then Bob moved in with him. Ray owned two houses in town and loved throwing dinner parties. I was often there, sometimes as a guest and sometimes as a bartender. Within a year of Bob and Ray getting together as lovers Ray bought two houses for Bob, one for him to live in and one for him to derive income from as a rental property. Ray knew a great deal about the cultivation of orchids and he and Bob eventually established nurseries in Fiji, the Azores, and Hawaii. They cultivated and hybridized over 1,500 new orchid species and, many years later, just before Ray became ill with kidney cancer, they started their own vineyard at their Dry Creek Valley ranch in the Sonoma Valley near San Francisco. Ray passed away in September 1993 and Bob continues to run the winery.

ONE OF THE MORE eccentrically interesting people I knew well was Harold Lloyd. He was one of those immensely talented "kings of comedy" during the era of silent movies. Harold was also one of the original thirty-six founding members of the Academy of Motion Picture Arts and Sciences. He owned a spectacular property called

"Green Acres" on 1125 Benedict Canyon in Beverly Hills. The gates and driveway to the grounds had first been pointed out to me by Walter Pidgeon the day he picked me up way back in 1946. The property boasted no less than forty-four rooms, twenty-six bathrooms, fourteen fountains, and at least a dozen individually tended gardens. Today it is listed on the National Register of Historic Places. The place originally consisted of nineteen acres but that was eventually reduced to twelve. Harold even had a stream on the property that he used as a canoe run. He built the place over a period of five years, between 1927 and 1931. It was a formidable undertaking. There was an enormous swimming pool, a multicar garage, a large movie theater with plush seating, a wine cellar, a hothouse, and a gymnasium. There were fabulous glossy green tiles everywhere, all handmade by an Italian glazer in Los Feliz, right here in Los Angeles.

I fixed Harold up with many girls over the years. They were all beauties and, I might add, all hookers. But he never touched any of them physically. All he wanted to do was photograph them in the nude with his special 3-D camera. The movies had made him very rich and he had a fabulous assortment of the finest photographic equipment. His nudie stereoscopic 3-D pictures of pretty girls were famous all over town and even became collector's pieces in New York, London, and Paris. Green Acres lent itself to the kind of photography he did. Dripping vines, beautifully carved stonework, carpets of living color, and a rich variety of wildlife all made for spectacular backgrounds. His pictures were breathtaking.

One day, at Harold's request, I brought a dozen young beauties over to Green Acres for him to photograph. While I was waiting for him to finish shooting them against groves of trees, amid beds of flowers, against waterfalls, or at the poolside, I was invited inside the house by his wife, Mildred. She always glided about the place in skimpy outfits. She liked her booze and by midday she was already as high as a coot. There was an enormous year-round Christmas tree inside the house festooned with fancy, expensive ornaments. I screwed Mildred at the base of the tree, in the parlor, and in her bed-room, and was invited back many times to repeat the favor. Harold was never the wiser and, even if he was, he was far more interested in his three-dimensional nude photography than he was in sex with his wife.

A VERY POPULAR GUY in my collection of male tricksters was a porn star by the name of John Holmes. John was a legend. While flaccid his penis was said to be nine to eleven inches long and perhaps an inch or so longer when erect. However, the real truth will never be known. Every source lists a different statistic. But whatever length it was, John was gifted with a mighty long schlong.

I once introduced John to George Cukor. After an hour with him George called me up and said, "Yes, well, interesting, but . . ."

"But what, George?" I prodded.

"Well, he is certainly beautifully hung but the poor boy really doesn't know what to do with it," he said.

George went on to say that poor old John had trouble getting an erection and also couldn't ejaculate. When I asked George why he thought that was he said that John was probably so addicted to stuff like coke and heroin that he had permanent erectile dysfunction and could no longer achieve a hard-on. I knew that John had a drug habit, and a very bad one at that. But then George jokingly went on to say that John probably had so little gray matter upstairs that any blood that flowed from his tiny brain to his gigantic penis may have caused him to pass out. George was not bereft of humor.

John Holmes was not gay, but he did anything for money, in-cluding gay porn movies. Lots and lots of them. As he was totally ad-dicted to drugs he did whatever was requested of him either in front of or behind a camera to pay for his habit. He often bragged that he had slept with over ten thousand women and that he had made well over a thousand porn movies but I firmly believe both figures are gross exaggerations. As time went by John became totally broke. He had innumerable affairs and was married twice but he ended up a lonely, broken, and impoverished man. Drug dependency, the demands of the pornographic industry, and a lack of inherent intelligence were an unfortunate combination.

John eventually joined a crime group known as the Wonderland Gang. They were responsible for various thefts, extortion rackets, and drug dealings. In the early eighties he got on the wrong side of the gang and they began to threaten him because of money that he owed them. At about the same time he developed a relationship with the notorious L.A. drug dealer and nightclub owner Eddie Nash. When threatened by the gang John told them that Nash had a large stash of money and drugs in his house. In June 1981 he engineered a robbery in which the Wonderland Gang broke into Nash's home. Although John himself did not personally take part in the robbery Nash accused him of it. Forcing John to confess that the Wonderland Gang was responsible for the break-in, Nash arranged to have four of the gang's members murdered. It was never determined whether John himself took part in the murders but, for all intents and purposes, his career as a porn star was over after that. He was jailed for a short time and then released for lack of suitable evidence. He was later arrested again and charged with all four murders but finally acquitted. In the mideighties he married again and spread rumors that he was suffering from colon cancer. The truth was that he had AIDS. He died on March 13, 1988, at the age of forty-three, a totally impotent and impoverished has-been.

The whole tragic escapade taught me one thing: I had to be extra cautious about who I included in my little black book of tricksters. Fortunately, I did not arrange tricks for John once he became a big porn star, but the sad story of John Holmes's downfall still made a lasting impression on me.

27

The Seventies

As the sixties began inching toward the seventies my daughter Donna grew into a lovely young lady. A few years before she started college at Cal State University in Northridge I had bought her a brand new Volkswagen Bug. She treasured that car the same way she had looked after her dolls and toys as a child. Donna was a loving, beautiful person. She lived at home with Betty until she was twenty-two and then I set her up in her own little apartment near the college campus, from where she finally graduated with a teaching degree. I was so proud of her.

One hot summer afternoon in 1970 I went to check up on Betty at our North St. Andrews Place house. As I drew up I saw Donna's Volkswagen parked outside. *That's good,* I thought. Donna was visiting her mother. I was going to see both of them, a rare occurrence now that Donna had an apartment of her own. As I opened the front door I heard Betty whimpering in the kitchen. When I found her she was crying over a pot of soup that she was stirring on the stove. When I asked her what was wrong she told me that Donna had taken ill and was lying down in her old bedroom.

As I opened Donna's bedroom door I saw that the curtains were closed and the room was in darkness. I didn't want to wake her but when Betty came in with a bowl of soup Donna stirred and sat up. I opened the curtains, only to get the shock of my life. Poor Donna looked awful. Her face was pale and she was obviously in great pain.

When I asked her what was ailing her she began to sob uncontrollably. Then she came out with it. She had gotten pregnant and had gone to have an abortion that morning. Clearly, it had been a botched back-street job because she was bleeding badly and had a high fever. We summoned an ambulance immediately but two days later she went into a coma and never revived. Forty-eight hours after arriving home my darling Donna was dead.

The event resonated on the deepest level with me. The tragedy was all the more difficult to bear because my own mother had been twenty-three years old, the same age as Donna, when she had given birth to me. And in an even harsher twist of fate, my brother Donald had been killed in battle on Iwo Jima when he was twenty-three. And Donna had even been named after him.

It was a devastating time. Betty and I shared our grief but the pain was almost intolerable. We both suffered terribly. After that awful event, whatever remained of the relationship between Betty and me became even more strained, more distant, more detached. I continued to care for her, of course. We still had a home together. But little else remained between us. We had separate bedrooms in our little house and, on those very infrequent occasions when I did sleep at home and not with some trick or other, Betty and I never had sex.

I was overwhelmed by a feeling of guilt brought on by how little I had really seen of my daughter during her brief life. She had been such a sweet, loving, good-natured person. And now she was gone.

Betty was forty-five years old and I was forty-three. In the years to come she would slowly retreat into her shell, living out her life in quiet solitude at North St. Andrews Place. As for me, I hid my pain deep down inside and came to terms with the fact that, no matter what, life had to go on.

ONE OF MY VERY GOOD FRIENDS at that time was producer Ross Hunter. I had first met him back in the fifties when he was producing low-budget romantic comedies for various studios, many of them starring Doris Day. Ross had so many successful pictures under his belt that one of the studios regarded him as a profitable asset worthy of a special gift, so the studio bought him a gorgeous house on Truesdale Place in Beverly Hills. Ross was gay and lived with his longtime lover, the set decorator and later producer, Jack Mapes. Because it sounded more classy and trendy, Jack went by the French version of his name: Jacques. He had worked on many good movies, including *Singin' in the Rain*. I often used to fix up tricks for both Ross and Jacques, but always together. They were a couple in every way, but when it came to sex they often enjoyed indulging in a ménage à trois or a foursome. I had lots of willing participants for them to choose from.

Among Ross's many credits were *Flower Drum Song, Madame X, Thoroughly Modern Millie,* and, in 1970, the film that made a fortune for Universal Studios, *Airport.* The night he screened it in his large home theater Doris Day, Rock Hudson, and many other big Hollywood names were there. Even though my proper place was really at the wet bar at the back of the room Ross insisted that I sit down and enjoy the show with everyone else. He was always like that. At the end of any screening he would go around the room asking for feedback and opinions, and he always included me. One night in 1972 he threw a dinner party and announced that he was going to produce a musical remake of the classic 1937 fantasy adventure, *Lost Horizon,* directed by the great Frank Capra and starring Ronald Colman, Jane Wyatt, and my good friend Edward Everett Horton. Later that night, when all his guests left, Ross and Jacques were sitting in the kitchen sipping a nightcap as I packed the last of the glassware away.

I turned to Ross and said, "Ross, you surely aren't serious about remaking *Lost Horizon,* are you?"

Ross squinted at me over his brandy and said, "Sure, I am. Why ever not?"

"Because," I retorted, "the original was a classic. You can't trivialize it by turning it into a musical."

But it was a case I wasn't going to win.

Ross told me that he had already lined up British director Charles Jarrott to direct it. Jarrott had recently won acclaim for his direction of *Anne of the Thousand Days* and *Mary, Queen of Scots.* He said that Burt Bacharach was already writing the music for it. Russ said he was confident that the movie was going to be a hit. But I wasn't sure. The whole idea just didn't ring true. It turned out my hunch was right.

Despite the inclusion of stars like Peter Finch, Michael York, John Gielgud, Charles Boyer, George Kennedy, Liv Ullmann, and Sally Kellerman, when the movie was released in 1973 it turned out to be worse than a disaster. It was a complete flop. The critics loathed it and the public didn't go to see it. But Ross held his guns. He never admitted his error and he certainly never said that I was right. Nevertheless Ross was a good guy and I always had a soft spot for him.

IN THE SEVENTIES pornography finally burst forth from the closet and made its way into mainstream America. In addition to *Playboy* you could now buy explicitly sexual girlie or boy magazines at certain news sellers and bookstores. In New York City *Screw* magazine, founded by porn publisher Al Goldstein in 1968, was available on most downtown street corners. But to see movies you had to go to a theater. Triple-X-rated cinemas began to proliferate in areas as conspicuous as Times Square in New York and on Hollywood Boulevard in Los Angeles. Most of the movies were appallingly bad productions with terrible camerawork, pathetic lighting, ghastly editing, and substandard soundtracks, and featured actors who were atrociously untalented. And then one single film came along that changed everything. It boosted porno movie making to new heights of technical and creative accomplishment. It also made porn more popular and profitable than ever. The year was 1972 and the movie was *Deep Throat*. It was made by a guy called Gerard Damiano and starred a pretty dark-haired and little-known twenty-three-year-old porn actress by the name of Linda Lovelace. It became a worldwide phenomenon and went on to make a fortune.

Linda played a girl with an anatomical anomaly. In the story she never enjoyed sex. She could not climax. A medical examination revealed that the poor girl was without a clitoris. However, closer investigation proved that she did have one, but it was situated in an unusual place, at the back of her throat. The only way for her to achieve an orgasm was to stick an erect penis down there, then vigorously thrust up and down on the shaft to stimulate her clitoris. The results of this activity are not too difficult to imagine. After the movie was released Linda became a popular talk show guest. She made headlines not only in the counterculture world and in the underground press but in newspapers nationwide and abroad. One night I got to meet her at a Beverly Hills party and we became quite good friends. Everyone wanted to meet her, including my pal, British-born motion picture director Tony Richardson.

Tony was in his midforties at the time and was fresh from a slew of highly successful films that had garnered critical acclaim. In 1961 he won a BAFTA Award for Best Film for *A Taste of Honey* and, in 1964, Hollywood's Academy of Motion Picture Arts and Sciences had honored him with two Oscars, one for Best Picture and another for Best Director for the raunchy period film *Tom Jones* starring a very young Albert Finney. In fact, under Tony's direction Finney would be nominated for an Academy Award, as would many other actors who worked under Tony on later productions, including Laurence Olivier and Jessica Lange. Tony was a masterful director.

His credits included intelligent, thought-provoking movies like *The Entertainer, Charge of the Light Brigade, The Loneliness of the Long Distance Runner, The Loved One,* and *Ned Kelly.* When I first met him he was still married to lovely British actress Vanessa Redgrave. However, it was a short marriage, only five years, ending in divorce in 1967 (the couple had been blessed with a delightful little daughter by the name of Natasha).

I did not know Vanessa Redgrave very well, although I had met her at various parties in town. Tony was another matter. I knew him intimately. He was gay and, once he had moved to L.A. from England, he settled down in a nice little rented place on King's Road in Hollywood. I often worked for him there as a bartender. Also, I was constantly arranging tricks for him. When *Deep Throat* came out Tony was extremely anxious to meet Linda Lovelace. He was curious about her talents and techniques. One day he called me up and told me that he was having a party for some of his friends. He said that he had had a brainstorm: he wanted to treat them to a lecture by Linda. He thought she could offer them valuable tips regarding oral sex. I told him that he must be kidding. I said no one knew more about oral sex than gay men. What on earth could she teach them? But Tony was adamant. He insisted on meeting Linda. I duly introduced the two of them and, for a fairly steep fee, Tony booked Linda to come and give a talk at a party at his home. About twenty-five movers and shakers in the gay community were invited and Tony asked me to come along and bartend. On the night of the party Linda showed up with a large latex dildo so that she could demonstrate the best techniques for fellatio. As her talk and demonstration got under way you could hear a pin drop. Every single male in the room was utterly fixated by every word she said.

She was very experienced at what she did but I have to admit that twenty minutes into the demonstration I leaned over to Tony and whispered, "Tony, old buddy, this is about as useful to this bunch of guys as having a ranch hand explain how to milk a cow to a gathering of dairymen. Sucking dick is what these queens do all the time, for cryin' out loud. She's not teaching them anything new. I think you've wasted your money."

Tony shrugged, chuckled, and continued to listen intently as Linda carried on with her demonstration. Well, needless to say, when it was all over some of the guys went over to Linda and politely sat her down to offer *her* one or two tidbits of advice, and, out of courtesy and appreciation, most of them thanked her profusely for her time and advice.

Days later I was working at an afternoon cocktail party at a fashionable Beverly Hills women's social event. Most of the ladies present had blue-dyed hair, were wealthy, bedecked in pearls, and in their late sixties to eighties. One of them told me that she knew Tony Richardson and his ex-wife, Vanessa Redgrave. As we chatted I mentioned Linda Lovelace's lecture at Tony's place. Well, it didn't take long for the news to spread around the room. As I was leaving one of the more elderly of the women came up to me and pulled an address book from her purse.

"Do you think you could write down Miss Lovelace's telephone number for me?" she enquired very demurely, with just a trace of embarrassment.

"Sure," I said as I dug into my pocket for one of my little black books. Rummaging through it I found Linda's number and scribbled it into the woman's address book. She thanked me, placed the book back in her purse, and left to find her chauffeur-driven car. Two weeks later Linda called to tell me that she had just been paid a very attractive fee to give a demonstration of oral-sex and hand-job techniques to a large group of wealthy, dainty old ladies in Beverly Hills. Just goes to show. When it comes to sex, it is never *ever* too late.

28

Kew Drive

Kew Drive is located on a precipice high in the Hollywood Hills. It is about 2,000 feet above Sunset Boulevard and commands an unsurpassed sweeping view of the entire Los Angeles basin. To the east you look over the downtown area with its cluster of soaring skyscrapers, ribbons of freeways, and glittering nightscape. To the west lies Santa Monica and the shimmering Pacific Ocean. In between those two extremes stretches Hollywood, Century City, and most of Beverly Hills. Beyond all that sprawls an endless carpet of cities and suburbs, including Long Beach, Orange County, and Anaheim. The view is unique, probably the best in all of L.A.

I knew the place well because an old friend of mine, choreographer Jack Cole, lived on Kew Drive. Jack's major claim to fame was that he was the one who taught Marilyn Monroe how to dance in the 1953 movie *Gentlemen Prefer Blondes,* in which she hoofed it opposite the great Jane Russell. Jack had an impressive résumé. Among his other credits are *The Jolson Story, David and Bathsheba, River of No Return, There's No Business Like Show Business, Kismet, Les Girls,* and *Some Like It Hot.* Getting up to Kew Drive was not for the faint of heart. You had to negotiate a maze of narrow twisting roads, barely wide enough to accommodate one car. Meeting an oncoming vehicle was a major challenge and could take up to ten minutes to resolve. But frankly, the difficulty in getting there and the isolation of the place were part of its charm for me. My favorite property on the road was number 2114, owned by another friend of mine, Dale Orr.

Dale bought the property just before World War II, probably around 1936 or 1937. Dale was gay and had been an army pilot during World War I. Whenever I went up to see him or to take a young trick up there to spend the night with him I always cast envious glances at his charming and cozy two-bedroom house, its garden, guest cottage, and two small empty plots, one on either side of the property. I coveted the place more than anything else in the world. I began going to see Dale often, just so that I could be on that plot of land. As Dale aged he decided to move to something a little more accessible. He set his heart on a small lot behind a grove of avocado trees down the coast near the U.S. Marine Corps base of Camp Pendleton, just outside the town of Fallbrook. When I heard about his plans I went up to see him straight away. I was determined to buy that fantastic Kew Drive property from him.

"No problem, baby," he said. "I'll sell you the house for $9,000, plus the two empty lots next door for $3,000. Twelve grand for the lot. It's a steal. Whaddya say?"

I looked at Dale and thought about it, but felt despondent. I just didn't have the cash. Nor did I have adequate assets, collateral, or income to approach a bank for a loan. It was a great price, a near giveaway, but I couldn't cut it. When I told this to Dale he sat me down, looked me straight in the eye, and said, "No problem, buddy boy. I understand. Give me a thousand now and then a hundred bucks a month."

However, even at those ridiculously low prices, I still couldn't quite manage it and had to walk away from the deal. I was broken-hearted, but what could I do?

As it turned out, Dale never did move out of the house. Then, in 1952, he passed away, and in his will left the property to a mutual friend of ours by the name of Jack Gard. Jack lived in it for a couple of years, then rented it out, and in the early seventies he decided to sell it. By then the asking price had gone up to $60,000. And that's when another good friend of mine, the actor, Beech Dickerson, came into the picture.

Beech had been in *The Dunwich Horror* and a bunch of Roger Corman cult classics, such as *Attack of the Crab Monsters, War of the Satellites,* and *Creature from the Haunted Sea.* In the course of his career he had invested wisely and had made a lot of money. He already owned a dozen or so houses in the area, which he rented out. When he heard that Jack was selling his prime real estate on Kew Drive, plus the two adjoining plots and the little guesthouse below the main property, he immediately snapped it up. He and I had known one another for many years, and I had done the odd handyman job for him so he hired me to do general maintenance on most of his properties, including this latest acquisition on Kew Drive. Whenever there was a faucet leak or a broken hinge or an electrical circuit that needed attention I was called in to take care of it. Beech himself moved into the Kew Drive house and subsequently developed both adjoining properties. I sometimes used his guesthouse, located just below the 2114 lot. When I wasn't in it I would help find him short-term tenants for it. I was so grateful to be able to spend time on that property. It was like living out my fantasy. Eventually I landscaped the garden for Beech and personally dug a hole and installed a tiled swimming pool for him there. It was situated in front of the living room, off of which I added a small terrace with tables, chairs, and a barbecue. This made it possible for folks to swim or sunbathe and enjoy a unique view overlooking all of L.A. below. It really was stunning. We had many skinny-dipping parties and evening get-togethers there.

In 1977 one of the short-term tenants who rented Beech's little guesthouse off and on was the Spanish-born cinematographer, Néstor Almendros. He was in L.A. for a month from New York. Néstor and I had known each other for a couple of years; he was a quiet, unassuming man who moved from Spain to Cuba at the age of eighteen to be with his father, who had been exiled because of his anti-Franco political activities. Néstor had discovered his love of cinema in Havana. He founded a film society there and began to write film reviews. Further studies in film took him to Italy, and then, on his return to Cuba, he began to make short, experimental films. He was noticed by the critics in New York and so he went to the Big Apple to make a couple of acclaimed shorts. In 1959 his life changed dramatically. The Cuban Revolution took place. Fidel Castro came to power and Néstor returned to Cuba. Two of the films he made there were banned by the new Communist regime so he moved to France, where he soon began shooting films for major French directors such as François Truffaut. Néstor rapidly gained a reputation as a master of motion picture lighting. He didn't use light to illuminate his subjects, he painted with it. He liked subtle light sources such as candles, oil lamps, the rays of a weak late-afternoon sun, diffused shafts of light as they shone through lace curtains, dark skies, twilight, the delicate play of light as it reflected off surface textures. His images were masterful, every frame of every film a true work of art. It wasn't long before Hollywood noticed him, even though Néstor much preferred living and working in New York.

In 1978 director Terrence Malick hired Néstor to shoot his epic romantic drama, *Days of Heaven,* starring Richard Gere, Brooke Adams, and Sam Shepard. Néstor spent a lot of time in L.A., especially during the preproduction and postproduction processes. He shot camera tests, checked out color filters, oversaw the laboratory work as the film was processed, and supervised the color timing and printing of the film. Néstor was gay and, even though he was a fairly shy and private person, there were times when I would arrange tricks for him with other guys or even trick him myself.

In March 1979 an extraordinary thing happened. To Néstor's absolute shock, when the fifty-first annual Academy Awards nominations were announced, his name was on the list for Best

Cinematography for *Days of Heaven*. Néstor could not believe it. What's more, he was in the running against four of the giants in the world of cinematography, Oswald Morris for *The Wiz*, Robert Surtees for *Same Time, Next Year,* Vilmos Zsigmond for *The Deer Hunter,* and William Fraker for *Heaven Can Wait.* Every one of them had either previously been nominated or had won an Oscar, whereas Néstor was the new guy on the block. He didn't think he stood a chance of winning.

The awards ceremony was scheduled to take place April 9, that year. If memory serves me correctly, I was puttering around Beech's garden that day while Beech sat on a deck chair reading the morning newspaper. At around noon Néstor came sauntering up from the guest cottage below, dressed in shorts, a T-shirt, and flip-flops. He greeted us and then lay back on one of the chaise lounges on the lawn at the side of the pool. Nominees, presenters, and guests at the Oscars were required to arrive at the Dorothy Chandler Pavilion in downtown L.A. by around four that afternoon. The pomp and circumstance of the so-called "red carpet" arrival was scheduled to take place at five o'clock and the actual awards ceremony at six. The timing was crucial, as it was going to be televised live, starting at five o'clock local time and at eight o'clock on the East Coast. Yet, here we were, all three of us hanging around the garden as if we didn't have a care or a concern in the world. Time was ticking relentlessly into the afternoon hour yet Néstor was behaving as though he didn't intend to budge. I noticed that he hadn't even shaved yet.

"Aren't you going down to the Dorothy Chandler for the awards tonight, Néstor?" I asked.

"You crazy?" he replied. "You know I can't beat any of those other four guys."

Beech and I immediately ganged up on him, scolding him for not wanting to go. Then Néstor came up with the lame excuse of not having anything decent to wear. Beech and I looked at each other in disbelief. Here was this guy who had come all the way from Spain,

Cuba, and Paris, made it big, and then become internationally recognized for his first major Hollywood feature film. How could he *not* go to the Academy Awards? He had been nominated for the highest goddamn award that the world's film industry could bestow on anyone. He *had* to go.

"C'mon, Nessie," I yelled. "Inside. *Now!*"

Suddenly Beech and I were in sync. We managed to drag him inside, pulled off his shorts and T-shirt, bundled him into the shower, and got him cleaned up. As Beech rubbed him down with a towel I ran a razor over his beard stubble. Beech rummaged through his wardrobe and found him a dark suit and a nicely pressed white shirt. We forced him into the clothes, then found an appropriate tie and some black socks. We shoved his feet into the socks and a pair of shoes, combed his hair, and looked at him.

"You'll do," said Beech. "Scotty, start the car."

Before I dashed outside I realized that they would never let Néstor into the auditorium without a ticket. I shook him, demanding to know where it was. He said he thought he had left it in the glove compartment of his rental car.

I dashed out to his rented car, rummaged through a pile of old papers in the glove compartment, and, miracle of miracles, there it was. I dashed back into the house, grabbed him, and, with Beech's help, shoved him into my own car. With the engine spluttering we pulled off, kicking up a cloud of dust as Beech stared after us, his hands on his hips.

How we made it down Kew Drive to Outlook Mountain Drive and then onto Laurel Canyon Boulevard heading south without careening over the edge of the cliffside or slamming into any other traffic I have no idea. We screeched onto Hollywood Boulevard and gunned it towards the 101 Freeway, often tearing through traffic lights split seconds before they turned red. Thank heavens the cops weren't around. Most of them must have been downtown at the Music Center directing a steady flow of stretch limousines to and from the Dorothy Chandler Pavilion. As we swerved onto the 101, exceeding the speed limit by at least twenty-five miles an hour, I yelled to Néstor to think of something to say in case he won. Clutching the dashboard as though he were on a rollercoaster hell-bent on his way to certain destruction he merely whispered, "I won't."

"Won't *what*?" I yelled back at him.

"Win," he squeaked.

I left it at that and concentrated on my wild ride downtown. By the time we pulled up outside the Dorothy Chandler Pavilion the crowds had thinned. The press corps had left and taken their places inside the auditorium. The hundreds of fans who had stood outside were drifting away. The ushers were closing the main doors. On one of the monitors in the courtyard I caught sight of the master of ceremonies, Johnny Carson, beginning his opening gambit to the awards proceedings. Shit! Were we too late? I flew out of the car, yanked Néstor out of the passenger seat, bulldozed him toward the entrance, shoved his invitation into his hand, yanked open one of the doors that an usher was trying to close, and pushed Néstor into the foyer.

With a few dozen people staring at me in my shorts, T-shirt, and flip-flops, I yelled at the usher through the glass doors. "He's a nominee! Please get him to his seat!" Then I raced back to my car and, with my head pounding like a sledgehammer, I drove back to Beech's place.

When I got there Beech was in the living room watching the ceremony.

I was just in time. As the commercial that was airing faded out the cameras cut back inside the auditorium and the next category was announced. It was the one for Best Cinematography. Beech and I shot a nervous glance at one other. The name of all five nominees were called out, short extracts of each of the films were shown, and then the envelope containing the name of the winner was torn open.

"And the Oscar goes to . . ." announced the presenter and then, for a moment that seemed like an eternity, time stood still.

Everything froze. I couldn't believe it as Néstor's name was called out. Beech and I looked at each other in utter shock. The complete outsider had beaten out all his seasoned competitors.

In the wee hours of the following morning as Beech and I dozed in front of an old movie a cab pulled up and Néstor crawled into the house, drunk and exhausted. He promptly passed out in the living room. In his hand he clutched a magnificent thing, a beautiful, gleaming, gold-plated Oscar statuette. Beech and I were so proud of him. I grabbed him by his feet, Beech took him by his arms, and we dropped him on the couch. He slept for hours. When he awoke he begged for coffee and then proceeded to proclaim that the Oscar belonged more to us than it did to him. He said we were the ones who believed in him, far exceeding his own faith in himself. As far as he was concerned, he thought it was essentially my win for getting him downtown. He couldn't thank me enough.

Néstor went on to carve out a spectacular career for himself. He photographed films as diverse as *Kramer vs. Kramer, The Blue Lagoon, Sophie's Choice, Places in the Heart, Imagine: John Lennon,* and *Billy Bathgate*. Sadly, he passed away in March 1992. While the newspapers called it cancer, the real cause of death was complications due to AIDS.

Not long after he died a letter and a package arrived from a lawyer in New York. The letter explained that in his will Néstor had left his Academy Award to me and in the parcel was the carefully wrapped Oscar statuette. I treasure it, but I confess that I regard myself purely as its custodian. It still belongs to Néstor and it always will. What it does do is remind me constantly of my close friendship with him and with all those other wonderfully creative and talented people in the motion picture and television industry whom I have known over the years. Fabulous people, all of them.

SOON THE SEVENTIES turned into the eighties. Movie genres had undergone a metamorphosis. The great romantic musicals had virtually disappeared. For want of a better term, the movies had lost their innocence. A new type of in-your-face violence was becoming popular. I didn't care too much for the overt cynicism and darkness that defined so many of the newer films. I longed for movies that underlined life, love, and lust rather than death, doom, and destruction. Nevertheless, the town that I adopted as my own remained the creative capital of the world and fantastic motion pictures were still coming out of it. Despite what are known as "runaway productions," when films are shot in places such as Vancouver, Toronto, and states on the East Coast where tax breaks created new incentives for cheaper location filming, Hollywood continued to thrive.

I was in my sixties and as active as ever. I was blessed with good health. All my physical attributes were still functioning at peak efficiency. Praise heaven, my libido was as strong as ever. I was arranging tricks for others, of course, but happily still tricking people myself, as well as bartending and serving folks at dinner parties. Life was good. Fresh young faces graced the screen and the social scene. New people were in town. However, a lot of my friends from earlier decades were gone by then, reduced to names carved in white marble on mausoleums and on gravestones around town. The names of some were now enshrined on the sidewalk along Hollywood Boulevard's "Walk of Fame." But a lot of the people I had known for many years were still holding on. Even though their careers had not made the transition in lockstep with the changing times, they were still around. Some clung to the past, others to their dreams, and a few just kept a tight hold on their memories. Sadly, however, one guy who had simply let go of everything was my old pal, actor William Holden.

I'd known Bill since 1950 when he rocketed to stardom playing opposite Gloria Swanson in *Sunset Boulevard*. He and I had met on the set when Gloria invited me over to watch filming. Ever since then we had seen each other at numerous parties and, on occasion, Bill had called me up to arrange for a nice young bit of tail to be sent over to his place to keep him company. Bill was as straight and as masculine as they come. He had a daughter out of wedlock with actress Eva May Hoffman in 1937. In 1941 he married actress Brenda Marshall. The marriage lasted thirty years but it was never a happy union. They both had many affairs and there were periodic separations. They had two sons together, and Bill also adopted Brenda's daughter from her first marriage. The couple divorced in 1971. Ever since, Bill had played the field. Most women found him exceptionally attractive.

Bill was the quintessential all-American male movie star. His list of credits was astonishing. He made more than seventy movies and was good in every single one of them. He won an Academy Award in 1954 for Best Actor for *Stalag 17* and was nominated for one in 1951 for Best Actor for *Sunset Boulevard.* He also starred in *Golden Boy, Our Town, Love is a Many-Splendored Thing, Picnic, The Bridge on the River Kwai, The World of Suzie Wong, The Wild Bunch,* and *Fedora.* He was tall, athletic, intelligent, good-looking, had a great voice, and was always an asset to have around at parties and social gatherings.

In 1952 he was the best man at the wedding of Ronald Reagan and Nancy Davis. Both Jacqueline Kennedy and Grace Kelly were hot for Bill. In fact, I personally saw him visit Princess Grace once when she was out here from Monaco and staying at my friend Frank McCarthy's place. He arrived in the late afternoon and didn't leave until the following morning. Bill had a lovely home in Palm Springs where he kept his collection of Oriental art, but he also had a little pad in Santa Monica. He would use it when he was shooting on soundstages at various studios around town. In later years he would simply go there to escape and hide, to chill out. As Bill's career wound down he became a somewhat wounded and reclusive man.

As starring vehicles became fewer and fewer and as loneliness began to take its toll on him, Bill began to drink. There were times when he called me up to arrange for some young lady to go over to his apartment in Santa Monica and when she got there the place was in total darkness. It would often take ten or fifteen minutes before Bill answered the door, usually staggering and swaying. He was sometimes wearing little more than a soiled pair of boxers or had a dirty sheet or towel draped around his waist. He invariably reeked of alcohol. I went around there a couple of times to see him and the place was a cesspool. Empty bottles lay cluttered all over every room. It was obvious that there were moments when Bill had bowel and bladder movements but hadn't even bothered to go to the bathroom. He just did what he had to do on the floor or in bed. It was painfully sad to see. There were periods when he didn't bother to wash or bathe for days or weeks at a time. It was a terrible tragedy. He had no friends. Nobody called on him anymore. The only people who came around were those girls I sent over to trick him. But often he wouldn't even answer the door to let them in.

Eventually he accused me of emasculating him by denying him the right to see women when I had no other alternative but to stop sending them over. Besides, even if he did let them in he was in no condition to do anything with them. He had become totally impotent and he was always drunk. He couldn't get it up if he tried. Bill died in November 1981 at the age of only sixty-three. I was notified about his death by, I think, someone who worked in film producer Howard Koch's office at Paramount Pictures. The coroner said that Bill had suffered a severe laceration to his forehead and had bled to death. It looked like he tripped over a rug and hit his head on a table or the floor. Details about whether that was true and whether he was drunk at the time were never made public. Bill's death was a real loss, not only to me as his friend but to the industry he loved, to his colleagues who had worked with him, and to the worldwide audiences who adored him.

29

Looking Back

By the time the mideighties arrived things had changed dramatically in Hollywood. The mysterious illness that first went by the ominous name of "gay cancer" or "gay plague" was making a lot of people sick. Many were dying. Eventually, the insidious thing was identified as the human immunodeficiency virus or HIV, the first stage of the killer disease that was wiping out an entire generation of people, not only in the gay community but also in heterosexual societies worldwide. AIDS had launched itself in a vicious war against humanity. It brought an end to the sexual freedoms that had defined much of life in Tinseltown ever since the birth of the movies. I, too, underwent a major change. Tricking—whether for others or doing it myself—gradually slowed down to a snail's pace. Sex used to be about having fun and a good time. The advent of AIDS didn't change that per se, but now sex could come at the cost of your very life. So, things changed. A lot. The wild and wooly days were over. The drag parties and gang bangs and swingers' evenings and orgies became a thing of the past.

But life went on.

One evening in 1981 I was with some friends at Alberto's, a fancy little piano bar on Melrose Avenue between Doheny and Robertson in West Los Angeles. A very attractive woman with a lovely voice was on stage singing "*Looking Through the Eyes of Love.*" She was no spring chicken, probably in her midforties, but she was trim, with a very appealing figure, a finely chiseled face with an infectious smile, pearly white teeth, and gorgeous blue eyes. She had soft, silky blonde hair. I was immediately taken with her. After she got off stage I cornered her and was surprised to learn that she was unaccompanied. I took her over to a table in a corner and we began to chat. Her name was Lois Broad. It turned out that she wasn't a professional singer but was simply at the bar that evening to while away a couple of hours. She had beautiful diction—which was not surprising because, as she explained, she was a professional speech therapist. She had come out to California from New York eighteen months earlier to teach in the public school system. She was clearly a very smart and educated lady, a graduate of Cornell and Columbia universities. While living in Manhattan she had been teaching and working in speech clinics. Lois, a divorcée with a daughter in Texas, wasn't your run-of-the-mill Hollywood type. Ten years younger than me, she wasn't in the least bit extravagant and was simply a sweet, uncomplicated woman with no ambitions of a career in show business. She was real. She was genuine. She was undemanding and easy to be with. And so we began to date.

Breaking a pattern of committed bachelorhood that I had zealously guarded for over sixty years, Lois and I got married on a summer day on July 8, 1984. The ceremony took place in a park overlooking the Pacific Palisades, not too far from the ocean. A Protestant minister officiated and about fifty or sixty guests attended. Lois was renting a comfortable apartment in Brentwood and so I moved in with her. Needless to say, Betty knew nothing of this new arrangement. Lois, on the other hand, knew all about Betty and was very understanding of the fact that I needed to put in regular appearances at my house on North St. Andrew's Place where Betty was living.

My life remained as gypsy-like as ever because I divided my time between Lois and Betty, still spending many evenings sleeping over at friends' or at the homes of clients after a dusk-to-dawn party. I also spent the odd night at the homes of people I knew well and continued to trick. In addition, I often slept in the guest cottage at Beech Dickerson's place on Kew Drive. Despite my marital status I maintained my bartending schedule and continued to serve dinner and repair picket fences and fix roofs. I also fed the wild raccoon and the cute little skunk and the itinerant feral cat that lived in the bushes of the St. Andrews Place property. As I had long ago entered the twilight of my life, my friends became more important to me than ever. Even though AIDS loomed over us, there were many who still asked me to arrange tricks for them. For a while I continued to do so, but I was never sure whether adequate protection and safeguards were being used. I always insisted that a guy assure me he was going to use a condom with his trick, be they male or female, but who knew whether or not he did so? It was all becoming too risky, too dangerous. As we inexorably headed toward the nineties I knew far too many people who had become HIV-positive or who had died of AIDS. It was obvious that my days of arranging tricks for others were over. It was too unsafe a game to play anymore. That wonderful era had come to an end. Period.

IN THE EARLY SUMMER OF 1999, Momma died in her little house in the town of Ottawa, in Illinois. She was ninety-nine years old. Now there was just my sister Phyllis. She was seventy-four and chose to remain in Ottawa. I continued to send money to help support her and we kept in regular touch with one another. Before I knew it the calendar had shed more pages and we had entered the bold new world of the twenty-first century.

Five years into the new millennium, on December 7, 2005, my dear friend Beech Dickerson passed away. A week or so after the funeral I was summoned to his lawyer's office. As I sat at his desk he read Beech's will and I was stunned to learn that he had left two of his prime properties to me. One was a home on Stanley Hills Road in the Hollywood Hills and the other was the Kew Drive property that I loved so much. According to the stipulations of the inheritance I was permitted to sell the Stanley Hills Road home, which I did. I received a substantial payment for it but most of the income from the sale was swallowed up by Uncle Sam in the form of back taxes and estate duties. However, the magnificent Kew Drive property was now mine. I was given permission to live in it for the rest of my life. According to Beech's will, on my death the property will go to Corbin Bernsen, the ruggedly good-looking actor who is Beech's godson and who appeared in TV shows like *Ryan's Hope, L.A. Law,* and *The West Wing.*

At the beginning of 2006 I moved into the house overlooking the great City of Angels with Lois. I was eighty-three and Lois seventy-three. We settled into our new Kew Drive home together with my beloved dog, a border collie mix named Baby. It was instant domestic bliss. Lois and I still sleep together, with Baby curled up at our feet. Lois and I still have sex regularly. Provided you are blessed with good health and share mutual affection for one another you cannot put a good man or woman down!

During all the years that I had been married to Lois it is doubtful that Betty ever found out about her. Certainly she knew I lived a multitiered life. She was always aware of the fact that I was screwing around with a lot of people and arranging tricks for hundreds more. The phone at our home at St. Andrews Place had rung incessantly. Exactly *how* much she really knew about my other life—or *lives*— will remain a mystery, but to some degree or another she was very much aware of it.

Betty never mentioned the subject and she continued to live alone in our house at St. Andrews Place while Lois and I made our home up on Kew Drive. However, I saw Betty just about every day. I went down to St. Andrews Place to check on her, to pick up mail and messages, and to feed the wildlife in the garden. And then, in 2008, something terrible happened.

One afternoon Betty slipped on the stairs outside the kitchen and shattered her hip. She was in agony but by some miracle she managed to crawl back inside the house. I arrived that evening to pick up the mail and to check on her, only to find the poor woman writhing on the kitchen floor. Trying to be as gentle as I could I picked her up, took her to my car, and rushed her over to Glendale Memorial Hospital. She was there for about a week and then they released her to another facility where she remained for a month. Following a short recuperation she returned to the house but it quickly became evident that she was too incapacitated to live alone. She was going to need constant care and supervision. After trying a couple of places I eventually found her a clean, comfortable, and efficient retirement home in North Hollywood. She was well looked after there and all was well. Until pneumonia set in. On August 5, 2008, precisely on her eighty-seventh birthday, she slipped into a deep sleep and never woke up.

Betty and I had not had a normal life together for longer than I could remember. But we had been together for sixty-three years, ever since I met her when I came ashore as a young Marine in Seattle after the war. She was the one who had come down to California with me. She had been the mother of my late darling daughter, Donna. I hurt deeply because I still cared for Betty. How could I not? I had spent two-thirds of my life with her. You don't just walk away from something like that without feeling anything. Though our paths had meandered far from one another she was part of who I was. Even though Lois and I had officially and legally tied the knot—Lois diligently filed away and locked up our marriage license—Betty was a part of my being. She must have known more than she ever let on about my double life, my sexual life, my tricking world, my other world. We had not been to bed together or had sex with one another for decades, not since Donna died from the botched abortion. And yet we had remained together. She was part and parcel of who I was. Her death hurt.

Now that I have reached my late eighties, Lois and I continue to live on Kew Drive. I'm still as busy as ever. During the day I keep on doing odd jobs around other people's houses. I repair roofs and drainpipes; I take care of plumbing, carpentry, and simple electrical problems; I trim trees. I've been in this town so long now that I know scores of people who call me up regularly to do handyman chores for them. And hardly an evening goes by that I don't don a nice clean white dress shirt to serve dinner and bartend at parties at people's private homes. In that regard, Beverly Hills, Bel Air, and the canyons remain my main beat. However, my clients are no longer only Hollywood personalities. Among those I work for now are doctors, lawyers, museum directors, art collectors, accountants, corporate executives, and industrialists. But show business people still make up a large proportion of those who employ me. In fact, I've been around for so long that I now do gigs for the second, third, and even fourth generation descendants of original clients who have long since passed on.

Even though I've been a bartender, caterer, waiter, handyman, general repairman, and, at the start of my career, a gas station attendant, most of what I did for six decades was to keep people happy. And, as I have revealed to you, I accomplished that by arranging sexual liaisons. Starting with that initial group of guys and gals who used to congregate at my gas station on Hollywood Boulevard I went on to develop a long list of wonderful, attractive men and women who were available to trick folks for fun and for profit. Whatever tip, gratuity, or financial transaction that may have passed hands was of no concern to me. I never made or wanted a dime out of the tricks that I set up for others. I just wanted to see people enjoy themselves. I wanted folks to experience what we as humans were naturally designed to do. In other words, to derive pleasure by being the sexual beings we are.

Oh, they were good days and I do miss them so!

At the height of my tricking days—in other words, during the gas station period and the years following—I was setting up an average of fifteen to twenty tricks a day. This was a 24/7 operation, extending over a period of, say, thirty to forty years. As for tricks that I performed personally, I was often seeing two or three people a day. How many sexual encounters does all that add up to? Who knows? The statistics aren't important. To be candid, I think of myself as being blessed. And I have to admit that I enjoyed every single one of those experiences. In retrospect I hope I provided as much pleasure as I derived myself. Starting with that little session back with my neighbor, old man Joe Peterson, I look back on it all with warmth, gratitude, and affection. I had fun. I enjoyed it. I regret none of it. Not once have I felt shame or guilt or remorse about what I did. Quite the contrary. It's been a fantastic life.

Now, almost in my eighty-ninth year, I share my life and my home with Lois and my dog, Baby. The other evening, just before I set out for a bartending job, I said good-bye to Lois. As I left the house I looked up at a sky that was so beautiful it took my breath away. I walked over to the edge of my Kew Drive property, leaned on the fence, and gazed out at the twilight view of the great Los Angeles basin. From the skyscrapers downtown to the beaches and ocean in the west, a wash of golden light brought a magic to the city that I have grown to know and to love so deeply. I leaned on the fence and stared at the panorama before me. Down in the south an endless line of twinkling lights that looked like glittering diamonds in the sky snaked from the east towards LAX, Los Angeles International Airport. Each one of those little shimmering dots was an airliner on a path heading toward one of the busiest airports in the world. It was captivating. Just south of the airport lay Long Beach, the largest and busiest port in the nation. The Los Angeles area is now one of the most culturally diverse and cosmopolitan places on earth. Billboards proclaim it the "Creative Capital of the World." With the vastness of the movie, television, and music industries centered here, there is undeniable truth to that statement. And then there is publishing and software and fine art and theater and opera. Not to mention heavy industry and science and manufacturing and aerospace. Compared to when I took my first tenuous steps here as a rookie Marine during my boot camp days back in World War II, the City of Angels has certainly come of age.

I took a deep breath, glanced at the skyline one more time, ruffled the fur behind Baby's ears, yelled out another good-bye to Lois, and got into the car. Moments later I was negotiating those winding, curving, treacherous twists and turns of Kew Drive as I headed down the mountain to my party.

I thought some more about myself, about my life, about the people I was going to see that night. No doubt I would know them all. They were probably folks I had seen and served for longer than I can remember. The hostess was a widow of a successful stockbroker who had lived in the same house for over forty years. She was a pretty woman and she would be dressed in all her finery, as she always was. I could even smell her French perfume already. I had no idea what brand it was but she had been using it for as long as I had known her. She was in her late seventies, perhaps even her early eighties. She was still an attractive woman. A ripple of excitement tingled in my loins as I pictured her and I felt myself getting hard. Admittedly I'm not sixteen anymore. I'm not even twenty-six or thirty-six or forty-six. But for me sex is as alive and important as ever. However, unlike the old days, I knew I would not be spending the night with the hostess. When the party was over I would help pack things up, put away the booze, assist the maid in tidying up the kitchen, stash away the glasses and the dishes, say good night, get into my car, and drive home. To Kew Drive. To Lois. And to Baby. They are my family. That is where my life now lies. And I am content.

ACKNOWLEDGMENTS

This book would not have seen the light of day were it not for our mutual friend, Joan Allemand. She was responsible for initially hooking us up and coercing us to collaborate on the project. We are deeply grateful to her.

Our thanks go to Gore Vidal who provided so much encouragement and for introducing us to Jeff Sharp. Jeff's enthusiasm was infectiously helpful and he, in turn, linked us up with our agent, David Kuhn, to whom we owe so much. David was supportive and constructively astute throughout the process of refining the manuscript. Whilst many publishers balked at the prospect of taking on a subject as potentially controversial as this, Morgan Entrekin was the exception. We owe him a great debt of gratitude for bringing the book to fruition, thereby continuing the long tradition of Grove Press for braving new frontiers where others feared to tread. We are thankful to our editor, Peter Blackstock, with whom it was always a pleasure to work. Thanks go to Lee Silton for reading an early draft of the manuscript and for her inspiration and creative insight. Thanks also to Diana Friedberg who was always patient, tolerant, and understanding during the many hours and days that we spent recording and documenting the many memories and recollections that form the nucleus of this book.

Scotty Bowers
Lionel Friedberg
Los Angeles